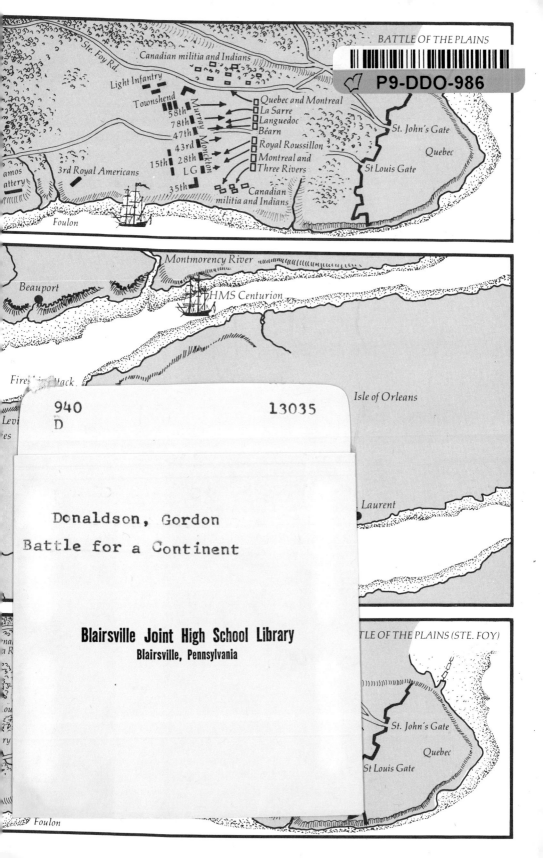

P9-DDO-986

Ste Foy Rd.

Canadian militia and Indians

Light Infantry

Townshend

58th

78th

47th

43rd

15th 28th

LG

35th

Murray Monckton

Quebec and Montreal
La Sarre
Languedoc
Béarn
Royal Roussillon
Montreal and
Three Rivers

St. John's Gate

Quebec

St Louis Gate

3rd Royal Americans

amos
attery

Canadian
militia and Indians

Foulon

Montmorency River

Beauport

HMS Centurion

Fire ship attack

Isle of Orleans

Levi
es

Laurent

na
a R

ou

ry

St. John's Gate

Quebec

St Louis Gate

Foulon

Battle for a Continent
QUEBEC 1759

Gordon Donaldson

Doubleday Canada Limited, Toronto, Ontario
Doubleday & Company, Inc., Garden City, New York
1973

940
D

Design: Brant Cowie
Endpaper artwork: Julian Cleva
Printed and bound in Canada by T. H. Best

To Timmie

CONTENTS

Chapter 1

Night
On The
River

At two o'clock in the morning the tide turned at Cap Rouge. It began to ebb strongly downstream, rippling past the two hundred foot high wall of rock that shielded the bastion of Quebec, past the Beauport shore where the defenders massed, and on toward the great Gulf of St. Lawrence and the sea from whence the invaders came. It was a chilly, gray-black night in mid-river. There was no moon, and the mists of early fall veiled the faint starlight.

Major-General James Wolfe clambered down a ladder on the starboard side of the 50-gun flagship HMS Sutherland and settled his long, painfully-thin frame in the stern of a crowded flat-bottomed boat. Under his gray cloak he wore the new bright-red uniform that he had laid away in his sea-chest throughout the summer campaign. He had been saving that uniform for this day — September 13, 1759 — when he fully expected to die in it.

Languidly, he waved the cane he carried into battle in place of a sword. A navy captain barked an order and a second lantern was hoisted to the main topmast shrouds of the Sutherland. As that dim orange signal bobbed aloft, the thirty flatboats that had been heaving and grinding, gunwale to gunwale, were cast off from the ship's side. With a tense, silent cargo of 1,600 soldiers they began to drift down towards the stronghold of France in the New World.

The next few hours would decide who would rule North America.

It was Wolfe's last chance of victory in this, or any other year. The harsh laws of the Canadian climate and his own state of health had determined that. As the tide tugged his boat away he was sick, nervous and afraid — not of death, but of defeat. He had only partly recovered from a long bout of fever. He had asked his surgeon to "fix him up" for the two or three days he needed to carry out his last, seemingly-desperate plan. After regular bleedings and hefty doses of drugs he was, for the moment, fixed up. But still his bladder and kidneys ached, he itched from traces of scurvy, and his long, tapered fingers plucked constantly at the cuffs of his red coat. "My constitution is entirely ruined", he had declared in a despondent letter to London four days earlier, "without the consolation of doing any considerable service to the state and without any prospect of it".

For four months he had laid siege to Quebec, shattering the town with cannon fire, and burning the surrounding farms and villages. But he had failed to get at the French army, entrenched along the rocky shoreline, or lure it out to fight. Now his time was running out. His admiral, Charles Saunders, had brought 141 ships — one quarter of the entire Royal Navy — up the treacherous river. He had to get them out again before the ice of winter clutched and held them. Already thin patches were forming in parts of the Gulf, and Saunders was anxious to leave. Two weeks at most, the admiral said.

Even if he survived the voyage home — and his three previous Atlantic crossings had nearly killed him — Wolfe knew he would be finished. His patron, William Pitt, would abandon him and he would revert to his permanent rank of colonel — an eccentric, awkward, too-young officer distrusted by his aristocratic superiors. Far worse, he would have missed the glory and immortality he had worked and waited for throughout his thirty-two years. For Wolfe was a hero to the manner born. Since his time nations have bestowed their highest honours for valour upon soldiers who stormed enemy positions in moments of zeal, madness or drunken frenzy. Wolfe was no such momentary, accidental hero, although he could be impetuous. He studied heroism as a craft, worked at it, and was to practise it, coolly and perfectly, on the Heights of Abraham. In Wolfe's opinion, it was the duty of an officer to impress his courage upon his men, and the more senior the officer, the more he was required to flaunt himself before the enemy. Four years before, when he was a lieutenant-colonel, he told his mother: "As I rise in rank people will expect some considerable performances and I shall be induced, in support of an ill-got reputation, to be

Wolfe points the way. From a contemporary sketch by one of Wolfe's aides, with the engraver, Richard Houston, supplying a dash of imagination to the background.

(Royal Ontario Museum, Toronto)

lavish of my life, and shall probably meet that fate which is the ordinary effect of such conduct."

Now he was ready for his ultimate performance.

Ten tarry-pigtailed seamen lowered their oars into rowlocks muffled by strips of canvas and pulled gently to give the boat steerage way. On benches between the rowing thwarts sat thirty picked men of Wolfe's elite Light Infantry, crowded back to back, holding their muskets upright between their knees, shivering in the light westerly breeze. Occasionally they sipped at the extra rum ration — one gill per man — mixed with water in their canteens. They were forbidden to talk; but the officers spoke quietly and the navigator of the lead boat, Captain James Chads, grunted his orders, keeping the fleet in the middle of the river, a full mile from the French watchers along the north shore.

The general sat stiffly in the sternsheets, his curious triangular profile pointing bird-like ahead. His plans were complete; for the next two hours he had no decisions to make. He must rely on Captain Chads and the navy to find their way down the dark river and hit the chosen landing place. As the boat creaked and gurgled along, he thought of death and glory, the rewards of his profession and goals of his short, pain-ridden life. He remembered a passage from the small, leather-bound volume his fiancee Katherine Lowther had given him that spring — Thomas Gray's recent poem "Elegy Written in a Country Churchyard":

> *The boast of heraldry, the pomp of power*
> *And all that beauty and wealth e'er gave*
> *Await alike the inevitable hour*
> *The paths of glory lead but to the grave.*

The words, which he had carefully underlined, seemed to match the immensity of the occasion, and convey the magnificent resignation that the young military romantic lived and breathed but could never express.

According to a famous story he recited the verse softly to his officers and added: "Gentlemen, I would rather have written these lines than take Quebec."

Later historians have scoffed at the story, but later generals have lived by it. Wolfe, son of a general, had chosen the paths

Louis-Joseph, Marquis de Montcalm, painted by Sargent. "What a country" Montcalm wrote from Quebec to his wife in France "where rogues get rich and honest men are ruined."

(Public Archives of Canada)

of glory as a lad of fifteen. Having been through the slaughter of Dettingen and Culloden, he did not need a poet to tell him whither those paths led. He had burned homes and butchered men to order. But now, as he sensed that his hour had come, he welcomed the reminder that it was inevitable.

The day before, he had taken the miniature portrait of Katherine Lowther which he wore in a locket under his shirt and given it to his friend Captain Jack Jervis, telling him to return it to Katherine if, as he expected, he died in the assault.

Now he could abandon himself to the tide which was pulling him swiftly downstream to Quebec and destiny. He had just eight hours to live.

Camp fires flickered along the Beauport shore, twenty miles downriver from Cap Rouge. The Marquis de Montcalm's French regulars had spent the night in their trenches, peering over stout log barriers at the dark basin below Quebec where most of the British fleet lay. They could see signal lanterns being raised and lowered on the halyards of Saunders' great three-decker ships of the line, and faint moving shapes that might be frigates approaching. Just after twilight the big ships had blasted broadsides at the shore, splintering birch trees and chipping off chunks of rock; at that point the Marquis had ordered them out of their tents, warning that the British might try to land. The cannonade was duly followed by the sound of splashing oars and sailors' cheers, but no attack came. Still, the British were obviously awake and up to something. Their lanterns waved and their threats and curses carried across the black water.

Montcalm paced slowly and thoughtfully by the river's edge with his Scots aide-de-camp Lieutenant James Johnstone (later the Chevalier de Johnstone). He had no thought of sleep — that was a luxury to be snatched briefly by day. He had not taken his clothes off at night since the siege began on June 23 and sometimes, in his black moments, the weariness showed. He was a Provençal, small, dark-eyed and excitable, with a temper that could flame into rage and cool again in minutes to serene arrogance. His moods might range from cautious optimism to deep despair, but at heart he was profoundly disillusioned. He thought he could save Canada, but only for another year or two. The appalling Canadian winter, which had been his enemy for his three miserable years in the quarrelsome little colony, was coming to defeat the British. But they would be back next spring and the spring after that and eventually the colony would crumble through its own corruption and the indifference of Madame de Pompadour's court in France. Montcalm, his duty done, would go home to his lovely wife Angélique-Louise, their six children and the gentle olive and almond trees of gracious Chateau Candiac in sunny Provençe.

He would have no regrets. "What a country", he had written, "where rogues get rich and honest men are ruined."

Meanwhile he awaited one last assault by Wolfe. From what he had heard of the young Englishman, he was not the sort to sail home without making a final, dramatic effort. Montcalm reckoned it must come within the next month, probably less. His superior, Governor Vaudreuil, gave Wolfe less than a week, but Montcalm considered Vaudreuil an idiot in military matters and a swine personally.

Pausing on the path above the low, broken Beauport cliffs, he told himself for the hundredth time that this was where the attack must come. Wolfe would try to land somewhere along the seven miles of accessible shoreline between the St. Charles and Montmorency rivers. If he succeeded he would march to the St. Charles, force a crossing, and take Quebec from its soft, northern landward side. The only logical alternative for Wolfe was to sail twenty or thirty miles upstream, land on the north shore and march back. To prevent this, Montcalm had sent young Chevalier de Bougainville with three thousand men to follow the British ships upriver and pounce on any landing parties.

Montcalm had little fear of a direct attack on the town itself or on the heights above it. They were shielded by miles of almost-vertical cliff face which no army could climb. The few tiny paths up the cliff were blocked and defended by Canadians. No, Wolfe was not crazy enough to try there: the English did not have wings.

Montcalm knew far more military history than his opponent. He had studied old campaigns for most of his forty-seven years, reading the classical accounts in Greek and Latin. It was a family tradition; the Montcalms of Candiac had been soldiers as far back as anyone could remember and had served France honorably,

Brigadier General, the Honourable George Townshend. "I have never served in so disagreeable a campaign as this."

(McCord Museum)

if unluckily, almost as long as France had existed as a nation. They were good and loyal officers, but so many of them had died through the mistakes of others that superstitious peasants on the chateau lands still whispered, "War is the tomb of the Montcalms". The present marquis followed the military logic of his ancestors and he, too, was to die, partly through the mistakes of others and partly through his own.

He walked back with Johnstone to his headquarters in the de Salaberry manor house. As the two men reached the gate they heard the boom of cannon coming from upriver, just above Quebec.

Brigadier-General the Honourable George Townshend stood on the poop-deck of the frigate Lowestoft, watching with an air of grim detachment as Wolfe's first wave of landing-craft slipped away from the nearby Sutherland.

It wasn't really his battle. As second of the three brigadiers — after the Honourable Robert Monckton, the unlettered,

Wolfe's distinctive triangular profile is very much in evidence in this malicious cartoon by Townshend. Wolfe was not amused.

(*McCord Museum*)

easy-going son of Viscount Galway — he was to command the second wave. In one hour's time the Lowestoft, with 300 men of the 15th regiment aboard, would glide downstream, followed by two more frigates, a sloop and five smaller vessels. By the time Wolfe's returning boats met them and took the troops ashore, it would be daylight and the glory, if any, would be gone.

By then it would be clear to all whether the Heights of Abraham were, in fact, scaleable: or whether James Wolfe had blundered into another disaster like his attempt to storm the cliffs at Montmorency six weeks before. Townshend faced the outcome with equanimity and his customary sardonic smile. He was no admirer of the chinless young general, his inferior in years and social position, who had for reasons known only to the incompetents in London been given command of the expedition.

"General Wolfe's health is but very bad," he had written to his wife, Charlotte, five days before. "His generalship, in my opinion, is not a bit better . . . this just between us."

If he had kept his opinions to himself and his dear Charlotte, feelings among the senior officers might have been better. But that was not Townshend's way. In his laconic, drawling manner, he said what he thought of the jumped-up, self-educated soldier's son. His malicious cartoon drawings of the gangling general had found their way into the officers' messes. Wolfe had seen some of them, and was not amused.

The careers of the two men had run parallel for years. They had fought in the same battles — Dettingen, 1743, Culloden, 1746 — but Wolfe was usually in the front line, while Townshend held staff jobs. The Townshends were a great Whig family, immensely rich and important. George got his name from his godfather, King George I; he owed his political connections to his uncle, the Duke of Newcastle, who was the king's first minister, on and off, for forty years, and to his brother Charles, who was to crown a brilliant career in the Commons by imposing a tax on tea for the American colonies. All in all, George was a very well-connected, very superior person and could afford to indulge his patrician sense of humor, even at the expense of his commanding officer.

The one quality shared by the cynical brigadier and the ardent general was bravery under fire; yet while Wolfe's troops admired his courage, Townshend was generally disliked. His coolness was legendary. At the battle of Laufeldt he was standing with some allied staff officers when a shell knocked off a German colleague's head, splattering its contents over his uniform. Townshend gave a foppish wave of his lace-trimmed handkerchief and wiped his chest with it. "I never knew before", he drawled, "that Scheiger had so many brains."

Throughout the summer siege of Quebec he had grown increasingly bitter at Wolfe and come to regret ever agreeing to serve under him. He was still furious over an incident early in July when the general had sneered at him for turning his camp into a "fortress". When the campaign was over, he planned to launch a parliamentary inquiry into Wolfe's conduct. He knew at least one of the other brigadiers would back him up, and probably the admiral, too.

What rankled most with all of them was the man's infernal secretiveness. Not until the last week in August had he even consulted the brigadiers on plans of attack; and apparently that was because he was sick and had no plan of his own.

Townshend remembered the day they surveyed the spot finally selected for today's landing. Wolfe had stood for a long time on a rock on the south bank of the river, telescope to his eye, looking at a crack in the cliffs on the enemy side. As an artist, Townshend appreciated the heroic scene and later sketched it. Silhouetted against the blue river and the savage forests alive with their autumnal yellows, oranges and reds stood the gaunt motionless figure, his drab grenadier's greatcoat carelessly flung open to reveal the brilliant red uniform it was supposed to conceal from the French spyglasses opposite. As an officer, Townshend considered it a picture of hopeless military indecision. The background of fall colors was a reminder that the general had to attack or turn tail and flee the Canadian winter. But Wolfe said nothing, closed his telescope and was rowed back to the flagship. Not until a few hours before the landing craft sailed did he tell the brigadiers that they were to land at that particular crack in the cliffs, where he believed there was a path. In order to get even that information they had been forced to write a joint letter of protest. They had been kept in the dark like common soldiers. It was incredible. Whatever happened now, no one in London could blame the brigadiers. And in a few weeks, Townshend would be there to tell his story. He could hardly wait. "I have never served in so disagreeable a campaign as this", he had told Charlotte. "I shall come back to Admiral Saunders' ship and in two months shall again belong to those I never ought to have left."

The capstan creaked on the Lowestoft's foredeck as sailors fitted the wooden bars into their slots and heaved them around in straining circles to raise the anchor. Despite his doubts and cynical suspicions, Townshend felt the tug of combat as the Lowestoft headed for the battle he was soon to command.

Pierre-Francois Rigaud, Marquis de Vaudreuil-Cavagnal and Governor of New France was writing a letter to his minister in Paris. "I shall do the impossible to prevent our enemies from making progress in any direction", he promised, "[I] will fight them with an ardor and even a fury which so exceeds the range of their ambitious designs."

He sat in his farmhouse headquarters overlooking the St. Charles river, one mile from Quebec and out of range of the heavy British siege guns that continued to batter the broken and

Pierre-Francois Rigaud, Marquis de Vaudreuil-Cavagnal and Governor of New France. In accordance with custom, the artist Henri Beau dressed Vaudreuil in medieval armour to emphasise his martial ardour.

(*Public Archives of Canada*)

starving town. He had long since abandoned his palace inside the walls. His style of life was shrinking along with his domain. In one year he had lost territories from Lake Ontario south to the Gulf of Mexico, and the eastern fortress of Louisbourg. He was now bottled up in the St. Lawrence between Quebec and Montreal.

But he remained optimistic. The losses were the fault of Montcalm, the snappy little general foisted on him by Paris. The victories, such as the recent defeat of Wolfe at Montmorency, belonged to the governor alone. Eventually, he was sure, the general would be recalled and the lost lands restored.

Unlike Montcalm, Vaudreuil could not imagine the possibility of losing Canada. He was a Canadian, born in Quebec. He was attuned to the country, its seasonal changes of mood, the steadfast simplicity of its people, whom he regarded as his children, and the hideous cruelties of man and nature which were sent to afflict them. Ever since he was one year old — and that was sixty years ago — French kings had been threatening to abandon the colony as a needless expense. Even before Voltaire said it, they viewed Canada as "a wretched country . . . covered with ice eight months in the year, inhabited by barbarians, bears and beaver."

Vaudreuil was no barbarian. He was the son of a French-born governor who had administered New France wisely and firmly from 1703 to 1725. He had the same stature and presence, but his father's tolerance had declined into laxity; he could be manipulated, and he was.

He had been appointed in 1755 as the result of fears in Paris that if the Canadians didn't get their first native-born governor some kind of revolution would break out. In a century and a half they had developed a character of their own, and with it a distrust of new arrivals from France. Vaudreuil's appointment only deepened this division between the new France and the old. With all his faults, he was firmly on the side of the Canadians. A tall, roundish figure with a large nose and folksy manner, he was full of quick quips and farm jokes. But behind the wink and the shrug and the paternal pat on the habitant's shoulder lay an enormous conceit — a naive and quite unjustified belief in the abilities of the Marquis de Vaudreuil.

He disliked Montcalm long before he met him. He had told Paris he did not need a French general. Frenchmen did not understand the way his Canadians fought. This proved to be true: the officers from France threatened the Canadian troops with sticks and swords, and insisted on being carried on the men's backs across rivers and over rocks. The Governor kept a file of complaints against Montcalm, including charges that he struck Canadians in outbursts of rage. In the lower ranks, the white-coated regulars despised the ill-clad militia and the colonial marines.

The marines — *Les Compagnies Franche de la Marine* — looked strange to European eyes. Their *mitasses*, leggings cut in Indian style, were often decorated by Indian beadwork thongs. Few of their battered tricorn hats still retained their jaunty black cockades, and their regulation swords had been eagerly swapped for hatchets and tomahawks. Their stiff boots had long since worn out and been replaced by deerskin moccasins, which did little to increase the impressiveness of a force made up of men with teeth and over four foot ten — the only conditions of enlistment. The French white-coats looked down their noses at both the Quebec troops and the Quebec civilians and were heartily despised in return. The blackened walls of Quebec bore scrawled slogans, "Frenchmen go home and leave us alone."

The King of France was a vague symbol to the militiaman, whose loyalty was to his land, his seigneur, his priest and his Governor. In his own kind of guerrilla warfare he could outfight any outsider. Like his Governor, he knew nothing of the elaborate ritual of killing and dying in formation on a set-piece European battlefield. Only Vaudreuil's vast conceit convinced him that he could lead them, if he had to, in a conventional battle against a professional English army.

He had tried to convince the French Court of this but had failed. That spring Vaudreuil had received orders from Versailles to defer to Montcalm in all military matters and not to set foot on any battlefield unless the general invited him. He was told to pass this instruction on to the general. But he seems to have kept it to himself, for Montcalm continued to defer to him according to his original orders of three years before.

As the "ambitious designs" of the British unfolded, no one was in absolute command of the French and Canadian defenders.

An hour before the first shots were fired above Quebec, Vaudreuil had signed his letter and gone to bed. He slept soundly — a round, self-satisfied, overblown man.

✠ ⚜

At two o'clock, François Bigot was concluding his night's entertainment in his great stone chateau in the woods. Another hand of pharo and he would retire to bed, leaving a handful of fellow plunderers and their women draped around the gaming rooms.

As Intendant, he managed the business and finance of the colony and in ten years he had created a system of fraud and corruption so vast and all-pervading that it touched everyone in the colony from the Governor down. He had raked off millions of livres for himself, but he was not a selfish man; there was loot for all but the poor, and occasionally even one of them got rich. Bigot was generous and well-liked by everyone who mattered. His hospitality was fabulous. He seldom ate dinner without inviting at least twenty guests. The nightly dancing and gaming in his palace by the St. Charles continued well into the siege of Quebec. Lest the hungry townspeople feel left out of things, they were invited to stand up in the gallery of the great hall and watch the gentry gyrating in stately fashion under the chandeliers — gentry grown fat on the rations the Bigot organization had stolen from them. When the last of Quebec's dogs and cats were being killed and eaten outside, Bigot's guests still dined on fowl fattened by corn seized from the farmers in the name of the King.

Now five hundred buildings had been burned or pounded to rubble by the British guns and the Intendant had moved out of town. He divided his time between army headquarters at Beauport, where there were still profits to be made, and the Chateau Bigot, in the woods of Charlebourg, about five miles away which, with fine irony, was nicknamed the Hermitage. The stories of wild debauchery that circulated in the ruins of Quebec would have made the stoutest hermit blush.

The Intendant wiped his florid, pimply face and his red mane and sighed with a comfortable expansion of girth. His cohorts told him Monsieur Wolfe was planning another river assault. Perhaps he could still take Quebec before the ice came. Perhaps not. It was a serious question — but no more serious than the turn of the next card, which could cost him ten thousand livres.* If the

*A livre was the equivalent of a franc, worth about ten pence, or slightly less than an English shilling. For a comparison with present currency in North America, think of it as roughly twenty cents.

The court of Francois Bigot, Intendant of New France. Despite the siege and bombardment, the revelry continued, while the common people starved.

(Public Archives of Canada)

English conquered the colony, the Intendant would depart, with appropriate speed, to luxurious retirement on his estates in France. He would lose money, yes, but the troublesome investigation of the colony's accounts would cease. The books would be lost along with the colony and in the confusion of defeat there would be no proof of wrongdoing. Suspicions, yes, but no proof.

If the English gave up and went home, the French ministers would be happy. They might decide that Canada was worth preserving after all. They might withdraw their threat to stop payment of the annual drafts that supported Bigot's paper currency. Then he would be safe for another year. Business would go on as usual. There were millions more to be made.

Either way, things would work to the Intendant's advantage. They always did.

Meanwhile, the siege was proving profitable. The Commissary-General's men were collecting food from the farmers to provide rations for two thousand militiamen who had already deserted. This was being sold back to the farmers at huge prices. The Commissary-General, a base-born butcher's son called Joseph Cadet, was too greedy for his own good. Bigot had trained him, and elevated him to a grand position which allowed him to carry a dress sword instead of a meat-cleaver. Now he was even richer than Bigot, and stealing much too blatantly. But, then, Cadet didn't know how to live. He couldn't handle women like the sixty-year-old Intendant. *Mais non!*

Which reminded him, he must check on the building of the new bomb shelter at the house of Madame Péan. He had diverted several of the few remaining horses and carts to the project. She made demands, did his dear young mistress Angélique. He had given her a monopoly on flour and vegetable supplies and paid off her husband, the ungallant Major Péan, with a commission to buy and sell grain at a tremendous, assured profit. But she was well worth it — not too pretty, but gay and charming. She presided at the Intendant's court with the flair of a younger Pompadour.

With a lively step for a man of his years, Bigot headed for bed. As he left the cardroom he heard the rumble of cannon fire over to the west. The noise seemed to come from the French side of the river, a mile or so above the town. Bigot knew the area and the state of the French defenses. If M. Wolfe was trying to land there he stood a very good chance of success.

👑 ⚜

Duchambon de Vergor, a captain of the Canadian colonial marines, was a typical Bigot crony — a dull, uneducated petty crook, who had once done the Intendant a favor by saving him from the risk of a duel in a scandal involving an officer's wife.

As a reward, Bigot had taught him the rudiments of large-scale fraud. "Profit by your place, my dear Vergor", he had written. "Clip and cut — you are free to do as you please — so that you can come soon to France and buy an estate near me."

That was four years ago, when Vergor commanded the important French fort at Beauséjours on the neck of land leading to Nova Scotia. After selling off the bulk of the supplies sent from Quebec to feed the local people, he surrendered to the English before they had time to attack. He was courtmartialled for cowardice but acquitted, largely because Bigot removed some of the evidence against him and packed the court with his friends. Now he was back in Quebec, restored to his rank and ready for the principal act in his disreputable career. On the morning of September 13, he commanded the heights above the cove known as Anse au Foulon and guarded the vital pathway up the cliff.

He had been there only a few days. The Governor had sent him to replace a French regular officer, Captain St. Martin, who had been Montcalm's choice. He commanded, in theory, one hundred men; in fact, only thirty were there that morning. Capt. St. Martin had insisted that they stay at their post, but Vergor, in the Bigot tradition, allowed them to go home and work on their farms — on condition that once they had gathered their own harvests they would work, free, on Vergor's own farm.

While Montcalm was accustomed to sleep in his uniform and boots, Vergor preferred a nightshirt and bedsocks. He was comfortably tucked up in his tent on the clifftop when Wolfe's boats approached the cove below.

👑 ⚜

So the principal characters in the drama of Quebec passed the final hours before the battle . . . the hero, the soldier, the cynic, the fool, the knave and the coward.

And a thousand miles to the south the man who would eventually profit most from the outcome slept comfortably in his home at Mount Vernon, Virginia, with Martha, his bride of eight months. If he dreamed at all, it was probably of his new method of crop rotation. At 27, Colonel George Washington had put all thoughts of war behind him.

Chapter 2

The Rock

Even today, the Rock of Quebec is a daunting sight. When Wolfe first saw it from the river below it looked utterly impregnable.

On two sides blank gray cliffs glared at the intruder. They soared up to form the prow-shaped pinnacle of Cape Diamond with its frowning fortifications and rows of black-mouthed cannon. On the slopes behind sat a cluster of imposing stone buildings — palaces, convents and churches crowned by shining spires — and down along the St. Charles river, the humble homes and rickety warehouses of Lower Town were well guarded by shore batteries and floating gun platforms.

The Rock stood where the St. Lawrence narrowed, controlling the great waterway into the continent that led to the canoe routes through the lower Great Lakes to the Mississippi and down to Louisiana, or westward to Lake Superior and the vast, fur-rich hinterland. It guarded what was left of France's huge stake in North America, which had long exceeded the British nibblings along the eastern seaboard and the Spanish remnants in Florida.

It was the heart of Canada and had given the land its name. The original *Cannata* ("village" or "settlement" in the Iroquois-Huron language) was the Huron village of Stadaconé on the site of Lower Town, where Jacques Cartier, the first white explorer, wintered in 1535-36. In some unknown crevice in that rock lay the bones of Samuel de Champlain, sailor's son and royal geographer, who founded the first successful French settlement in 1608. He had sensed even then, from Cartier's reports and Indian tales, that Quebec, (from the Huron *Kebec*, "the narrowing place") was the key to all the vital water routes of North America. He planned to grasp the entire continent for France, and the only way to do it was by boat and canoe. It was impossible to travel any great distance on foot, through the dark, bewildering forests and choking bushlands.

So Champlain built his little *habitation* at Quebec — three two-storey wooden buildings surrounded by a palisade — on the waterfront at the foot of present-day Mountain Street. He was to spend the rest of his life defending it, expanding it, losing and regaining it. He made twenty-five weary voyages across the Atlantic in attempts to persuade the rulers of France that it was worth keeping, but found no enthusiasm there. France had made three previous efforts to colonize Cartier's discovery. Criminals had been sent out in chains, but even they refused to stay. The French court showed even less interest in Champlain's grand scheme than the English displayed in the efforts of their first starving settlers to win a foothold in the wilds of Virginia.

The merchants of Paris were interested only in the fur trade. Canada was a land populated by furry animals and so it should remain. Settlers drove away the animals and upset the trappers. So, over the years, a series of trading companies received monopolies over the fur trade, but deliberately refrained from sending the settlers their charters demanded.

Champlain founded Quebec with thirty-two colonists, four of whom had to be arrested, and one hanged, for plotting to kill him. When he died twenty-seven years later there were fewer than 300 whites in the whole of Canada. Yet in the same period the English colonies increased their population from near zero to nearly 7,000. This ratio of more than twenty English to one Frenchman was to remain about the same throughout the history of France in America.

Yet there *seemed* to be more French, because they moved about so much. While the English inched their way inland from the Atlantic, laboriously clearing the bush, hacking and planting, the French ranged the wilderness in thousand-mile sweeps, exploring, trapping, running wild with the Indians. Theirs was a new breed of man, as far removed from the narrow Norman or Breton peasant as from the gloomy, godly English colonial.

In the early years, few of them were rooted to one spot. The first truly determined settler was Jacques Hébert, physician and apothecary, who arrived in 1616. He led his family up the steep path to the summit of the Rock, where he had been granted 10 acres. They spent their first night under a tree, then began to build the first stone house in Canada, a single-storey structure thirty-eight feet long and nineteen feet wide. Around it, Hébert

The Rock of Quebec seen across the St. Lawrence from the south east, by J. F. W. DesBarres.
(Royal Ontario Museum, Toronto)

planted the apple trees and the vegetables that were to save his family and other colonists from starvation and scurvy.

Some time later he acquired a neighbor, Abraham Martin, known as Maître Abraham, a river pilot who cleared the plateau to the west of Hébert's farm and innocently gave his name to a battlefield.

But the younger men scorned this pretence at civilization. Rather than huddle in Champlain's wooden shacks, waiting the chance to pick a bride from among the poor, bewildered "daughters of the King" who were to be shipped over as breeding stock, most of them took to the woods. And while the English were nervously sharing corn and turkeys with the Indians, naked Frenchmen, daubed with paint, were cheerfully mating with squaws, roving and hunting in the terrifying but exhilarating freedom of the huge, cruel land.

These *coureurs de bois* were to be damned by the priests and outlawed by the authorities, but they were never crushed or brought back into "straight" society. Each spring they would appear at Quebec or the later settlements of Montreal and Three Rivers, their birch-bark canoes heavy with pelts. They would sell their cargo, drink, gamble and whore away their profits, then vanish again along the rivers, to spread new trails of debauchery across the continent.

The clergy were hot on their trail. In 1620 the first four Recollets landed at Quebec and Father Jean d'Olbeau celebrated the first mass heard in Canada. They paused just long enough to build a log cabin and an altar, then paddled forth to Indian country to save the savage souls. Father d'Olbeau, a frail figure with the pallor of the monastery cell still upon him, spent his first winter with the primitive Montagnais. He could not communicate with them; he was partly blinded by the stinking smoke of their loghouses, but he stayed.

The zest for discomfort of the gentle, gray-robed Recollets was only exceeded by the lust for martyrdom of the fiercely militant Jesuits who arrived later. In their way, the priests were as reckless as the *coureurs de bois*. Champlain, the dignified, goateed geographer, was reckless, too. With one musket shot he decided once and for all the allegiance of the Indian tribes in the French-English wars that would inevitably come. And he chose the wrong Indians.

The Hurons and Algonquins were his closest neighbors, roving the north bank of the St. Lawrence. They became middlemen in the fur trade, and were thus chosen to be bribed and cajoled into alliance with the French. To the south lay the territory of the Five Nation Iroquois confederacy, the most powerful and best-organized Indian empire of all. The *Ongue Honwe*, "Men of Men", guided by a workable democracy and ruled by a Great Immutable Law which declared all members to be free and equal, had maintained mastery of the seaboard since the time of the legendary Daganawidah and his successor, Hiawatha. They were taller and fiercer than the northern Indians. No man alone could defeat them — it took a man with a gun and a barrel of liquor.

Champlain made his great mistake in June, 1609. With two other Frenchmen and several dozen canoe-loads of Huron, Algonquin and Montagnais braves he advanced into Iroquois territory. Near Ticonderoga between Lake Champlain and Lake George, they met two hundred of the "Men of Men" in their distinctive elm-bark canoes.

Both sides landed and formed lines on the shore for a formal confrontation. Champlain put on his polished breastplate and a casque with a white plume. As the Iroquois chiefs stared curiously at this god-like figure, he set up his arquebus on its stand on the sandy ground, lit its slow fuse, pulled the trigger which connected fuse and breech powder, and fired the four bullets he had rammed into the muzzle.

That one shot killed two chiefs and felled a third. A second Frenchman fired and the astounded Iroquois fled, with the despised Hurons whooping in pursuit, relishing their new role as victors.

The sudden arrival of white gods with death-dealing fire sticks was something to be pondered by the Five Nations during interminable meetings in the smoky long-houses. The unwritten tale would endure for generations, and the Iroquois would remember. Later, when they, too, had fire-sticks, they would have their revenge. The Five Nations would remain enemies of France long after the Hurons had been wiped out and the Algonquins and Montagnais had ceased to count.

In 1620, Champlain built a stone citadel on the heights of Quebec to ward off Indian attacks. It was 120 feet long, with four turrets, and it so impressed two Iroquois braves who came to inspect it in the guise of a peace mission that no war parties followed. Yet the Rock's defenses were barely strong enough to repel warriors with bows and arrows and stone tomahawks. They could not withstand a well-armed attack.

In 1629, British privateer Captain David Kirke and his two brothers arrived in the St. Lawrence with letters of marque from Charles I instructing them to root out French settlements. Champlain had sixteen skinny men and 50 pounds of gunpowder with which to defend his colony. The original wooden buildings were leaky and sagging; the stone citadel was crumbling and two of its turrets had collapsed. Supply ships from France had been captured by the British and the colonists were chasing squirrels and picking seeds from Hébert's farm to keep alive. As the Kirkes anchored off Lower Town, Champlain surrendered and the British flag was raised for the first time. It was all done with the greatest politeness and, as both sides discovered later, this was just as well. Champlain went bird-shooting with the Kirkes on the river, then he and his colonists, now fattened by British salt pork, sailed for internment in England. The batteries he had so laboriously installed were fired for the first time — by British gunners, saluting the departure.

The Kirkes dropped anchor triumphantly in the Thames, preened themselves and stepped ashore to present their king with the glorious gift of Canada, its leader and most of its population, all in one shipload. Minutes later they learned that they were no heroes and probably pirates. Peace had been signed with France three months ago. Champlain went to the French embassy, demanding that his colony be restored.

He waited for three years. Then a thought entered the scheming head of Charles I — the head that was soon to be parted from the royal body in England's only republican revolution. He had dismissed his troublesome parliament and was thus unable legally to collect taxes. In his poverty he remembered that the French still owed him much of the dowry that was supposed to have come with his French wife, Henrietta Maria. For the equivalent of $240,000 cash he would return Quebec (which, according to the peace treaty, was not his anyway) plus the French colony of Acadia, which he had won in war.

The wily Cardinal Richelieu, who was now running France, knew a bargain when he saw one. $240,000 for most of the northern New World, plus the route to China which, everyone assumed, began just west of Lake Michigan. Done!

So, in 1633 Champlain sailed back to Quebec to reclaim his citadel and rebuild its fallen towers. He was now sixty-six, a worn old prisoner of his faith, his Rock and his dream of empire. His young wife, Hélène, had left him years before. After spending four winters in the harsh little settlement she had returned to France to enter a convent.

Still he labored on, planning campaigns against the English, the Iroquois and the Dutch on Manhattan Island. But no troops arrived from France to fight them. Nor did the shiploads of sturdy peasants he had hoped to lure over, to transform the fierce land from a hell of drunken savages and lecherous plunderers to a haven of peace and delight to his God. Only a trickle of colonists came.

He died on Christmas day, 1635, in a small room in his stone fort. His last view was of the bleak, gray ice below, clamping the Rock once again in the death grip of winter.

Quebec under siege, 1759. This picture is based on a sketch made by one of Wolfe's officers, Captain Hervey Smyth, aboard H. M. S. Vanguard.

(*The National Gallery of Canada, Ottawa*)

It was fitting that the founder of Quebec should be buried by black-robed Jesuit priests. For during his exile in England these diamond-hard soldiers of Christ had moved into Canada, elbowed out the milder Recollets, and taken over the spiritual life of the settlements and the conversion of the Indians.

Unlike the Recollets, a Franciscan order who worked among the poor, these were middle and upper-class Frenchmen, arrogant and fanatical, brave as the Iroquois and capable of in-credible feats of endurance. The early arrivals were the first in a series of supermen whose exploits shine through the fog of stupid-ity and corruption that clogs the history of New France.

Father Jean de Brébeuf, a lumbering giant of a man, be-gan missionary work among the Hurons, hoping that if they could all be converted, the faith would spread to the other Indian nations. "They are frightened by the torment of hell", he reported. "Enticed by the joys of paradise, they open their eyes to the light of truth . . . We have baptized more than 90". The Hurons listened to the zealous Black Gowns and were awed by their magical machines — a chiming clock and a magnifying glass. They could even command the moon in the heavens — as they proved by predicting an eclipse on the night of December 31, 1638. But they were never entirely welcome.

"It is the prayer that kills us", an old chief complained. "Before you came we were happy and prosperous; now your books and your strings of beads have bewitched the country. Your charms kill the corn and bring sickness and the Iroquois".

And they did bring the Iroquois, now armed with firesticks and loyal to the English and their West Indian rum. In 1648 they invaded the Huron country north of Lake Ontario and destroyed the Jesuit missions and the Huron nation.

Father Brébeuf was boiled, roasted, scorched and flayed for four hours before he died. His thin, sickly companion, Father Gabriel Lalemant, held out for eleven hours. The braves fought for the chance to eat the hearts of men who had died so well, then looked around for more.

More came. The letters sent home by the fathers, published in vellum in the Jesuit *Relations* started a wave of missionary fervor in France that brought more priests, then Ursuline nuns, frail and pallid, but immensely courageous and ripe for suffering. Many died, but by 1665 — when young Louis XIV subdued the Iroquois by sending "one good regiment of infantry" out from France — one quarter of the population of Quebec (550) consisted of priests and nuns. New France was taking its peculiar shape.

It was now a crown colony, governed by a troika system that would remain, despite its inherent weakness and confusion, until the English conquest. The system merits examination, since it had much to do with Wolfe's victory. The governor commanded the army, the intendant controlled the finances and the administration of justice, and the bishop ruled the Church. All these functions overlapped, and the functionaries quarrelled constantly.

For 29 years, God was represented by Bishop Francois de Laval-Montmorency, fanatic and tyrant, whose long, lugubrious face hid a scholarly mind tinged with mysticism. He spent his nights praying on the clammy floor of his cathedral or sleeping in flea-bitten squalor. During the day he preached holy war against the Iroquois who, he had decided, could achieve salvation quicker by fire than by holy water.

The King's man, Governor Saffray de Mézy, was soon outwitted by the Bishop, who tricked him into holding a form of democratic election to oust three of the Bishop's men from the colonial council. Louis, the Sun King, would tolerate no such democratic nonsense. De Mézy died just in time to avoid humiliation before the King, having first confessed his sins to his holy opponent.

While the Bishop and the Governor were locked in combat, the representative of Mammon, Intendant Jean Talon, stamped his imprint forever upon the colony. The Great Intendant was a pleasant, soft-faced young man with a twirly mustache and a well-ordered bureaucratic brain.

He saw to it that all dogs were locked up by nine p.m. and all chimneys regularly swept. He supervised the handing out of the King's bounty (20 livres as a wedding present to youths of twenty or under and girls of sixteen or under, and pensions of 300 livres a year for producing ten children); he also collected fines from fathers who had not married off their daughters by the age of sixteen or their sons by twenty.

These financial blandishments, plus the efforts of the priests to encourage procreation, were the foundations of the staggering birthrate of French Canada, which was to continue for three hundred years.

Talon tried to put the colony on a business footing. He started small industries — the production of tar, woollen cloth and shoes. He built a ship to show the Canadians how it was done. He founded a brewery, and taxed imported wines from France. The Jesuits declared beer to be "wholesome and not injurious", and to this day Quebec remains largely a beer-drinking area. He was less successful in enforcing the King's rule that only dark brown bread be baked and eaten. Louis thought it was more nutritious than other breads, although he didn't touch it himself and the colonists shared his distaste for it.

It was, and remained, a totalitarian state, under Louis' policy of "One King, one Law, one Faith". Farmers were ordered to stay on their farms, under pain of a fifty livres fine and confiscation of all their goods. Nobody could go back to France without per-

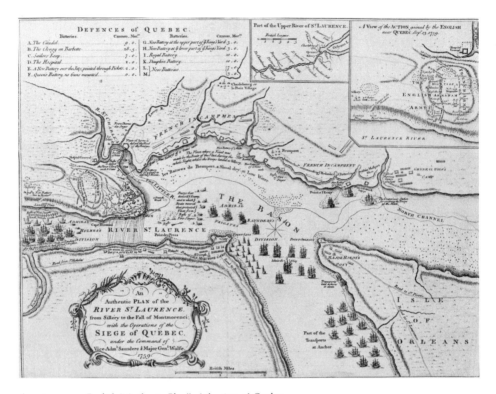

A contemporary English "Authentic Plan" of the siege of Quebec.

(Archives Nationales du Québec)

mission, which was seldom granted. No resident could drink at a local tavern and no farmer could own more than two horses and one foal. Blasphemy was punished on an ascending scale — the pillory for the fifth *"Sacre bleu"*, branding for the sixth and seventh, while the offender's tongue was cut out after the eighth. All books other than approved religious works were banned. All work was forbidden on Sundays or the many church holidays and saints' days.

The energetic Intendant was always at the dockside when the King's Daughters arrived from France. He examined each one to make sure she was "free from any natural blemish or anything personally repulsive."

As many as 150 would arrive in a shipload. They were mostly peasant girls from the country districts in the west of France, broad-beamed with strong legs and backs. The prettier but fragile city girls were scorned. All had been certified as spinsters by their local priests before embarkation. The few previously-married ones who were caught were whipped, or half-drowned on the ducking stool, and then sent home.

They staggered weakly off the ships, dressed in their poor best — the hooded woollen cloaks in which they had survived the voyage. They had no silks or whalebone stays.

The young men gathered in a tense crowd on the wharf in their wool hats and red home-woven coats, ready to choose their brides and be married on the spot. Each couple was entitled to an ox and a cow, a pair of chickens, two barrels of salted meat and eleven gold crowns. The wife became the husband's property; she could claim a separation only if he beat her with a stick thicker than his wrist. If a King's Daughter refused marriage, or was passed over as too repulsive she would be consigned to domestic service for the rest of her despised life. But if she missed her chance at Quebec she could be shipped upriver to Three Rivers or Montreal, to try her luck there.

The Baron de Lahontan described the selection process about 1665: "Several ships were sent hither from France with a Cargo of Women of an ordinary reputation under the direction of some old stale Nuns who ranged them in three classes. The Vestal Virgins were heap'd up (if I may so speak) one above another in three different apartments, where the bridegrooms singled out their brides, just as a butcher does a ewe from amongst a flock of sheep . . . the fattest went off best, upon the apprehension that these, being less active, would keep truer to their engagements and hold out better against the nipping cold of the winter . . . the officers, having a nicer taste than the soldiers, made their application to the daughters of the ancient gentlemen of the country, or those of the richer sort of inhabitants."

So the good seed was sown and scattered throughout the angry land. Beyond the little towns and the lonely farms, the wilderness beckoned. The Indians formed new alliances and plotted eternal vengeance. And the *coureurs de bois* roamed ever farther, rotting the tribes with cheap French brandy before the late-coming English got at them with their cheap West Indian rum.

When de Lahontan wrote his account there were as many *coureurs* as settlers in Canada. A few were captured and sent to slave in the King's galleys and at least one was hanged, but succeeding governors, intendants and bishops never brought them to heel. The government, swayed one way by the priests who were losing converts to the grape, and the other by the businessmen who lost furs without it, alternately banned and authorised the sale of brandy.

The great governor Louis de Buade, Comte de Frontenac, fought with Bishop Laval over the brandy question and was accused of being in league with the *coureurs*. In a way, he was. For in Frontenac was reborn the spirit of Champlain — the urge to seek out and possess the continent's waterways for France.

He arrived with a flourish in 1672, sweeping ashore in scarlet and gray, his wig perfectly curled below a dashing, wide-brimmed hat, his imperious jaw cleaving the air before him. The Indians, the nobles, and the settlers recognized at once that here was a man of strength. The Iroquois chiefs were shocked and resentful when he summoned them to a council and called them his children instead of brothers. But they came and were awed by the mighty figure who sat on a gilded chair beneath a great white and gold banner, smoked the peace pipe and spoke the flowery language they understood. They called him Onontio, their father, and for a time they ceased their attempts to divert the fur trade to the English.

Frontenac encouraged supermen. He supported Daniel Greysolon, Sieur Du Lhut, known as King of the Woodsmen, in the western forays that were to give his name to the city of Duluth, Minnesota. He listened to Robert Cavalier, Sieur de la Salle, who planned a line of forts along the entire length of the Mississippi to the western sea that he expected to find at the river's mouth. With the governor's help La Salle reached his "western sea" which was actually the Gulf of Mexico, raised a cross and royal flag and claimed the territory of Louisiana which extended as far west as the explorer's mind could imagine. Like most of New France, Louisiana was a vision, a shaded area on a vague map, never to be properly occupied or colonised by Frenchmen. But in 1687, five years after he planted his cross, the determined La Salle returned in an attempt to found a colony. He was murdered by one of his own men and left to the buzzards under the open skies of what is now Texas. The rest of his colonists died of heat or malaria or were killed by Indians.

Although La Salle claimed about a third of the continent and is justly famed, an equal role was played by two ragged rascals in a canoe — Médard Chouart, Sieur des Groseilliers (Squire of the Gooseberries) and his brother-in-law, Pierre Radisson. They discovered the fur treasury of the great north-west and effectively founded both the giant British Hudson's Bay Company and its French opposition, *La Compagnie du Nord*.

"We were Caesars, being nobody to contradict us", Radisson wrote. And so they were, although both the British and the French swindled them and they changed allegiance with dizzying frequency.

They paddled their canoe the length of Lake Superior and northward to the fringes of Hudson Bay, returning to Quebec with a heavy load of pelts and tales of immense profits to be made. But the governor of the time, Sieur d'Avagour, inspired by the Jesuits' hatred of *coureurs de bois* and his own greed, arrested the pair and confiscated most of their cargo.

That one act of quasi-religious thievery brought about the birth of a British empire in the north-west. Radisson and Groseilliers took their tale, first to the New England colonists and then to Charles II in London. Groseilliers, in the Nonsuch, sailed through Hudson Strait into the Bay and brought back nineteen thousand pounds worth of furs. Impressed, the King chartered the Governor and Company of Adventurers of England, Trading into Hudson's Bay (1670) which was to become one of the world's most profitable businesses. But Radisson and Groseilliers, the real foundders, got little more than a gold chain and a medal apiece. So they went to France and helped to found a French company to challenge the new British "Lords of the North."

Radisson captured a British fur ship and was cheered as a hero in Quebec. But the priests had not forgiven him, Frontenac had been recalled and the new governor, Le Febvre de Barré, fined him and sent him back to France. Groseilliers disappeared to his gooseberry patch at Three Rivers and Radisson turned his coat for the fourth time. He rejoined the Hudson's Bay Company, became a shareholder, and led profitable voyages until he died in London, aged 76.

Like most of the supermen he had been baffled and defeated by stupidity in Quebec and Versailles. The British colonists of the period had no heroes to match Champlain, Du Lhut, La Salle, the valiant Jesuits, Frontenac and their successors such as d'Iberville and de la Mothe-Cadillac, founder of Detroit. But they had numbers — 200,000, compared to 10,000 Canadians — and they had the Iroquois. While Frontenac languished uselessly in Paris,

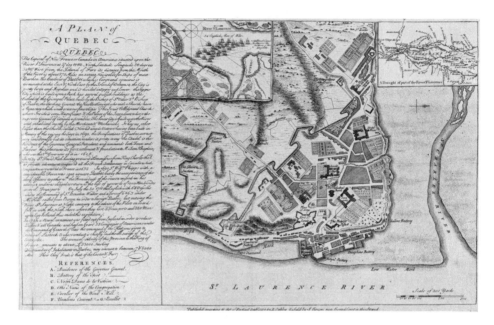

A detailed plan of the city of Quebec "Published according to Act of Parliament October 1759."
The accompanying caption reads, in part: "The Upper city which is built upon a rock has sev-
eral publick buildings . . . which would grace our finest cities . . . . The Fortifications of
Quebec are not very considerable, but its situation renders it pretty strong."

(Archives Nationales du Québec)

having lost a power struggle with Bishop Laval, fifteen hundred
warriors massacred the inhabitants of Lachine and terrorized Montreal. One hundred and twenty prisoners were carried away to the
torture stakes. The Montreal garrison troops panicked and refused
to fight. The western Indian tribes showed signs of joining the
Iroquois to wipe out New France. With the colony in danger, bick-
ering over religion and brandy ceased. The King sent Frontenac
back to save the situation.

He was seventy years old, but fierce and domineering
as ever, when he returned to the Rock in 1689. England and France
were at war once more, so he decided to strike directly at the New
Englanders, whom he blamed for the Iroquois uprising.

In the dead of winter, three war parties of untamed
Christian Indians and half-wild *coureurs* padded through the snows
to invade New York, New Hampshire and Maine. The raids were
brutally successful.

In the little town of Schenectady, thirty-eight men, ten
women and twelve children were carved to pieces by tomahawk

and scalping-knife, while all the buildings were burned.

"You cannot believe", Frontenac wrote, "the joy that this slight success has caused, and how much it contributes to raise the people from their dejection and terror." The raids restored the Indians' respect for old Onontio, their father. But they convinced the disunited, quarrelsome British colonists that they must destroy Canada or be destroyed. So began the series of wars that would last for seventy years.

On October 16, 1690, a second fleet of ships flying the British flag dropped anchor in the river off Quebec. Sir William Phips, a ship's carpenter who had struck it rich by salvaging a million dollars from a wrecked Spanish treasure ship, had brought thirty-four vessels and two thousand men up the St. Lawrence to challenge the old governor in his lair.

A junior officer, sent ashore under a flag of truce, was blindfolded and led through Lower Town, up Mountain Street to the stone fort on the heights. There, in the governor's reception room, his blindfold was removed and he faced the great men of New France.

They wore their richest silks and finest lace but below the powdered wigs, their hard, lined faces told of their violent life in the wilderness, and well-used swords jutted out below their flared, velvet coats. Six of the mighty Le Moyne brothers were there, including d'Iberville, who would complete the work of La Salle. Nicholas Perrot, voyageur and chronicler of the north-west stood beside Du Lhut, king of the *coureurs*, and the Marquis de Vaudreuil, father of Wolfe's opponent.

"The men were dressed so splendidly" the subaltern later reported "that it made small difference taking the cloth from my eyes. I was dazzled by looking at them." Most splendid of all was the old governor. He glared savagely at the awed messenger and threw his demand for surrender on the floor. "I will answer your general only by the mouths of my cannon", he declared.

The New Englanders landed on the Beauport shore, intending to cross the St. Charles river and storm Lower Town, while their ships bombarded the city. But the defenders, led by Ste. Hélène Le Moyne, held them at the river and Frontenac's cannon drove back the ships. After three days, Phips gave up and retired downriver. He had expected a quick and easy victory like that of the Kirke brothers and he lacked the stamina and the supplies needed for a siege.

Worse than that, he had underestimated the quality of the French leaders. He had challenged the supermen at the peak of their strength. In twenty years they would all be gone and New France would not find their like again. Future attackers would discover that the awesome Rock was only as strong as the spirit of the men who defended it.

Chapter 3

Braddock's Chest

Robert Stobo was not quite a gentleman, but definitely a man of substance. He rode to war with ten personal servants, a squad of hunters and a covered wagon containing 300 guineas worth of personal equipment, including a 126-gallon butt of madeira.

He wore a newly-tailored blue coat, faced with scarlet and trimmed with silver, a scarlet waistcoat and blue breeches. At his belt was a new sword, chased with gold, and in his saddlebag lay a copy of Humphrey Bland's "A Treatise of Military Discipline."

It was spring, 1754, and 27-year-old Captain Stobo was enjoying his first command. Behind him straggled his company of the Provincial Virginia Regiment — fifty rangy farm boys, all without uniforms and some without shoes or shirts. He had been given the company by his distant relative Robert Dinwiddie, Lieutenant-Governor of Virginia, a man whose motives he well understood; for they were both sons of Glasgow merchants.

Stobo had arrived in the colony in his teens and established a sound business in Petersburg, importing from Scotland useful everyday items like cloth, tools, and kitchenware, and Indian trading goods such as mirrors, laced hats and jew's harps. Now he was off to fight the Canadians and, while he was about it, reap some profit from the development of the Ohio wilderness.

Dinwiddie had similar ideas on a grander scale. He had begun as a customs clerk and advanced in His Majesty's service to become chief officer of the oldest, largest and most comfortable of the North American colonies. (There was a Governor of Virginia, but he governed in name only: he lived in England and took no interest in the colony).

Despite his sixty-one years, Dinwiddie was still too dourly aggressive to waste time relaxing in the pleasures of Williamsburg — the dancing, drinking, gambling and gaiety so abhorrent to the Puritans up north. He believed the Canadians were determined to occupy the frontier lands to the north-west, and for reasons patriotic and commercial he intended to drive them out.

He had promoted the Ohio Company of Virginia, an "association of gentlemen" which had received a Crown grant giving vague title to half a million acres in the Ohio valley. The associates included prominent Virginians such as the Lees, the Washingtons, and Dinwiddie himself.

Six months earlier he had sent the adjutant-general of his militia, 21-year-old Major George Washington to order the Canadians off the land. The major had ridden through the snows of Pennsylvania to a Canadian fort on the Allegheny river and politely requested "the peaceable departure" of the garrison. The commandant had been polite, too, (England and France were, for the moment, at peace) but had not departed.

Now Dinwiddie was sending Washington back with all the militiamen he could raise — about 150 out of 170,000 free, white Virginians — and orders to establish a presence, build a fort and defend it.

The scene was set for the opening of the final struggle between the stay-at-home British colonists and the roving Canadians. As Horace Walpole later put it "a volley fired by a young Virginian in the backwoods of America set the world on fire." Washington fired the famous volley at a Canadian patrol near Fort Duquesne (now Pittsburgh). It killed ten men, including the French leader Coulon de Jumonville, and brought on the counter attack by a much larger Canadian force that led to Washington's surrender at Great Meadows. He was allowed to march home with the remnants of his men. But first he had to sign a surrender document admitting to *"l'assassinat du Sieur de Jumonville"*. Washington, who knew no French, thought he was agreeing that Jumonville had been killed — not murdered — but the words would return to haunt him in the wars ahead.

Captain Robert Stobo carried the surrender papers over to the Canadian lines. He had volunteered to remain as hostage for ten weeks until Washington returned twenty-one Canadian prisoners. With him went a French-speaking Dutchman, Captain Jacob Van Braam, loosely draped in a splendid uniform he had just purchased from Washington for twenty-five pounds. (Van Braam was

The young George Washington, painted by Stearns. "A volley fired by a young Virginian in the backwoods of America set the world on fire."

(Public Archives of Canada)

fairly tall, but came nowhere near Washington's six foot three inches).

As the Virginians never did return the Canadian prisoners, Stobo and Van Braam were to spend the next five years in Canada. And Stobo would re-appear to play a mysterious role in the final drama of Quebec.

Washington's defeat led to the first attempt to bring about a union of the thirteen colonies. A convention met at Albany in June 1754, but only seven colonies bothered to send representatives. A delegate from Pennsylvania named Benjamin Franklin offered what he called "short hints" on how to achieve a confederation, which he felt was essential to hold back the authoritarian power of Canada. The colonies, he felt, must be bound together by an Act of the British Parliament so that none would be free to secede. The suggestion failed. (More than a century later, the Canadian provinces would adopt it as the basis of their nationhood under the British North America Act.)

As the battle lines were drawn between the English and French colonists, there were incredible miscalculations on all sides. The thirteen colonies now had a population of more than 1,500,000, including about 200,000 slaves; the total white population of New France, including the Louisiana settlements, was less than 80,000. There were 200,000 white Americans of military age, compared to about 20,000 Canadians. Yet the majority of Indian chiefs, viewing the adaptability and venturesome spirit of the Canadians, gambled on them to win. The leaders in Quebec were confident before and after the Albany convention that the American rabble could never agree on anything. And the gouty courtiers in London and Paris decided that the battles of the backwoods could best be fought by traditional European methods. Both England and France sent out regular armies, and both armies were defeated by the country and its natives.

Major General Edward Braddock was a model Guards officer — short, rubicund, obstinate and fearless. He arrived in Virginia with 1,000 magnificently-disciplined redcoats, collected the best of the blue-coated Virginians, and marched off stoutly into the woods. He followed Washington's route to Fort Duquesne and took Washington along as staff officer and guide. But where the Virginian had slipped through the trees, Braddock's fine force needed a roadway for its gun-carriages, wagon train and herd of cattle. Three hundred axemen went ahead, hacking a twelve-foot wide path. It took eight days to cover the first twenty miles, 32 to reach Fort Duquesne.

Drums rolled and bugles screeched as the army forded the Monongahela in parade-ground formation. Discipline was everything to Braddock. From the woods ahead, the first hail of musket-fire hit them. Six hundred Indians with one hundred and fifty Canadians and seventy-five French Regulars were behind trees, sniping at the resplendent red and white targets.

The fall of Braddock. The end of a model Guards officer. Engraved by J. B. Allen, New York 1859.

(Public Archives of Canada)

Braddock stormed up and down his ranks, lining his men up stiff and straight, beating them with his sword when they tried to take cover. For two hours he refused to retreat while his men fell in heaps around him and four horses were killed beneath him. He was rearing up on his fifth, still waving his sword and cursing, when a bullet brought him down. He died muttering "We shall better know how to deal with them another time."

Washington led the remains of the army homeward. The Canadians captured General Braddock's military chest, which contained the British plans for the North American campaign. They showed that the next move would be an attack by colonial troops on Crown Point, the French fort commanding the Lake Champlain water route between the St. Lawrence and New England. With the plans was a drawing of Fort Duquesne and a letter describing conditions in the fort and how it could best be attacked. It was signed by Robert Stobo, the hostage Washington had left behind a year before, and had obviously been smuggled out to the British. It would bring Stobo a death sentence for spying.

The French Regular army — 3,000 whitecoats led by the German general Baron Dieskau — landed at Quebec while Braddock was marching to his doom at Fort Duquesne. Like Braddock, the Baron was accustomed to handling seasoned troops and marching them in straight lines. From what he had heard in Europe, the English colonials were pacifist, hymn-singing farmers, useless in war. They lacked both the discipline of the regular and the savagery of the woodsman.

"The more there are", he declared, "the more we shall kill." When news reached him of the war plans found in Braddock's chest, he embarked his force in canoes and hurried to Crown Point to surprise the attackers when they arrived.

They arrived late. It had taken the Massachusetts governor William Shirley all spring and part of the summer to get five New England contingents together. The five legislatures had provided the money for the force, and each wanted a share in the command. The newly-created general, William Johnson of New York, had harangued his Iroquois allies for four days before throwing down the war belt and pouring out the King's rum. When the wardances were over, only 300 Indians actually took to the warpath.

They were given long sermons, translated into Mohawk, one of which took the text "Love thine enemies". While the Indians puzzled over that, the colonial militia divided their time between prayer and drill.

"We are a wicked, profane army", wrote Colonel Ephraim Williams. "Especially the New York and Rhode Island troops. Nothing is to be heard among a great part of them except the language of Hell. If Crown Point is taken it will not be for our sakes, but for those good people left behind."

Late in August, 1755, the expedition began hacking its way through the woods to Lake George. Dieskau, impatient for battle, moved in to meet and ambush them. His first volleys from the trees crumpled the leading regiment and sent the column reeling back to the barricades of a small fort they had built. The Baron left the safety of the woods and attacked the barricades. Hit twice in the leg, he sat down behind a tree a short distance from the American line, refusing to be carried to the rear. To his surprise, his force was routed and he was captured.

The American militia, he said, fought like good boys in the morning, like men at noon and like devils in the afternoon. Like Braddock, he had learned something new about war; but, like Braddock, he would not be able to use the knowledge. He was taken to New York and escorted in gentlemanly fashion aboard a ship bound for Europe.

For, despite the slaughter in the forests, England and France were not yet officially at war.

After his victory, Johnson fell into the sort of lassitude that seemed to afflict every commander who won a North American battle. No one pushed on after a defeated enemy to wipe him out. This was not because of French gallantry or British sportsmanship; the Indian allies had to satisfy their greed for scalps, which they obtained from the wounded, the dead and the already-buried.

Johnson's excuse was that his men were tired, sick and discontented. In fact, five hundred of them had yet to fire a shot. The general himself was sick and the militia organization had collapsed once again. The officers, chosen by democratic election, could not maintain discipline. Johnson compared them to "heads of a mob." By mid-October, the army was still at Lake George and the men were freezing in their summer clothes. The officers held a council of war and decided to go home for Thanksgiving. So Johnson's militia melted away, insulting their colonels as they left. It was the American way.

The half-victory was celebrated in a 1756 poem entitled "The Christian Hero, or New England's Triumphs", designed "Chiefly to Animate and Rouse the Soldiers": —

> *Their Dieskau we from them detain,*
> *While Canada aloud complains*
> *   And counts the number of their slain*
> *And makes a dire complaint;*
> *   The Indians to their demon gods;*
> *And with the French there's little odds*
> *   While images receive their nods,*
> *Invoking rotten saints.*

Defeat ran in Vergor's family. His father, Governor Duchambon, had commanded the supposedly invincible fortress of Louisbourg and had managed to lose it to the New Englanders in 1745. Vergor had been with his father at the time and had learned that surrender was not the end of everything. He had studied graft and corruption at the feet of the master, Bigot, who was then Intendant at Louisbourg. He learned how to charge the King for non-existent supplies purchased, while selling off the actual supplies sent by the King. He knew how to profit from the miseries of the Acadians — the French colonists of what is now Nova Scotia. Food sent to them from Quebec would vanish on the way. With cheerful cynicism luxury items such as damasks and satins were bought at great cost to the King for shipment to the starving Acadians, who, of course, never saw them. The Bigot ring would buy them up for next to nothing and send them back to Quebec to be sold at their real value.

Vergor was not particularly bright, but he mastered the Bigot system and Bigot liked him. So he was given command of Fort Beauséjours at the neck of the Acadian peninsula, and with it, the Intendant's advice "Profit by your place, my dear Vergor . . ."

The fort was the strongest French position left in Acadia, which was now nominally under British rule. The colony had been founded by Champlain four years before he reached Quebec and had been shuttled back and forth between the British and French flags for more than a century. The English took it in 1613, handed it back in 1697 and got it back in 1713. The 9,000 Acadians kept their language and Roman Catholic religion, but remained miserable pawns in the diplomatic games played between Paris and London. By 1755 most of them had made their crosses under a conditional oath of allegiance to King George, but their priests told them these marks were meaningless. The Abbé Joseph Louis Le Loutre threatened them with slow death at the Indian torture stake, followed by eternal perdition, if they forsook France. This violent fanatic kept small bands of Indians and Acadians at constant war with the surrounding English. He offered 100 livres for each English scalp and recorded payments of 11,000 livres for scalps over two years. The Abbé presided personally at scalpings, tracing the path the knife should follow on the victim's head. When a punitive English expedition drove him out of his church at Beaubassin he burned it and the village, and led his flock to Fort Beauséjours.

He was there, terrifying the easily-terrified Captain Vergor, when the English attacked the fort.

Two thousand New Englanders and a few British regulars, all led by Brigadier Robert Monckton, landed unopposed and began a leisurely preliminary bombardment. One shell fell through the roof of a "bomb-proof" shelter, killing six French officers at breakfast. This so alarmed Vergor and Le Loutre, who were sitting in the next shelter, that they promptly raised the white flag.

EXILE OF THE ACADIANS FROM GRAND PRE.

The expulsion of the Acadians: "the affair looks odd."

(Public Archives of Canada)

Monckton hid his surprise and contemptuously accepted the surrender. Le Loutre escaped in disguise and Vergor, his nerve restored, entertained Monckton to supper while his Canadian officers drank and looted their way through the storerooms. Two years later he faced a court martial for cowardice, but Bigot arranged an acquittal.

The unfortunate Acadians did not get off so lightly. They had been a conquered people for a generation, and most of them had grown up under the British flag, but they showed no signs of settling down.

Governor Charles Lawrence of Nova Scotia summoned their elected delegates to Halifax and demanded that they take a new, unconditional oath of allegiance. They refused. "Then", said Lawrence, "you are no longer subjects of the King of England but of the King of France. You will be treated as such and removed from the country."

Throughout the summer and fall of 1755 the Acadians were summoned to their churches and surrounded by English bayonets. The young men were taken from their families and prodded aboard the ships that waited for them. The older people followed when the ships were ready to sail. It was a long drawn-out, wailing process that wracked the emotions of the soldiers who carried it out. The New England colonel John Winslow wrote to Monckton that the affair "looks odd, and will appear so in future history."

There is no record of Monckton's reply. The 28-year-old Irishman wrote as little as possible, for he was barely literate. He conducted the operation without remorse or enthusiasm; to him all colonials, French or English, were insignificant.

By the end of the year about 6,000 Acadians had been carried off to be distributed among the English colonies down the Atlantic coast. The rest had joined guerrilla bands in the bush, or made their way to Canada.

The English colonies did not welcome the stinking shiploads of bothersome Roman Catholics. Virginia, South Carolina and Georgia rejected them outright and shipped their consignments off to England. New England divided them into tiny groups and scattered them as widely as possible to dilute the contamination of popery.

Many of those shipped south wandered the long road to Louisiana to find fellow-Frenchmen. Others reached Quebec, and some eventually returned to what had been Acadia. Nowhere were they well received. The English were hostile and the French indifferent.

The Acadians faded away. The name itself is now half-forgotten. But for Longfellow's poem "Evangeline" and the Louisiana word "Cajun" it might be gone entirely. They were gentle peasants, not as adventurous as the Canadians. They were never a menace to anybody; only a nuisance. A later generation of New Englanders would shed tears over Longfellow's version of the Acadian tragedy, but the colonists of the period thought they were well treated in the circumstances. At least they escaped being butchered and eaten like the Scotch-Irish and German frontier families of Pennsylvania, Maryland and Virginia.

While the French were losing Acadia and Baron Dieskau, their Indian allies were chewing the fruits of their victory over Braddock. They howled, unchallenged, along the Ohio frontier, torturing and burning the settlers who did not escape in time. In the space of three days, Washington counted three hundred wagons fleeing east, and the road Braddock had built through the forest was soon beaten flat by moccasined feet. Canadian officers accompanied the Indians. They were given impossible orders to prevent the torture of prisoners while encouraging the war parties to destroy English settlements. The result was horror. Children were scalped alive; women raped and mutilated. Often the men escaped: they would be out in the woods, hunting deer or wild turkey to feed their families until their dismal little clearing in the bush could support a crop. They would come home to find a burned-out cabin and the mangled remains of a wife and children.

"It is really very shocking", a settler wrote to the Governor of Pennsylvania, "for the husband to see the wife of his bosom, her head cut off and the children's blood drunk like water by these bloody and cruel savages."

Captain Jean Daniel Dumas, commandant of Fort Duquesne reported in July, 1756: "I have succeeded in ruining the three adjacent provinces, Pennsylvania, Maryland and Virginia, driving off the inhabitants and totally destroying the settlements over a tract of country thirty leagues wide . . . I had six or seven different war-parties in the field at once, always accompanied by Frenchmen." So many scalps were brought in to the fort that it took him eight days to hand out the payments for them.

The raiders came within fifty miles of Philadelphia — at that time the largest English-speaking city in the world, after London — yet the Quaker leaders of that city believed that it was a sin to fight, particularly against Indians and in defense of Presbyterian and Catholic settlers. Quaker preachers took to the streets, denouncing war, while a cartload of freshly-killed settlers' bodies was dumped in front of the Assembly building.

Farms were burned sixty miles from Boston and along the borders of Georgia and the Carolinas, but still the colonies could not agree on a common defense. Those in the South were afraid to send their men off to war in case their black slaves or indentured whites rebelled at home. Maryland, which had refused to raise troops because of the expense, responded to the murder of its people by offering 50 pounds for the scalp of any enemy male Indian over the age of ten.

Apart from Washington and his Virginia regiment of 1,000 (later 1,500) men, there was no one to stop the massacre. And the regiment consisted mainly of sullen malcontents who resented any form of discipline because they felt it infringed upon the liberty of free white men and put them on the level of the Negroes.

Washington wrote to Governor Dinwiddie describing the plight of the settlers: "The supplicating tears of the women and moving petitions of the men melt me into such deadly sorrow that I solemnly declare, if I know my own mind, I could offer myself as a willing sacrifice to the butchering enemy, providing that would contribute to the people's ease."

The killing went on until there were few frontier families left.

👑 ✳

War between England and France became official in the spring of 1756. It was part of a complex European entanglement that began in the blue and gold boudoir of the Marquise de Pompadour's summer home at Bellevue.

Frederick the Great of Prussia had drawn upon himself the wrath of three mighty women — the Pompadour, mistress of Louis XV of France, Elizabeth, Czarina of Russia, and Maria Theresa, Empress of Austria. He had sneered at Madame de Pompadour's bourgeois origins ("I do not know her — this is not the land for swains and shepherdesses") and named his lapdog Pompadour. He had made venomous jokes about the Czarina's fondness for sturdy guardsmen and he had seized Catholic Silesia from the pious Catholic Empress of Austria. So when the Austrian Ambassador arrived in the Pompadour's boudoir with instructions to flatter her outrageously, she soon agreed to promote an alliance between France and Austria. Frederick sent his ambassador to flatter her even more, but he only succeeded in boring her, and the friendless Prussian king had to settle for a pact with his hated uncle, George II of England.

By October the Seven Years War was under way, with England and Prussia ranged against France, Austria, Russia, Saxony and Sweden.

The alliance and the war were to be disastrous for France. Although this was by no means the fault of the Pompadour alone, she was the one who collected the blame from the perfumed cynics of Versailles and the rabble of Paris. It was eleven years since

Madame de Pompadour, the real ruler of France. When he visited Paris, Wolfe found her "extremely handsome."

(Public Archives of Canada)

she had first seduced the virile Louis after the Ball of the Clipped Yew Trees in the great gallery of the Palace of Versailles. At the ball she and the King had been seen together, unmasked and happily giggling, and after it her carriage had been observed still parked indiscreetly outside the palace at eight in the morning. She had progressed from a small flat in the private sector of the palace, linked to the King's private room by a secret staircase, to a huge apartment on the ground floor, crammed with her art treasures, her pets and her collection of china animals. It also contained 58 servants and the red-lacquered office in which she conducted the King's diplomacy.

About five years later she had given up hope of satisfying Louis in bed. She pleaded ill-health and religious duties and passively watched him perform his public going-to-bed ceremony in his huge draughty bedroom, ill-heated by a smoky fire, then patter off barefoot in his nightshirt to his private brothel at the villa Parc aux Cerfs, from which he would return in time for his public rising ceremony in the morning. But in those active years she had become more than an overused sex object; she had become a power behind the throne. The King's enemies called her the real ruler of France.

She was now 35, still attractive but aging beyond her years. She could act, sing and dance, paint and play the clavichord;

she was amusing, while Louis' real Queen, who had learned to accept her, was dull. While the courtiers spread vicious "Fish" stories, based on her name, Jeanne-Antoinette Poisson, she used the fish symbol proudly on her plate. Her position was unassailable, because she preserved the King from boredom — the one spectre that haunted the resolutely merry woodland court; mysteriously, Louis turned yellow when bored.

But clever as she was, she remained a woman who could be charmed and cajoled by attractive and attentive men. And her influence upon the war, exerted in the long, peaceful afternoons with Louis in the red-lacquered room and the even longer days when he was out killing stags, was often disastrous. She picked ministers and generals according to her personal likes and dislikes and their ability to amuse the King. Bigot, she felt, must be a good intendant because he was such an amiable, ugly man.

She took little interest in North America, and when the war began her favorites all sought the glamorous commands in Europe. There was no rush for Baron Dieskau's job on a distant front which was now, more than ever, a sideshow. So the choice of a successor was left to the Minister of War. He chose a soldier — Montcalm.

At first, the soldier was reluctant to go. He carried on his short, rolling frame five sabre scars and a large musket wound, relics of thirty years' service. He had just spent the seven happiest years of his life, resting with his family at Candiac.

Angélique-Louise tried to persuade him to evade the appointment. She was related to Talon, the great intendant, and had heard family tales of the hazards and corruption of Canada. But Montcalm's tough old mother, the Marquise de St. Véran, would not hear of such nonsense. When a King spoke (or his minister, or his mistress) the Montcalms obeyed.

The Marquis hesitated, but only for a moment. Soon he was planning his departure. He would wear his embroidered coat with new badges of rank as major-general. The King had promised him 25,000 livres a year, the same pay as Baron Dieskau, and 12,000 livres for his equipment. He read a book about Quebec by the Jesuit historian Pierre Charlevoix who gave "a pleasant account". And he made his will.

He was pleased with his staff. As second-in-command he had Gaston François, Chevalier de Lévis, an impressive figure

The Chevalier de Lévis, second-in-command of Montcalm's forces. "I like him", said Montcalm, "and I think he likes me".

(Archives Nationales du Québec)

of tremendous pedigree. The Lévis family, supposedly descended from the tribe of Levi, was older than France; a remote ancestor even claimed direct descent from the Virgin Mary. The Chevalier, aged thirty-six, was gentle, unaffected and capable, if not brilliant. "I like him" said Montcalm "and I think he likes me."

The third officer was Colonel François Charles Bourlamaque, a quiet reserved man of Italian descent whom Montcalm described as "steady and cool, with good parts." As first aide-de-camp, he had Louis Antoine, the twenty-five-year-old Comte de Bougainville, a scientific prodigy making his first overseas foray as a soldier. He was already widely known for his treatise on the integral calculus. Despite his youth and nationality, he had been elected a Fellow of the Royal Society of England. Yet for all his brilliance, Bougainville retained a cheerful innocence that was to brighten the fearful voyage.

"What a nation is ours", he wrote. "Happy he who commands it and commands it worthily." The genius of the integral calculus knew little of Louis XV, who commanded unworthily, if at all. He watched two battalions of the Royal Roussillon and La

Sarre regiments board their ships "with incredible gaiety", and the small fleet lurch forth from Brest and into the Atlantic gales.

Five weeks later, it reached the St. Lawrence. Three hundred of the 1,200 troops were so sick they had to be carried ashore at Quebec. Montcalm survived by sipping tea and lemonade, but wrote Angélique: "I have taken very little liking for the sea . . . . We heard Mass on Easter Day. All the week before it was impossible, because the ship rolled so that I could hardly keep my legs. If I had dared, I think I should have had myself lashed fast. I shall not soon forget that Holy Week."

Bigot staged a grand welcoming banquet for the new commander. The Intendant's palace rustled and fluttered with the gay silks of the colony's élite. Forty guests sat down to a meal which, Montcalm noted, would have astonished even a Parisian — "such splendor and good cheer show how much the Intendant's place is worth . . . everything is horribly dear in this country. I shall find it hard to make the two ends of the year meet with the 25,000 francs (livres) the King gives me."

Evidently he missed the point that Bigot was trying to make — that there was no reason for a gentleman to stint himself just because the peasants were hungry; or to spend his own money when the treasury was there to pillage.

The Intendant smiled dubiously at the general. If this were, indeed, an honest man, how much honesty would he expect from others? Vaudreuil was not concerned about honesty. In his year as governor he had been charmed and flattered by Bigot. He could overlook a few irregularities — these were traditional in the colony — so long as he was accorded the deference that was his due.

He looked at the new general for signs of ready subservience and found none. The man was small, hot-eyed and obviously impetuous. If he could not be overawed or frightened, he must be outwitted. So the Governor smiled, as Bigot had smiled, and awaited an opportunity to discredit him.

Within a week, Montcalm was on Lake Ontario, preparing to strike at the last English toehold on that waterway — the forts at Oswego, near present-day Rome, New York. The English garrison there had starved all winter and were now so weak that sentries had to prop themselves up with sticks and often collapsed at their posts. The chief engineer, Major Patrick Mackellar, had examined the works and declared that they could not be defended. The two cannon protecting the exposed side of the principal fort had to be removed because they shook the walls down when fired.

Montcalm sailed in by night, dragged cannon ashore and pounded the shaky structure. The fiendish howls of his Indians and Canadians and the screams of the hundred-odd women of the garrison families did the rest. Oswego surrendered; the victors broke into the rum barrels and tomahawked a few prisoners; then the forts were burned. Mackellar was taken prisoner and sent to Quebec. He would spend a year there, collecting information and making sketches that, on his return, were to establish him as Wolfe's expert on the French defenses.

Montcalm led his army back to Montreal, to hang the captured British flags in the churches and sing triumphant Te Deums. Vaudreuil took full credit for the victory and wrote to Paris, accusing his general of an ineffective, halting performance.

Oswego gave Montcalm his first experience in handling Indians. To keep them from murdering all the prisoners he had to make extravagant promises of gifts which, he reckoned, would cost the King eight or ten thousand livres. But his victory established his reputation with the warriors. Since the death of Frontenac, the great Onontio, they had been looking for another mighty foreigner to open the trail to scalps and plunder. Montcalm could be the man. Chiefs came from east and west to look him over.

At first sight, he was a disappointment. This was not the towering, granite figure of the Onontio legends, but a short, roundish man with bright, dark eyes.

"We thought your head would be lost in the clouds", one orator began, "but you are a little man, my Father." He added diplomatically "Yet when we look into your eyes we see the height of the pinetree and the fire of the eagle."

The new Onontio began his rounds of Indian villages to rouse the northern tribes to war. It was a long, wearying business. At each council-lodge he had to sing the war song. The words were simple — "Let us trample the English under our feet". They were chanted over and over, hour after hour as the warriors swayed and stamped to the rhythm of it; on and on until they screamed and seized the tomahawk.

In this way he set two thousand braves from forty-one tribes on the warpath for his assault on Fort William Henry in the summer of 1757. On the eve of battle he assembled all the chiefs in one camp for a final harangue and gave them a huge belt of six thousand wampum beads. There were Christians and pagans, clothed Indians and naked ones, some with muskets and some with stone clubs. They celebrated the victory to come, managing in the process to set their camp on fire and burn themselves out by morning.

Next day the priests called the Christian Indians to mass and found beside their cross an old coat and a pair of leggings hanging on a pole, symbols of the Huron great spirit, Manitou. This upset the priests, who wanted to cancel the mass, but Montcalm suggested they get on with it. He was tired of long-winded Indian arguments and tired of the war song. "One must be a slave of these savages" Bougainville wrote, "listen to them day and night, in council and in private, whenever the fancy takes them or whenever a dream, a fit of the vapors or their perpetual craving for brandy gets possession of them; besides which they are always wanting something for their equipment, arms or toilet and the general of the army must give written orders for the smallest trifle — an eternal, weary detail of which one has no idea in Europe."

Some tribes were beyond control. The Iowas spoke no language known to anyone else, marched when they felt like it, and stopped to make camp without regard to what the rest of the army was doing. The Ottawas were cannibals. A French missionary watched them roast pieces of a New Jersey man on sticks while the rest of him boiled in a camp kettle. Eight of his fellow prisoners were forced to look on. The missionary was invited to share the meat and was told by a French-speaking Ottawa "You have French taste; I have Indian. This is good meat for me".

The Christian Hurons carried mirrors to war, the better to arrange their war-paint, the feathers on their heads and rings in their ears and noses. Montcalm observed "They think it a great beauty to cut the rim of the ear and stretch it until it reaches the shoulder. Often they wear a lace coat with no shirt at all. You would take them for so many masqueraders or devils."

A coureur de bois *and a* war-painted Indian ally. *Both groups were splendid guerrilla fighters but, as Montcalm discovered, there were drawbacks to their use.*

(*La Gravure Francaise*)

This mixed army of naked warriors and lace-trimmed French gentry descended Lake Champlain and Lake George and surrounded Fort William Henry, a log and earth fortification which blocked the Hudson river route into New York.

Its fall was inevitable. The English general, the Earl of Loudon, had withdrawn his best troops from Lake George for an abortive attempt to take Louisbourg. Every day Montcalm's trenches crept closer. When three hundred defenders had been killed, with food and ammunition running low, and smallpox raging within the walls in the August heat, the fort surrendered. The rum casks were smashed on the English commander's orders before the garrison marched out. Yet some of the troops, hating to see such waste, filled their canteens before they left.

Montcalm prepared for an orderly takeover. His Indian chiefs promised to restrain their braves, but he wondered what their promises were worth in the heat of victory. Bougainville wrote "We shall be but too happy if we can prevent a massacre . . . "

The braves swarmed over the rum-soaked ruins of the fort and found nothing to drink and no one to scalp apart from the sick and wounded in the hospital. These were butchered at once while the Canadian militia looked on, and their diseased scalps were carried off — to start smallpox epidemics in the Indian villages.

The 2,200 English troops were to be marched, under French guard, to the nearest English camp, Fort Edward, and there released. But they were barely out of the gates before the Indians fell on them. More than a hundred were tomahawked for their muskets or canteens of rum, and six hundred were carried off to be tortured. The French regulars at the head of the column said they didn't know that a massacre was going on at the rear.

Montcalm tried to stop the slaughter. He rushed in, shouting "Kill me, but spare the English who are under my protection," and personally wrestled a prisoner away from an Indian. By force, threats and promises of gifts, he retrieved about four hundred English. But the horror of Fort William Henry was long to be remembered in London and the colonies. It remains the one ugly stain on Montcalm's reputation. The memory of the chopped-up bodies on that forest path stayed with him and sustained his distaste for Indians, Canadians, and the revolting ways of the New World.

By the end of the 1757 campaign he knew he was winning his war. He had firm control of the approaches to Canada, and the English were cut off from the West. But he was far from happy. He wrote to Angélique: "My heart and stomach are both ill at ease, the latter being the worse."

Chapter 4

The Pomp Of Gout

Just when Britain's bungling of the war was approaching the disaster point and when the worldly-wise Lord Chesterfield could groan "We are no longer a nation", a leader surfaced in the swamp of indolence that was George II's London.

William Pitt the Elder was a manic-depressive, obsessed by delusions of grandeur. He was always in pain from gout and at times he was mad. Yet there raged within him a clarity of purpose and a sense of destiny. He declared, with passionate simplicity: "I am sure that I can save this country and that nobody else can."

If he did not personally save the country, he certainly saved the situation, bringing a series of victories that left London reeling with success and deafened by the clangor of bells and the blast of triumphal trumpets. And he was absolutely right when he said that nobody else could have done it. "England has long been in labor," said Frederick of Prussia, "and at last she has brought forth a man."

The England of 1757 had little to commend it. Religious passions had burned out a decade before when the last Jacobite leaders were hanged; libertarian notions were dormant. The poor could get drunk on gin for a penny, "dead drunk" for twopence. Londoners could attend the bear-baiting on Mondays and Thursdays at Hockley-in-the-Hole for nothing if they stole a dog to toss into the ring. The hangings at Tyburn, beside Hyde Park, were free; for a small tip to the keepers they could go and taunt the madmen in Bedlam, and by queuing for an hour outside the Bridewell jail they could get in to watch half-naked women being whipped. Such entertainments distracted the masses from the boredom and

William Pitt, later Lord Chatham. "I am sure that I can save this country and that nobody else can." From a portrait by R. Brampton.

(Public Archives of Canada)

discomfort of life in sludge-filled streets like Foul Lane and Melancholy Walk.

Henry Fielding, Bow Street magistrate and author of "Tom Jones", complained that lives were destroyed at Tyburn "not for the reformation but the diversion of the populace." The great Dr. Samuel Johnson defended Tyburn, rumbling "Sir, executions are intended to draw the spectators."

The leisured classes were carried to their coffee houses in sedan chairs to begin a long day of posturing, gossiping and gambling, primping their periwigs and sniffing their snuff, followed by nights of more gaming, flirting at masked balls, and whoring in town houses. The bribing, blackmailing and scandal-mongering necessary to politics was carried on in between times.

The great Whig families ran the government for the King, who was more interested in his German possessions, while the discredited Tories grumbled in the country, savagely pursuing stags and foxes. The names of the groups — it was too soon to call them parties — dated from the previous century. A "whig" had been the name for a cattle thief, or Protestant rebel against the Stuarts, and a "tory" was a Papist outlaw. The Duke of Newcastle, George Townshend's uncle, ruled the Whigs by virtue of his money and patronage. He had no other virtues; Macaulay describes him as "contemptible in morals, manners and understanding."

In the army, as in the church, promotion was achieved through family connections, political pay-offs and the purchase of commissions for hard cash. This system produced bloated, red-coated incompetents like General James Abercromby and the Earl of Loudon, who were losing the war in America.

William Pitt emerged as the champion of the long-impotent middle class which was to provide the country's missing backbone. Although vain and intolerant as any aristocrat, he did not come from the landed gentry. His money came from his grandfather, "Diamond" Pitt, a rough, piratical East India merchant who acquired the governorship of Madras and a famous jewel of 410 carats. So did his policy. Shorn of the shimmering oratory that enveloped it, it was equally rough and piratical. England could achieve greatness only by grabbing the lion's share of world trade. The greatest trading enemy was France, and she could be beaten through sea-power.

It was simple and effective, but it took a man of Pitt's blazing conviction and histrionic gifts to push it through. Macaulay describes his parliamentary performance in the early days of power:

He would arrive in the House "in all the pomp of gout", which had afflicted him since his schooldays. His legs would be swathed in flannel, his arm dangling in a sling. "His figure . . . was strikingly graceful and commanding, his features high and noble, his eye full of fire. His voice, even when it sank to a whisper, was heard to the remotest benches; and when he strained it to its full extent the sound rose like the swell of the organ of a great cathedral, shook the house with its peal and was heard through lobbies and down staircases, to the Court of Requests and the precincts of Westminster Hall . . . His play of countenance was wonderful: he frequently disconcerted a hostile orator by a single glance of indignation or scorn. Every tone, from the impassioned cry to the thrilling aside, was perfectly at his command."

Pitt achieved a form of power at the end of 1756, but was forced out the following April by the hatred of the King, Newcastle's Members of Parliament, and the army chief, the Duke of Cumberland. After three months, during which England lurched, leaderless, through a major war, a strange compromise was reached. Newcastle would remain as nominal head of government while Pitt, as Secretary of State (Southern), would lead the Commons and control the war.

For a man whose military career consisted of a few months as a cornet of horse, he showed a remarkable grasp of strategy. The way into Canada was not the painful, tree-chopping route taken by Braddock, or even the marching, paddling and portaging way along the lake and river highways, but the front door — the St. Lawrence. Once Louisbourg was retaken, the great estuary would be open for a direct strike to the heart, backed up by new efforts on the lakes.

He recalled the Earl of Loudon — who, Horace Walpole said, could be scared by a pop-gun — and reinforced the useless Abercromby with a young and unorthodox soldier, Lord Howe. He wiped out the irritating caste system which gave any regular British officer precedence over every colonial, regardless of rank. Looking around for new leaders, he found a young lieutenant-colonel who had distinguished himself during an abortive attempt to take the French port of Rochefort from the sea the year before.

James Wolfe didn't look like a hero. He was thin, clumsy and chinless. Only his startling, pale-blue eyes saved his features from downright ugliness. He wore no wig, and his red hair flamed against his womanishly-soft white skin. Like Pitt, he was chronically sick, forever fighting his own weakness. Like Pitt he had a vision of his destiny. It was a smaller vision, but equally certain. He would lead masses of soldiers — brilliant, two-dimensional red figures — marching in perfect formation towards ordered death and regimented glory. "I know nothing", he wrote, "more entertaining than a collection of well-looking men, uniformly clad, and performing their exercise with grace and order."

According to a genealogy published by the Quebec House Permanent Advisory Committee he was descended from Edward III of England and Sir Henry Percy, known as Hotspur. The Wolfes or Woulfes sailed from Glamorgan to Ireland in the fifteenth century, looking for the life of gentlefolk which Wales could no longer support. They settled in western Limerick, becoming, it is said, more Irish than the Irish, but refusing to intermarry with the peat-smelling natives.

One Woulfe became a Franciscan friar and was executed by Cromwell's Roundheads; his brother dodged over to Yorkshire, adopted the Reformed faith and dumped the superfluous 'U' from the family name. His son, Edward, joined the Marines, helped scourge the Jacobites in the 1715 rebellion, served with the Duke of Marlborough in Europe and ended a satisfactory military career as Lt-Gen. Wolfe, master of Spiers, a gabled Tudor house at Westerham, Kent, near the old Pilgrim's Way to Canterbury.

The general's elder son, James, was born at the Vicarage in Westerham on December 22, 1726 (Old Style) or January 2, 1727 according to the present calendar.

He was a pale, sickly boy with a severely receding chin, inherited from his Yorkshire mother, Henrietta. She dosed him regularly with two spoonfuls of her own recipe for consumption, made from green garden snails and sliced earthworms. Not surprisingly, he remained sick.

With his brother Edward, one year younger, he scampered through the old house with its winding staircase and hidden doors leading to secret passages, and sailed model ships in the nearby brook. And in the evenings, by the huge fireplace, he heard warlike stories told by brandy-smelling colonels of grim face and bloody attribute. His life was determined for him: he would be a soldier and die for his country in the most glorious manner conceivable. Dying was as important as killing in the military arts; both had to be done stylishly and well.

He answered the trumpet-call at the age of thirteen, embarking with his father as a "gentleman volunteer" in an expedition against the Spaniards at Cartagena. As soon as the ship rocked at anchor at the Isle of Wight, Jamie was seasick and had to be sent home. The sickness would occur every time he set foot on a deck, yet he would become, in Corbett's words, "the greatest master of amphibious warfare since Drake".

He went back to school at Greenwich, still determined to go to war as soon as possible. At fifteen he was commissioned as ensign in Colonel Duroure's Twelfth Regiment of Foot and at sixteen he was an acting battalion adjutant, fighting the French at Dettingen, twenty miles east of Frankfurt.

It was excellent battle with which to start one's career — the last in which a King of England personally led his troops. Wolfe watched George II mount his horse, wearing, with difficulty, the same powder-stained red coat in which he had led a cavalry charge at Oudenarde, thirty-five years before. He watched him dismount, after the horse had run away with him, and march to the head of

King George II, the Hanoverian king of England and the hero of Dettingen. Portrait by Thomas Hudson.

(Public Archives of Canada)

his infantry, waving his sword and shouting battle-cries in his thick, Germanic English.

The French were routed. But since the King and his fat son, Cumberland, stopped on the battlefield to receive the congratulations of all the generals and every ambitious courtier in sight, they were able to escape. The Twelfth Regiment lost 100 men, more than any other English unit. Wolfe's horse was shot and he lost his pistols. He was elated by his baptism of fire, but so exhausted that he stayed in his tent for two days, being bled, before he recovered and wrote home: "His Majesty was in the midst of the fight and the Duke (Cumberland) behaved as bravely as a man can do. He has a musquet-shot through the calf of his leg. I had several times the honour of speaking with him just as the battle began and was often afraid of his being dash'd to pieces by the cannon balls."

Cumberland remembered the young acting-adjutant. Two weeks later he was confirmed in his post and promoted to lieutenant. Three other young officers saw their first action at Dettingen — Jeffrey Amherst, Robert Monckton and George Townshend.

While Wolfe was writing excitedly about the bravery of his leaders, the eighteen-year-old Townshend wrote; "I could give such an account of the declining condition of our army . . . as would make the most indifferent person weep . . . the more I consider the situation of our armies and the temper of those who direct them, the conduct of the French from our first sight of them, the accounts I learn from the inhabitants of this country and the opinions of people in general, all seem to agree in the verdict: Inglorious."

Townshend had arrived at Dettingen in style as a volunteer staff officer with a personal letter of introduction from the Duke of Newcastle. He viewed the battle from a better vantage point and with a cooler eye than the romantic Wolfe. The gap between the two teenage officers in their attitude to war would remain and widen until the day, sixteen years later, when they stood together on the Plains of Abraham. Townshend's biographer, Lt.-Col. C. V. F. Townshend says of his ancestor: "I am afraid that throughout his service he never learned by experience the difference between the labors and dangers of staff and regimental officers on active service, which are — as Napier has so truly said — generally in inverse ratio to their promotion".

As the English line approached across the damp moor of Culloden Captain James Johnstone, the future Chevalier, stood with the Macdonalds of Glengarry. He wore a tartan sash over his Lowland cloth coat and swung a studded-leather Highland shield on his left arm. Although he was a Lowlander from Edinburgh, he had joined the Highlanders and their "Bonnie Prince", Charles Edward, in a last, desperate attempt to restore the Stuarts to the throne.

Like the gaunt, wild-eyed men beside him, he was hungry and exhausted. They had marched all night through sleet and rain with a biscuit each for sustenance. Some were asleep on the heather, wrapped in the all-purpose tartan blanket that was often the clansman's only garment — so tired that even the bagpipe rant of their clan could hardly rouse them.

The Macdonalds were bitter. The Prince had deprived them of their traditional place on the right of the line, which they had occupied in every Scottish battle since Bannockburn, four centuries before. Their complaints had gone unheard. The senior officers were busy trying to convince Charles that, considering the state of his army, it was madness to fight that day.

But the Prince curvetted merrily on his horse, lisping cheerful slogans in his soft Italian voice. Testing the edge of a clansman's claymore, he cried "I'll answer this will cut off some heads and arms today!"

Johnstone sensed that this might be the last battle, so he had decided to face it on the left of the front line with his friend Donald Macdonald of Scotus, instead of remaining in the rear with his own regiment, the Duke of Perth's. He was a soldier of independent means, a rich merchant's son who fought for whom he pleased, so long as his father kept sending him money. His early wanderings had taken him to Russia, where he obtained the Czar's commission to fight the Turks. He was back in Edinburgh when news came that Charles had landed from France and raised the flag of rebellion. In September, 1745, a month after the landing, he joined the rebel general Lord George Murray as aide-de-camp, later becoming a captain of artillery.

In the seven months that followed, he tasted victory at Prestonpans and Carlisle and marched with the rebels south as far as Derby, 130 miles from London, before the slow retreat began. The rebellion accomplished all that its sponsor, Louis XV, had hoped for. It drew Cumberland's entire army back from Flanders to defend England.

Now the hour of reckoning was near. Cumberland's drums were beating across the bleak moor, his three dense columns had wheeled into an immaculate red line. The flat ground the Prince had stupidly chosen was ideal for these steady, well-drilled veterans. Johnstone's Lowland canniness told him the clans didn't have a chance. Yet he charged with the recklessness of a Highlander, yelling the ancient cries of the Macdonalds in a tongue he did not understand.

Wolfe was with Barrell's battalion, at the other end of the English front line. He faced the Camerons of Lochiel, whom he called the bravest clan in the Highlands, and beside them Lord George Murray's Athollmen, the Stewarts of Appin and the Frasers of Lovat.

They stood, while the first rounds of English grapeshot tore hideous red ribbons in their ranks. Then they threw down their muskets, drew their claymores and charged through the sleety rain.

The Cameron piper shrilled his pibroch — "Ye sons of dogs, of dogs of the breed; O come, come here, on flesh to feed!" The elegant chieftains, their tenants, tacksmen and ragged humblies, rushed together in a screaming, terrifying horde, on to the steady bayonets of Barrell's and Munro's.

The wild claymore charge was the Highlander's only tactic. After earlier failures Cumberland's foot soldiers had been drilled in a new method of withstanding it. The clansman guarded his left side and middle with his target, or shield, while swinging his broadsword with his right arm. Once his sword arm was up, his right was unprotected. So the redcoat had been drilled to stick his bayonet, not at the warrior directly ahead of him and about to slice his head off, but at the one attacking the man on his right. It took immense self-control. While killing his neighbor's assailant, he had to rely utterly on the man to his left to impale his own attacker. Yet it worked. Barrell's men killed one or two Highlanders apiece with their bayonets, although their own losses — 125 out of 373 killed and wounded — accounted for more than a third of the total English casualties.

Barrell's was Wolfe's regiment but he was detached from it, standing slightly to the left with a group of staff officers when the Highlanders charged. This time he had a privileged position, as aide-de-camp to General Henry Hawley, while George Townshend was a regimental officer. Wolfe admitted later that Barrell's would have been destroyed if Cumberland's second line had not moved up and shattered the rest of the Highland charge with musket-fire. Townshend was with Bligh's in the second line, cool and methodical as ever.

James Johnstone saw his friend Scotus killed beside him. At the time he hardly cared, although he brooded over it afterwards. "Military men susceptible to friendship", he thought, "are much to be pitied." The Macdonalds, their charge halted, fell in scores. Pulteney's men shot them down, calmly and cheerfully, from twenty yards' range, while their young officers giggled with delight. Finally, after an hour, the survivors broke and ran. Johnstone ran with them, looking for a place to hide until he could find a ship to France and another lost cause.

The Prince was led away, in tears, as his army dissolved into the heather. The commander of his Life Guards shouted after him "Run, you cowardly Italian!" Minutes later, Cumberland's red dragoons thundered in pursuit of the fleeing rabble, trampling the dead and hacking the wounded.

Wolfe seems to have taken a grim delight in the murder that followed. "We had an opportunity of avenging ourselves", he wrote. "And I assure you as few prisoners were taken of the Highlanders as possible." But apparently he refused to kill prisoners with his own hands. According to a contemporary account he was riding with Cumberland after the battle when the wounded Fraser commander, Lt.-Col. Charles Fraser of Inverallochie, grinned defiance at the Duke.

Cumberland ordered: "Wolfe! Shoot me that Highland scoundrel who dares look on us with such contempt and insolence."

"Sir", said Wolfe. "My commission is at your Royal Highness's disposal, but I can never consent to become an executioner."

In reality, Wolfe may have ridden with Cumberland, but is more likely to have been with his general, the bloodthirsty brute known as "Hangman" Hawley, who certainly enjoyed killing helpless men. And if he did refuse such an order it was probably because he felt the task demeaned his rank; it was work for a common soldier. In any case, such fastidiousness did Fraser no good. A common soldier shot him.

In the months that followed, the nineteen-year-old Wolfe learned the business of cold-blooded killing, which was quite distinct from the noble slaughter of the battlefield. He hated Hawley, but remained on his staff. Hawley's baggage train included a full-sized portable gallows. Suspected Jacobites were despatched on the spot, or dragged off to be ceremonially hanged, disembowelled and beheaded, or transported to the West Indies or the frontiers of the Carolinas, Virginia, or Pennsylvania. Their houses were looted and burned, their families driven out, and their cattle, sheep and horses shared out among the English officers and men, according to rank. When Hawley resigned in June, Wolfe continued to ravage the Highlands with his own regiment.

Wolfe would spend six of the next ten years in Scotland. He crossed the Channel for two campaign seasons in Flanders, was wounded at Laufeldt (where Townshend was spattered by Scheiger's brains) but always returned to the land he detested. He disliked the Lowlanders, finding the men "civil, designing and treacherous" and their women "coarse and cunning . . . cold to anything but a bagpipe." The Highlanders, he wrote, were better governed by fear than favor. They must be kept in awe, terrified by sudden night marches, even tricked into attacking, if necessary, so that a clan could be wiped out.

"Would you believe that I am so bloody?" he asked his friend, Captain Rickson, after outlining one such scheme. "It was my real intention and I hope such execution will be done upon the first that revolt . . . "

He found time, however, for Highland ladies, whom he described as "wild as the hills that breed them". At a ball in Inverness he danced with the daughter of Macdonald of Keppoch, a chieftain killed at Culloden. And he met Simon Fraser, the young Master of Lovat, and discussed with him the possibility of raising Highland regiments to fight England's wars in North America. Fraser was interested, although he found it difficult to forget that the English had recently beheaded his 80-year-old father and looted his family seat, Castle Dounie. Later he did raise 1,800 men, clad them in a new tartan, probably in the drab, black "government" pattern and led them, eventually, to the battle of Quebec.

Wolfe was bored by peacetime soldiering. On his twenty-fifth birthday he wrote: "the winter wears away, so do our years and so does life itself; and it matters little where a man passes his days and what station he fills, or whether he be great or considerable; but it imports him something to look to his manner of life . . . . the fear of becoming a mere ruffian and of imbibing the tyrannical principles of an absolute commander or giving way insensibly to the temptations of power — these considerations will make me wish to leave the regiment before the next winter."

This gloom lifted when the weather improved. He rode the moors daily, shot game and fished for salmon. His only companions were his dogs.

His officers resented his constant attention to detail, his strictures on the need for military perfection and the extra duties he kept devising for them. Peacetime was a time for hunting, drinking and whoring. But their colonel spent his nights in his quarters, studying history, latin and mathematics. He drank little, disliked cards, and existed solely on the stodgy mess food. Sometimes he played chess or blew mournful tunes on the flute he had bought in Ghent.

"Our acting commander here is a paragon", one captain

wrote. "He neither drinks, curses, gambles nor runs after women."

"Gaming, eating and the pox", Wolfe declared, "are the vices of the effeminate and flagitious; and have loosened the morals and ruined the constitution of half our countrymen".

To set an example to the regiment, he spent two hours at kirk each Sunday. Privately, he considered them "lost" hours — "the generality of Scotch preachers are excessive blockheads, so truly and obstinately dull that they seem to shut out knowledge at every entrance."

He experimented with new and dreadful cures for his bladder and kidney troubles. For weeks he drank only goat's whey and took a cold bath every day. Then he tried scouring his insides with soapy water. These medicines did not help, and the baths gave him rheumatism.

On top of all this, he was lovesick. He wanted to marry Miss Elizabeth Lawson, a maid of honor to the Princess of Wales and niece of a useful and well-connected general, Sir John Mordaunt. She had, he wrote "won all my affections" — although he added critically that she was rather tall and thin and his own age. She came equipped with a dowry of twelve thousand pounds. But his parents had bigger plans for him. He was their only remaining son, Edward having died of consumption at sixteen. They had their eye on a Croydon heiress, Miss Hoskins, who was worth *thirty* thousand. The Wolfes made it clear that if he married Miss Lawson he could say goodbye to his prospects of promotion. Commissions cost money and so did the horses and servants that went with increased rank. Wolfe could barely support his present position as acting lieutenant-colonel. He got fifteen pounds a month, but by the time he had paid for board and lodging, his horse, servants and washing, he had only a shilling a day left for pocket money.

He rejected Miss Hoskins and pined for Miss Lawson who was far away in the south of England; this left him with only his chess, his studies and his flute. "If I'm kept long here the fire will be extinguished", he told Rickson. "Young flames must be constantly fed or they'll evaporate."

Before that could happen he went on leave to London, renounced Miss Lawson, quarrelled with his parents, and plunged into dissipation. The paragon who avoided strong drink and even abstained from "strong food", spent his leave in what he called "the idlest, most dissolute, abandoned manner conceivable." What kind of strong meat he tasted in the unholy gin mills of the capital has not been revealed. But he returned to Scotland cured of love and in better spirits.

"I have no very high opinion of love affairs, except they are built upon judgment", he told his mother. "Unless there be violence done to my inclinations by the power of some gentle nymph, I had much rather listen to the drum and trumpet than any softer sound whatever . . . there is great probability that I shall never marry."

He told Rickson that he had greatly recovered from "my disorder that my extravagant love for Miss Lawson threw me into, yet I never hear her name mentioned without a twitch . . ."

Having thus settled his romantic affairs and improved his mind by study, Wolfe took stock of his social graces. His regimental colonel, Lord George Sackville, told him bravery and devotion to duty were all very well, but not enough to take an officer to the top of his profession. Charm and polish were required, too. Wolfe was now the youngest lieutenant-colonel in the British Army and he still felt as awkward as he looked when away from the battlefield or the parade ground.

"The fortune of a military man", he mused, "seems to depend almost as much on his exteriors as upon things that are in reality more estimable and praiseworthy."

He must improve his dancing and fencing and put more style into his riding. Since war with France was off for the time being, he headed for Paris, where these arts had reached perfection. He entered the gay city grimly determined not to indulge himself. He was up at break of day and off to the riding academy, back to his room to study French verbs, off to fencing classes, then back and forth across the dance floor, home to dinner, and bed by eleven — just as Parisian society was roistering forth on the town.

A few weeks later he admitted in his letters that he had met "some of the prettiest women in Paris" but was wary of them, as women cost a great deal of money and "One terrible, frequent and almost natural consequence of not marrying is an attachment to some woman or other that leads to a thousand inconveniences. Marshal Saxe died in the arms of a little whore that plays upon the Italian stage — an ignominious end for a conqueror."

He found the French ladies wellbred, delicate and genteel but "a little inclined to gluttony and troubled with frequent

King Louis XV of France. "The Bourbons seldom speak to anybody."

(Public Archives of Canada)

indigestions." He visited Versailles twice, accompanying the British Ambassador, Lord Albemarle. The first time, it was Louis' annual New Year's Day reception, attended by every minor dignitary in Paris, and Wolfe was not impressed. It rained so hard that he missed the splendor of the gardens and he remained "a cold spectator" as "a multitude of men and women were assembled to bow and pay their compliments in the most submissive manner to a creature of their own species." He noticed, however, that the Marquise de Pompadour seemed to pay special attention to Albemarle.

The second time he was introduced personally to the King and Queen and their family — "all very gracious as far as courtesies, bows and smiles go, for the Bourbons seldom speak to anybody" — then reached the centre of power, the Pompadour's apartment. "Madame la Marquise entertained us at her toilette. We found her curling her hair. She is extremely handsome, and, by her conversation with the Ambassador and others that were present, I judge she must have a great deal of wit and understanding." Apparently she did not pay particular attention to the ungainly young colonel.

As his minuets and swordsmanship improved, Wolfe grew tired of Paris; the feeling towards Englishmen there was almost as hostile as it was in Scotland.

In April, 1753, he was called back to his regiment in Glasgow. He found morale low, discipline lax, and the officers sick and dejected. Even the women of the regiment were complaining. The petition of Anne White to Lt.-Col. Wolfe has been preserved:

"Collonel — Being a True Noble-heart'd Pittyful gentleman and Officer your Worship will excuse these few lines concerning the husband of ye undersigned, Sergt. White, who not from his own fault is not behaving as Hee should towards me and his family, although good and faithfull until the middle of November last . . . "

Wolfe told his mother he had a collection of such letters that would make her laugh. But he was too depressed for laughter. He brooded again about death:–

"I have hardly passion enough of any kind to find present pleasure or feed future hope, and scarce activity to preserve my health . . . .

"The warmth of temper which you so justly censure when it breaks out improperly, is what I depend upon to support me against the little attacks of my brethren and contemporaries, and that will find the way to a glorious or at least a firm and manly end when I am of no further use to my friends and country, or when I can be serviceable by offering my life for either.

"Nobody has perhaps more reason to be satisfied with his station and success in the world than myself, nobody can have better parents, and I have hitherto never wanted friends; but happiness or ease, which is all we can pretend to, lies in the mind, or nowhere."

There would be no happiness or ease for Wolfe until he went back to battle, four years later.

Lt.-Col. the Hon. George Townshend adapted easily to the pleasures of peacetime. He glided from the Flanders campaigns to the civilized life of a Guards officer in London, married Lady Charlotte Compton, daughter and heiress of the Earl of Northampton, and took a small country mansion a few miles from his family seat, Raynham Hall, in Norfolk.

He had no difficulty in slipping away from the regiment when he felt like it. A brother officer could always be found to mount guards for him or attend to other tiresome military details. Raynham was ordered and pleasant. The lands which the Townshends had owned since the twelfth century rolled off to the horizon. The Hall, a huge pink-brick palace built by Inigo Jones in 1630, sat squarely on its barbered lawns, overlooking an ornamental lake nearly two miles long. In its great galleries, rows of Townshend ancestors in court robes, knightly armor or doublet and hose, preened and frowned while the ghost of George's grandmother, Dorothy Walpole, Viscountess Townshend, flitted along the corridors.

Townshend was heir to these centuries of courtly splendor and military glory; soon he would inherit the Hall itself and before he died, a full-length heroic portrait by Reynolds of Field Marshal George, First Marquess Townshend, would take its place on those historic walls.

He had no need to prove himself in battle, improve himself by books or dancing classes, or flatter senior officers. He stood in no awe of H. R. H. the Duke of Cumberland, the old King, or anybody else. His place was secure, although he would do his duty, as Townshends always did, when the need arose. Meanwhile he would air his biting criticisms of Cumberland's conduct of the Flanders campaign. So began his quarrel with the Duke.

It intensified when Townshend, who, like many officers and gentlemen with time on their hands, was a Member of Parliament, introduced a Bill to raise militia regiments. Despite violent opposition from the government, the Bill passed. Townshend went off for a few days' fox-hunting with his friend the Marquess of Granby. On returning to his regiment he was — incredibly — placed under arrest by the colonel for leaving town without leave.

This was monstrous. Obviously, Cumberland was out to get him. So Townshend promptly resigned his commission and left the army in a dignified huff. A year later his good friend Pitt was in power and it was Cumberland's turn to resign as commander-in-chief. Townshend returned as a full colonel, feeling that the time had come for him to leave politics and the country life for a while.

His younger brother Charles, a famous parliamentary orator and wit, told their mother: "George seems more intent upon his command in the army than ever I saw him. The retreat of his formidable and abdicated enemy (Cumberland) the disreputation of almost all the senior officers hitherto employed, and the infinite honor naturally bestowed upon Commanders successful in this perilous time, all unite in indulging and inflaming his original Genius and uncommon talents for the army."

George was ready to go back to war. But on his own terms.

"For a man that does not feel the ship's motion, and whose nose is not too nice for the smells" Wolfe wrote, "this life for a little while is tolerable; it is then an easy, commodious conveyance for a distant place, and upon the quarter-deck of a ninety-gun ship a man may stretch and exercise his limbs. I have not myself been one hour well since we embarked and have the mortification to find that I am the worst mariner in the whole ship."

He wrote from the Ramillies on her way to attack Rochefort in the Bay of Biscay, in September, 1757. They had sailed from the Isle of Wight, where seasickness had deprived young Jamie Wolfe of his first adventure seventeen years before.

This time, sick or not, Wolfe showed more grasp of amphibious warfare than Sir Edward Hawke, the admiral, or any of his army superiors from General Sir John Mordaunt down. Because the admiral and the general could not agree as to when and exactly where the landing should be made, Wolfe, the sick sailor, was the one officer with the stamina to make a landing, reconnoitre the French fort, and suggest a plan of attack. But he failed to convince his general, and in any case generals avoided talking to admirals because the manners of the sea-dogs were too ferocious for normal communication.

Mordaunt's ten regiments were put into boats and left to toss for three hours on the offshore waves, awaiting a lantern signal to land that never came. Eventually they sailed home.

In the post mortems that followed, Pitt, King George and Frederick of Prussia became disgusted by the failure of the army and navy to cooperate in a simple landing operation. Hawke's sixteen great ships of the line had creaked uselessly offshore for two days, surrounded by a swarm of frigates, fireships and little bomb ketches. Mordaunt's men had got sick for nothing.

The conclusion was that the only man who had shown that he had the stomach for a sea landing was the man with the weakest stomach of all. Wolfe was plucked from the ranks of obscure young lieutenant colonels to be third brigadier under General Jeffrey Amherst in Pitt's sea assault on Louisbourg. That assault was to be the prelude to the conquest of Canada.

Chapter 5

A Stupendous Stronghold

James Johnstone, safely escaped from Culloden and now a lieutenant in the French colonial marines, arrived at Louisbourg in the rotting hulk of the Iphigenie, which had lost its mainmast and part of its forepeak on the crossing from France. While his shipmates kissed the rocky ground and muttered prayers of thanksgiving, he grabbed the ship's captain by the throat, flattened him with a blow, and began beating him with a barrel stave.

He had just learned that the unseaworthy Iphigenie was part-owned by Louisbourg officials who had fully expected it to sink, and whose plans to collect compensation from the King were well under way. It was his introduction to the ways of New France.

When he escaped to Paris after Culloden, Johnstone had hoped that Louis would back another Jacobite rebellion. Prince Charles had been successfully spirited across the water and was a guest of the French court, loudly and usually drunkenly proclaiming that he would return to Scotland. After Louis made peace at Aix-la-Chapelle in 1748 that hope ended. Charles Edward became a nuisance. Hints were dropped that it was time he rejoined his father James, the Old Pretender, in Italy. When the hints failed to register, Louis had Charles arrested as he drove to the opera, and he was escorted to the Italian border.

Johnstone, who had existed as an ardent fringe member of the Prince's court-in-exile, obeyed Louis' proclamation that all foreigners register for service with the armies of France. They were guaranteed the same ranks they had held in the Highland army, and most of them achieved this. But the stocky, argumentative Edinburgh man, like his Glasgow counterpart, Robert Stobo, was never quite a gentleman, and he was reduced to the rank of ensign in the colonial marines. Not for him the gracious life in the

Soldiers of the Marine Companies in which James Johnstone found himself serving at Louisbourg. Left, *winter campaign dress* centre, *full parade dress and* right, *summer campaign dress.*
(Drawing by Gerald Embleton)

French West Indies or French India. He was assigned to the chilly desolation of Louisbourg.

For accepting the rigors of that unpopular posting, plus the risk of drowning at the hands of the Iphigenie's rascally owners, he was promoted to lieutenant, and his natural air of authority reasserted itself. The Independent Companies of Marines (Les Compagnies Franches de la Marine) had been formed by Cardinal Richelieu in 1622 as shipboard troops. After 1680, however, units were stationed permanently in the French colonies in North America and the Caribbean. Their officers held naval ranks which were translated into army terms in shore commands; so Johnstone was more or less an army captain once more when he arrived in Louisbourg.

Seen from the sea, Louisbourg was a mighty structure, the strongest fortress on the continent. It projected bleakly over

the gray sea at Cape Breton Island on the northern tip of Nova
Scotia. The French had spent millions of livres to build up its stone-
works and moats. It boasted 219 cannon and seventeen mortars —
"a stupendous stronghold", according to the French-Canadian historian, the Abbé Casgrain.

Yet the ill-disciplined New Englanders, in conjunction
with a small British fleet, had knocked it over in a five-week siege
in 1745. The British government thought so little of it at the time
that they swapped it at Aix-la-Chapelle for the trading post of
Madras. Bigot learned his trade in Louisbourg. When the New Englanders took it he was commissary and the garrison had just mutinied and locked him up. The soldiers were demanding firewood
for their unheated barracks and an end to Bigot's "company-town"
system, under which they were all in debt to the canteens run by
their officers.

Another reason for this first fall of Louisbourg was that
the military bureaucrats in France had sent out cannon balls that
didn't fit the cannon. The New Englanders, who knew more about
weights and measures than soldiering, brought along their own
cannon balls, captured the French batteries across the harbor, and
bombarded the main fort into submission with its own weapons.

When the French got the fortress back, more shiploads
of gold and silver coins, engineers, tools and guns were sent out
from France. So much money was spent and so many tales told of
its incredible strength that Louis XV said he expected one morning
to look from his bedroom window at Versailles and see those great
walls clear across the Atlantic.

But it was never as strong as it looked, even from close
range. Good French stone was used for the houses of the governor
and intendant, but the outside walls were of soft stone, cheaply
quarried on the island. Somehow, the rest of the French stone
found its way to Boston. The mortar was mixed with beach sand,
and eventually gave way. The walls sagged and collapsed in places,
leaving gaps that were filled with logs. Louisbourg's real defense
was its frightening natural shoreline and the angry sea.

Johnstone hated the place — its narrow, swampy streets
lined with rumshops, the tawdry attempts of the corrupt officials
and their haggard women to ape the life of Versailles in draughty
stone ballrooms and makeshift theatres, and the unhealthy mixture
of pirates, smugglers, Indians and discontented troops.

The service of France, he found, consisted of "lazy officers who do no other service but pillage and rob the King and, being enriched by rapine, are received with open arms at the bureau in Versailles. My daily food during a year at Louisbourg consisted solely during the winter of codfish and hog's lard. In summer we had fresh fish, bad rancid butter and bad oil."

He awaited the English attack with equanimity. If the English captured the fort they would save him from his purgatory. He would escape to fight them again — in pleasanter surroundings.

👑 ⚜

The worst February weather in many years held up the English expedition. Admiral Edward Boscawen's twenty-three ships of the line were battered by waves and torn by winds even before they left Portsmouth harbor.

Wolfe lingered in the grimy port, reluctant to entrust his stomach to the sea until the last moment. He called it "an infernal den . . . where the condition of the garrison (or rather the vagabonds that stroll about in dirty red clothes from one gin shop to another) exceeds all belief. Disorderly soldiers of different regiments are gathered here . . . dirty, drunken, insolent rascals, not improved by the hellish nature of the place where every kind of corruption, immorality and looseness is carried to excess; it is a sink of the lowest and most abominable of vices."

The civilians were worse. Of the "diabolical citizens of Portsmouth", he wrote: "It is a doubt to me if there is such another collections of demons upon the whole earth."

Wolfe left them, thankfully, on February 19, 1758. He sniffed the brisk breezes of the Solent from the quarter-deck of the Princess Amelia, then staggered to his tiny cabin in the stern. Until May 9, he lay groaning on his bunk, staring at the planking a foot or so above his nose as the ship heaved and crashed through one of the worst crossings its older officers could remember.

In the sterncastle Wolfe had ventilation and a small, carved window to spare him the stink that rose from the bilges and swept through the 'tween-decks, where four hundred redcoats lay wedged together like heaps of dirty laundry. He never saw the foc'sle, where the fruits of the press-gang's labors huddled damply,

awaiting the next order that would set them swarming up the jud-
dering ratlines and fighting the savage canvas along the freezing
yardarms. Even the redcoats pitied the sailors, the tarry remnants
of village lads snatched from the streets and churches, or wretches
routed from jail or tavern in the navy's never-ending search for
men. For every one killed in action, nine died of scurvy and forty
deserted. Only the rare career sailor served willingly. For, as Dr.
Johnson remarked, navy life was just like jail, with the added risk
of drowning.

Wolfe, the constant sufferer, had never been so sick for
so long. It was mid-May, at Halifax, before he found the strength
to write a letter — "From Christopher Columbus' time to our days
there perhaps has never been a more extraordinary voyage."

He was still white and shaky two weeks later when he
joined Amherst and the other brigadiers on a reconnaissance of
Louisbourg. They tossed offshore in a longboat, viewing the fortress through misty rain. The surf boiled and foamed on the craggy
shore. Every possible landing-place for four miles was guarded by
log fortifications and gun batteries. Behind the fort, in the well-
protected harbor, stood the masts of five French ships of the line
and seven frigates, representing 3,000 men and 544 guns.

The governor who had succeeded Vergor's father, the
surrender-prone Duchambon, was a stout old veteran, the Chevalier de Drucour. He had been awaiting the English all spring. When
Boscawen's flock of sails appeared through the mist he was as prepared as he could be. In addition to the 3,000 sailors he had 3,800
troops, including three regular regiments. Every male inhabitant
from merchant to smuggler, pirate and drunk, had a weapon of
some kind. His middle-aged wife set an example by taking her
place at the gun embrasures and learning how to load and fire cannon. But Amherst had 12,000 men, mostly regulars, in his thirty-
nine ships. If they landed there could be no doubt of the final outcome. Drucour had to stop them in the surf.

The sea raged for a week. Gales followed snow-squalls
and violent rains. Twice the English troops got into their landing
craft but had to return to the ships. A frigate was driven on to the
rocks.

On the early morning of June 8, the sea calmed down
slightly and Amherst ordered the attack. It was the only time this

dogged, plodding general gave way to impatience. Throughout most of his career he was criticised for undue slowness and caution. But in this case even Wolfe, usually more impatient than anyone else, described the landing as "rash and ill-advised." His division was to make the main assault at Freshwater Cove, the small beach farthest from the fort, while the other two brigadiers pretended to attack two nearer coves.

It was no surprise attack. The gunners of the fleet pulled the wedges from under their cannon-breeches, tilting the muzzles to fire over the landing-craft, and sent broadsides of nine-pound balls flying at the shore, where a thousand defenders were dug in behind barriers of pine logs.

Wolfe found the sea much rougher than he had expected. As the breakers gripped his boats, the French opened up with their eight cannon and swivel-guns, followed by volleys of musketry.

Raked by shot, the sailors lost their oars. Boats tangled and smashed on the rocks. Some were shattered by cannon balls, while others turned over in the surf, throwing redcoats into the foam to gulp and struggle in their heavy uniforms. Volunteer James Thompson of the Fraser Highlanders saw shot tear holes in the side of his boat. The Frasers bundled up their plaids and stuffed them into the holes, but the water kept coming.

Wolfe stood, miraculously upright, as a cannon shot thumped past him and smashed the flagstaff. He waved and shouted, but no one could tell whether he was ordering a retreat or waving his men on. Three boats rode the breakers into shore and ground on a rocky beach where they were sheltered from the French fire by an overhanging rock. Pointing his cane at the beach, Wolfe jumped knee-deep into the waves and scrambled ashore. According to one story, he found time to seek out the two Frasers who had been first to land and present them with a guinea apiece. This sounds unlikely, but in view of Wolfe's insolent coolness in battle and his strange joy in flaunting himself under fire it is probable that he made some gesture, if only to restore his dignity after stumbling, bedraggled, from the hated sea.

Three months of agony were behind him and he was back, triumphantly, on dry land, sniffing blood and gunpowder. He clambered up a twenty-foot crag and began mustering the vanguard of his troops with the precision of Dettingen and Culloden. Their

Wolfe landing at Louisbourg. "The sea was rougher than expected".

(Public Archives of Canada)

muskets and powder were soaked, so they rushed the nearest battery with bayonets. More boats piled ashore and the French abandoned their cannon and took to the woods, circling back to the fort.

They had cleared the beachhead. Now the British
swarmed ashore in their hundreds, then thousands. They advanced
to a clearing in the pine trees, two miles from the ramparts of
Louisbourg and settled down to prepare a siege. After that, the only question was how long it would take before the fort surrendered,
and whether sufficient time would be left to push on to Quebec
that season.

The French ship Prudent is captured at Louisbourg. Painting by Francis Swaine.
(*Royal Ontario Museum, Toronto*)

It took 52 days. Long before the white flag went up, Wolfe was cursing Amherst for his slowness. The general was accustomed to long painful sieges in Europe, where forts were gradually starved into surrender. He never grasped the basic fact of war in Canada: that once the snows came everything stopped.

Wolfe did not wait placidly behind the siege guns. The frantic timepiece within him sent him parading and posturing, scurrying and scratching around the defenses, attacking here, probing there. His use of light infantry in loose, small parties, jabbing at the enemy and then retreating to cover, was to be hailed in Britain as new military brilliance. Actually he was using tactics laid down by a Swiss officer, Colonel Bouquet, who got them from the American ranger, Captain Robert Rogers, who got them from the Indians.

Wolfe declared grandly that he learned them from Xenophon — "but our friends here are astonished at what I have done, for they have read nothing."

Wolfe (left) at the siege of Louisbourg. "Our friends here are astonished at what I have done . . . "
(Royal Ontario Museum, Toronto)

Wolfe's darting and skirmishing around the perimeter of Louisbourg brightened the long, dreary days while the rest of the overwhelming British force inched towards the walls, dragging their big iron guns, and the French cannon thundered down upon them.

Inside the fortress the wooden houses of the poor were blazing. The gunners were collapsing from exhaustion, but the magnificent Madame Drucour continued to load and fire, contemptuously dusting with her handkerchief the holes in the battlements left by British shot.

Three of the French warships were hit and blew up, or were burned to the waterline. Others were sunk to block the harbor entrance. The last two were boarded and taken by 600 British sailors who rowed into the harbor by night.

Towards the end, the walls of Louisbourg drooped and crumbled, victims of the long bombardment and their own bad mortar. Governor Drucour asked Amherst for a ceasefire to evacuate the women and children. This enraged Wolfe who, like every British officer, still cursed the French for the massacre at Fort William Henry.

He wrote to Amherst: "When the French are in a scrape, they are ready to cry out in behalf of the human species; when fortune favors them, none more bloody, more inhuman. Montcalm has changed the very nature of war and has forced us, in some measure, to a deterring and dreadful vengeance."

Whereupon he moved a new battery closer to the walls and the bombardment went on.

A quite different Wolfe would write to his mother after the surrender: "I went into Louisbourg this morning to pay my devoirs to the ladies, but I found them all so pale and thin with long confinement in a casemate that I made my visit very short. The poor women have been heartily frightened as well they might; but no real harm, either during the siege or after it, has befallen any . . . I was determined to save as many lives and prevent as much violence as I could, because I am sure such a step would be very acceptable to you, and very becoming."

The dutiful son thus spared his mother the details of the scene. Twelve hundred inhabitants lay wounded or dying in what was left of the bombed hospital and the torn, roofless houses around it. The remaining women and children cowered in subterranean tunnels below the ramparts, half suffocated by the fires which had swallowed the wooden buildings. The stone chapel behind the King's Bastion had collapsed along with the officers' quarters, and only the governor's apartment remained. But Drucour and his men had saved Canada for another year. It was now too late for Amherst to move up the St. Lawrence and coordinate his attack with Abercromby's push up the New York lake route. It was also too late for Abercromby. He had been beaten by Montcalm at Ticonderoga.

👑 ⚜

Twelve hundred boats carpeted a stretch of Lake George (then Lac St. Sacrement) as Abercromby's 15,000 men glided towards Montcalm's fort on the rocky peninsula at the junction with Lake Champlain. The sun glittered on the diamond-bright waters ahead, and dusted the pleasant green mountains and the rocky little islets that sprouted like flower-pots with birch and pine.

The bandsmen happily banged their drums and blew trumpets and bagpipes. "I never beheld so delightful a prospect", an officer wrote.

The army landed comfortably at the head of Lake George. The gunners trundled their cannon off the big flatboats while the vanguard entered the sudden shade of the great evergreens and met the silent mystery of virgin forest. They soon lost their way and ran into a French advance force, also lost. The primeval silence was shattered by musket fire and Lord Howe died, shot through the chest.

That one shot wrecked the hopes of the fifteen thousand. Howe had been sent to do Abercromby's thinking for him. He had rapidly adapted the army to the realities of North American warfare. He kept the red coats, but cut off their tails to make bush travel easier. He made the men discard their powdered wigs, cut their hair and paint their musket barrels to cut down glitter. He eliminated some of the unwieldy baggage trains that had so encumbered Braddock. More than that, he inspired confidence. Wolfe called him "the noblest Englishman that has appeared in my time and the best soldier in the British army."

His death, said Major Rogers, the Rangers' leader, "seemed to produce an almost general languor and consternation through the whole army." Major Thomas Mante added "the soul of General Abercromby's army seemed to expire . . . neither order nor discipline was observed and a strange kind of infatuation usurped the place of resolution".

It was not just Abercromby's incompetence that worried the army. Armies had fought well in the past under poor generals. But Howe's death was an omen that struck the phlegmatic British regulars as deeply as it affected the God-fearing colonials and the darkly-superstitious Highlanders.

For one man it was a confirmation of doom already foretold. Ten years before, according to legend, Major Duncan Campbell of Inverawe had been awakened in his damp Highland castle by the ghost of his cousin Donald, whose murderer he had unwittingly shielded.

"Farewell, Inverawe," the vision cried. "Farewell till we meet at Ticonderoga!"

Campbell never heard the Indian name again until the day of Howe's death. His brother officers and clansmen, who knew the ghost story, told him the place they were to attack was called Fort George.

Montcalm and his officers at Fort Ticonderoga, July 1758.

(Gravure Francais au Canada)

But on the morning of battle he shouted at them: "You have deceived me! I have seen him. He came into my tent last night. This is Ticonderoga! I shall die today."

He did not die that day but was mortally wounded, together with hundreds of the best regulars on the continent. His regiment, the 42nd, or Black Watch, lost 500 officers and men, out of a total British casualty list of 2,000.

Abercromby made the mistake of hurling his great force against a fortified ridge two miles from the fort, without waiting for his artillery to be dragged up. Between one and seven o'clock on a witheringly hot July afternoon, he launched six attacks against a deep wall of logs, all pointing outward. Behind it, Montcalm, in his ruffled silk shirt-sleeves, hurried back and forth, directing his musketry and shouting *"Vive le Roi!"*

"Vive notre géneràl!" the whitecoats roared in reply as they loaded, rammed, aimed and fired, leaving the attackers moaning to death in the torn branches, trapped in the entangling brush, or blundering helplessly in the blood-spattered greenery.

From behind their logs, they tried a trick that would become a staple of Western movies — raising their hats on sticks to draw enemy fire. Even the dashing Chevalier de Lévis did it;

his plumed tricorne sustained two large holes. Bougainville was wounded slightly and Bourlamaque seriously, but the French losses were comparatively light — 377 killed and wounded.

Abercromby, who never went near the battle, panicked when he heard the result. Although he had thirteen thousand men left, and cannon that had never been fired, he fled down the lake towards New York. Two days later de Lévis reached his landing-place and found the army gone. Beside the piles of abandoned baggage were dozens of shoes, stuck in the mud. The best British troops yet seen in North America had run, some going barefoot in their hurry.

The Campbells were carrying the wounded Inverawe south from accursed Ticonderoga. He was to die nine days after the battle and be buried at Fort Edward.

The mercurial Montcalm went into transports of delight and exaggeration. He wrote to Angélique; "Without Indians, almost without Canadians or colony troops . . . alone with Lévis and Bourlamaque and the troops of the line, 3,100 fighting men, I have beaten an army of 25,000 . . . "

He raised a tall wooden cross on the battlefield, with the painted inscription which he composed himself:

> *Quid dux? quid miles? quid strata ingentia ligna? En Signum! En victor! Deus hic, Deus ipse triumphat.* (Parkman's translation: "Soldier and chief and rampart's strength are nought; Behold the conquering Cross! 'Tis God the triumph wrought.")

Wolfe was furious. Despite the debacle at Ticonderoga, perhaps because of it, he urged Amherst to push on to Quebec and finish off the Canadian "hellhounds". When the general refused to move, he threatened to resign. His letters grew violent: "Tho' I am neither inhuman nor rapacious, yet I own it would give me pleasure to see the Canadian vermin sacked and pillaged and justly repaid their unheard-of Cruelty."

Wolfe may have seen a few scalped corpses at Louisbourg but, at this stage, he had no first-hand experience of the true cruelty of colonial war. He had never watched torture at the stake

"View of the Plundering and Burning of the City of Grymross, 1758". Grymross, now Gagetown, New Brunswick, was one of the villages laid waste by Wolfe's men after the capture of Louisbourg. The painting was done on the spot by Lieut. Thomas Davies of the Royal Artillery.

(The National Gallery of Canada, Ottawa)

or been invited to eat a boiled human. He, himself, had done some sacking and pillaging and was about to do more.

He was sent, with seven warships and three frigates, to lay waste French fishing villages along the Gulf of St. Lawrence. His letters are shamefaced about this "great exploit" which, he wrote, consisted of robbing fishermen of their nets and burning their huts.

"We have done a great deal of mischief", he reported to Amherst, "and spread the terror of His Majesty's arms through the Gulf, but have added nothing to the reputation of them."

After this dubious episode, he sailed home with Boscawen's returning fleet. He arrived in London, sick as usual, to find he could have spared himself the agony of the voyage. Pitt had ordered him to stay on for next year's North American campaign, but he had sailed before the order reached him.

Over dinner with Lord George Sackville at White's Club he discussed the results of the summer's fighting.

The British had taken Fort Frontenac (now Kingston, Ontario), in a sudden swoop by 3,000 men. This meant the French had lost control of Lake Ontario and were threatened from the up-

per St. Lawrence, 200 miles from Montreal. A French supply fleet
of nine ships had been destroyed at the same time, thus starving
the defenders of Fort Duquesne, until they had burned and abandoned it. It was now being rebuilt as Fort Pitt, and would in time
become Pittsburgh.

With the capture of Louisbourg, that added up to three
British wins and one loss at Ticonderoga. Canada had lost the west,
and was now threatened from the east. The centre, the St. Lawrence, had yet to be attacked by a competent general.

Sackville had heard rumors that Wolfe was to be promoted. But only rumors. Nothing more. Wolfe said he would pre-
fer to fight in Germany where war was more civilized, but feared
that he was marked for Canada once again.

⚜ ✤

Montcalm's elation soon subsided. Worn out by work, battle and
the "miserable dissensions" that racked the colony, he asked to be
recalled to France.

Vaudreuil was jealous of his victory at Ticonderoga, especially because so few of his Canadians were involved. His letters to Paris grew nastier; "I cannot help warning you of the unhappy consequences that would follow if the Marquis de Montcalm should remain here . . . I pass over in silence all the infamous
conduct and indecent talk he has held or countenanced . . . "

The two men had a confrontation in the Governor's
house. While eight junior officers looked on in embarrassment,
Vaudreuil revived his old charge that Montcalm failed to follow up
his success at Fort William Henry the year before. The general controlled himself and said quietly that he had done his best.

"When one is not pleased with one's lieutenants," he
added coldly "One had better take the field in person".

Vaudreuil muttered that he might do just that. Montcalm said he would be delighted to serve under him.

Then Madame de Vaudreuil said what *she* thought and
the general's blood rose.

"Madame", he said, "saving due respect, permit me to
have the honor to say that ladies ought not to talk war."

She kept on.

"Madame, saving due respect, permit me to have the
honor to say that if Madame de Montcalm were here and heard me

talking war with Monsieur le Marquis de Vaudreuil, she would *remain silent."*

Alone in his quarters, Montcalm gave way to despair. He confided this, not to Angélique — for women should not know the miseries of war — but in emotional, almost illegible letters to his friend Bourlamaque:–

"I should like as well as anybody to be Marshal of France; but to buy the honor with the life I am leading here would be too much".

He describes the state of Fort Duquesne before it was abandoned — "Mutiny among the Canadians, who want to come home; the officers busy with making money and stealing like mandarins. The commander (Ligneris) sets the example and will come back with three or four hundred thousand francs; the pettiest ensign who doesn't gamble will have ten, twelve, fifteen thousand. The Indians don't like Ligneris, who is drunk every day.

"Forgive the confusion of this letter; I have not slept all night with thinking of the robberies and mismanagement and folly. *Pauvre Roi, pauvre France, cara patria!* Oh, when shall we get out of this country . . . When shall I see my chateau of Candiac, my plantations, my chestnut grove, my old mill, my mulberry trees?"

The letters trail off with plaintive requests that Bourlamaque burn them.

By daylight, Montcalm shook off his despair, but not his pessimism. The fall colors were burning their way along the banks of the St. Lawrence, heralding the end of another year's fighting. Soon all the armies would be settled down for the winter and only small bands of woodsmen would roam the blank wastes on snowshoes, leaving a few scalped bodies in the snow. Canada had survived once more, but only just.

Montcalm wrote to the Minister of War, withdrawing his request for recall (which the minister had already rejected) and declaring that he was prepared to die in the ruins of Canada. But, he said "the situation of the colony is most critical. Peace is necessary."

The Governor expressed it differently: "The people are alarmed and would soon lose courage if my firmness did not rekindle their zeal to serve the King."

Whichever way it was put, the French court had to be told that New France was in dire need of help. Despite his compulsive boasting, Vaudreuil realized this. He and Montcalm agreed to send Bougainville and the commissary of war, Doreil, to make a direct appeal to Paris.

They sailed in early November, armed with letters from Vaudreuil expressing his fullest confidence in them. They did not know, but probably suspected, that the Governor had sent a separate letter to the Colonial Minister, describing them as "creatures of M. de Montcalm" who didn't understand the true state of affairs in the colony.

Then the ice thickened in the river, sealing off Canada for six months. There would be no response from France until the first ship brought letters in the spring.

Chapter 6

"Mad, Is He?"

Since the Romans discovered the bitter waters of Bath in the west of England, prosperous invalids have hastened there, by chariot, carriage, train, bus or limousine to try their healing properties. In the mid-18th century it was the most fashionable of English spas.

Wolfe arrived by post-chaise in December 1758, took lodgings in Queen Square and embarked simultaneously on a cure, a romance, and the planning of his expedition.

He was a hero. His exploits at Louisbourg were the talk of the gentlemen's clubs in London and even the rubicund retired generals who nursed their gout at Bath deigned to recognize the pale young colonel. Beau Nash, the aging dandy who ruled Bath society, came to meet him, and the local ladies twittered over him.

Miss Katherine Lowther was staying there with her mother, the widow of a former governor of Barbados, and her brother, the enormously rich and unpopular Sir James Lowther. Wolfe had met her in Bath the year before; this time he plunged into courtship, and a betrothal was arranged within a few weeks. He does not mention his feelings towards her in his letters to his mother or anyone else. He had learned from his blighted love affair with Elizabeth Lawson that it was better to keep these matters away from his mother. But undoubtedly she knew of the Lowther engagement, and she resented it bitterly. She nourished a growing dislike of Katherine for no known reason except that she was becoming more stubborn and unpleasant with the years.

Katherine is remembered best by the famous miniature portrait she gave Wolfe to wear next to his heart. She was fluffily pretty in a chocolate-box way, her large, gentle eyes softening a long, sharp nose. We know little about her character. We can only hope that she was not like her brother, who became the first Earl of Lonsdale. Horace Walpole described him as "equally unamiable in public and private"; another contemporary called him "more detested than any man alive . . . truly a madman, though too rich to be confined."

While pledging his heart to Katherine, Wolfe pledged the rest of him to Pitt. "He may dispose of my slight carcass as he pleases", he told Rickson. "I am in very bad condition both with the gravel and rheumatism; but I had much rather die than decline any kind of service that offers."

Just after Christmas, the call came. Wolfe was summoned to Pitt's gracious country house at Hayes and given command of the next attack up the St. Lawrence, with the temporary rank of major-general. Amherst, as supreme commander in North America would advance from the south, via Ticonderoga. Wolfe would be given a free hand in organizing his own expedition. It was, he told his uncle, Major Walter Wolfe, "a greater role than he had expected or desired." Then he put modesty aside and took firm grasp of the long-awaited opportunity to plan his own campaign.

Townshend was staying at Raynham when a horseman cantered up the long, tree-lined driveway, bringing an urgent letter from the adjutant general at the War Office:—

My Dear George,
  I beg you will lose no time, but come to Town directly. I am not allowed to explain myself by this letter, but you may be sure my reasons are very cogent. I should not otherwise write in this manner, but it is highly important for you to lose no time.
                    Your faithful friend,
                    Richard Lyttleton
P.S. Lord Orford's game is not arrived.

Townshend hurried to London where General Lyttleton arranged for him to have a brigade in Wolfe's army. In a subsequent letter, Lyttleton praised him for his "magnanimous" acceptance and congratulated him upon the honor and glory he would obtain by it. He added the hope that "the short time you will be absent and the small risk you will probably run in this enterprise will in some degree reconcile Lady Ferrers (Mrs. Townshend) to it."

Whether or not Wolfe wanted Townshend with him, he accepted him and wrote a flattering letter; "Such an example in a person of your rank and character could not but have the best effects upon the troops in America and indeed upon the whole military part of the nation."

Brigadier-General, the Honourable Robert Monckton. From the portrait by Benjamin West.
(Public Archives of Canada)

He was allowed to choose the other two brigadiers himself. The Honourable Robert Monckton, who had captured Beauséjours and expelled the Acadians, was reliable and experienced in transatlantic wars. He was an easy-going Irishman, son of Viscount Galway, with no jealousy of burning ambition in him, and no pretence of intellect. He was only six months older than Wolfe; they had served together as boy officers in Flanders.

James Murray was a different proposition. The impoverished fifth son of Lord Elibank had a wider military experience than any senior officer — he had even served in the ranks, to the disgust of his family. He was fiercely ambitious, with a tiny, intense face and a ridiculous jutting chin. He and Wolfe had quarrelled violently in Scotland after Culloden — Wolfe still spoke of him as "my old antagonist" — but he had fought so well at Louisbourg that Wolfe forgave him. Murray never forgave Wolfe, alive or dead: he was too stubborn for that.

But the new major-general did not want friends with him on the campaign; he wanted soldiers. As commander, he had no intention of fraternizing with his subordinates, so friendship was unnecessary.

Thus out of three brigadiers, he got one who sneered at him and openly despised him, and one who hated him quietly and steadily. But even if he had known this beforehand he would probably have chosen the same men. He was a professional.

All three brigadiers were older than Wolfe and all were the sons of peers, which made for added awkwardness between them and the middle-class commander. But all knew before they sailed that social rank and the quality of blood to be shed were not so important in North America as on the fashionable battlefields of Europe where you allowed the enemy the courtesy of firing first. It was a middle-class place, ideal for the Wolfes and below the Townshends.

It was also below the cavalry, the aristocratic cream of the British army, who never appeared there. Shortly before he was given command of the Quebec army, Wolfe wrote wistfully that what he would really like would be a cavalry post in Europe. He must have known that, hero or not, the cavalry would never accept a soldier's son with no pedigree.

His two senior staff officers were both Irish and remarkable men in different ways. The adjutant-general, Major Isaac Barré, a large, swarthy man of appalling manners, was the son of a French refugee who lived in Dublin. He was to become a prominent parliamentarian later in the century — the first to call the American revolutionaries "sons of liberty".

The quartermaster-general, Colonel Guy Carleton, solemn, self-possessed and outspoken, thought little of Hanoverian soldiers and said so loudly enough for the Hanoverian king to hear. George disliked him so much it took three attempts at persuasion before he would sign Carleton's commission for the expedition. Later, as Governor of Canada, Carleton would hold the land for Britain and stop the American revolution at the 49th parallel.

Major Patrick Mackellar was chief engineer. After his capture by Montcalm at Oswego and imprisonment at Quebec he knew more about the fortifications there than anyone else in the British army. Wolfe distrusted him because of his ungentlemanly behaviour during the siege of Louisbourg, but he was the only expert available.

At forty-two, Mackellar was the oldest officer on Wolfe's staff. To mollify the veterans who had been passed over, the general and his brigadiers and colonels were given only temporary ranks. Wolfe got £14 a week as a North American major-general while Amherst who, though commander-in-chief, would play a secondary role, received a handsome £70 a week. Wolfe pointed out that a general, however local and temporary, must keep up appearances. The King was persuaded to advance him £500.

With his military preparations complete, the young general rattled back to Bath to say goodbye to Katherine. No wedding date was set because he could not say when he would return. With his own opinion of his health and chances of surviving two more ocean crossings, he could not honestly have promised to return at all.

There is no record of this final parting, no indication whether Wolfe loved her, or proposed to marry her for her money. He does not mention her in his subsequent letters, only in his will. So writers of the period gave their imagination full rein. Here is the parting, as described by Charles Johnstone, a wordy Irishman who claimed to have known the Wolfe family:–

> "Mistake not, O my love, the inconsistencies which anguish extorts from my bleeding heart. How can I say it? Our happiness is delayed — delayed but to be more exalted. Honor, the service of my country, call."
>
> "And am I to be left?"
>
> "But for a time, a little time, the pain of which shall be overpaid by the joy of meeting, never to part again. Oh, spare my heart, restrain those tears; I am not proof to such a trial. The interest, the glory of my country demand my service, and my gracious master has honored me with such a station, in which my endeavors may be effectual to accomplish his commands — nay, must be effectual — where love urges duty, where you are the inestimable reward."
>
> "Go! go! and Heaven guard and guide your steps" waving her hand and turning from him to hide her tears. "I shall no longer struggle with the sacred impulse that leads you on to glory . . . "
>
> "I go to certain victory; the prayers of angels must prevail!"
>
> Saying these words, he rushed out of the room, leaving her half dead with grief.

Perhaps the lovers of two centuries ago did talk like that in their private moments; Wolfe may have reserved his more extravagant phrases for Miss Lowther. To his mother he sent only a brief, businesslike letter, saying "I shall carry this business through with my best abilities." But according to another story, he could be carried away by heroics.

As Pitt's brother-in-law, Lord Temple, told it, he and Pitt entertained Wolfe at dinner in London on the eve of his departure for Portsmouth and the fleet. Suddenly the general lost his self-control, drew his sword and walked up and down the oak-panelled room, brandishing it in the candlelight and raving boasts and threats. His eyes glittered as he slaughtered imaginary Frenchmen by the fireplace.

Pitt, most theatrical of statesmen, sat frozen in embarrassment. Then, abruptly, Wolfe left.

"Good God", said Pitt. "That I should have entrusted the fate of the country and of the Administration to such hands!"

Temple's story was not printed until thirty years later and then it was surrounded by apologies for the reflections it cast on the hero. But it was the talk of the coffee houses at the time, and was used skillfully by Pitt's enemies. Temple's most damning observation was that Wolfe had taken very little wine. So the gossips assumed that if he wasn't drunk he must be mad.

The crafty Duke of Newcastle scurried to tell George II that he was sending a madman to Quebec.

"Mad, is he?" the King snorted. "Then I hope he will bite some of my other generals."

Admiral Sir Charles Saunders was a model leader of the silent service. He wrote little, said little, and carried out orders with dogged reliability and a rare tolerance of land warriors. He was forty-six when Pitt summoned him to take charge of naval operations in the St. Lawrence — a bulky man with fierce, baggy eyes and a great, square nose.

He had a solid reputation within the navy, but was little known outside of it. He had no outstanding sea victories to his credit, although he had joined the navy as a King's Letter boy of fourteen, and had sailed with Commodore George Anson on his

Admiral Sir Charles Saunders, in command of naval operations in the St. Lawrence.

(McCord Museum)

famous voyage around the world. He was, however, a seadog who could rise above the sordid horrors of life aboard ship and associate with civilized gentry ashore, and was even capable of original ideas. As his ninety-gun flagship Neptune stood out from Spithead, the admiral made an historic decision: he would go beyond his orders from Pitt, take his big ships as far upriver as Quebec, and fight alongside the army if necessary. He would order his sailors and marines to help Wolfe's redcoats and, if need be, permit the redcoats to help man his ships.

This was revolutionary thinking for a navy man of the period, and it establishes Saunders, not Wolfe, as the real father of combined land-sea operations. Pitt had ordered him to co-operate with the land forces, not merely transport them to their destination. But neither the war leader nor the general expected the entire fleet to take part in the assault. Wolfe assumed the line-of-battle ships would guard the Gulf against French warships while Saunders' sloops and frigates escorted the troop transports upriver. There was grave doubt whether large ships could navigate the St. Lawrence as far as Quebec.

Saunders decided to try. Before the fleet left English waters, a frigate overtook the Neptune with orders from Pitt to detach the sixty-gun Stirling Castle and another ship for use in other operations off the Spanish coast. Saunders refused to relinquish the Stirling Castle because, he said, "she was handy for rivers."

But true to navy tradition, he did not tell the army how far he was prepared to go. On the ten-week voyage to Louisbourg he kept his own counsel, standing firmly on his heaving quarterdeck, his square frame in its blue coat with white and gold facings steadfastly bucking the wind. On blue water, there was no need to talk to landlubbers.

Wolfe suffered alone in his cabin. When he could get out of his bunk he spent the time poring over Mackellar's map of Quebec and the sketchy reports available on conditions there. He had little to say to Townshend and Carleton, although they lived a few feet away from him in the sterncastle and passed one another regularly on their way to the breezy gallery outside the ship which was the officers' lavatory.

It was a bad crossing, stormy and very cold. As the Neptune approached Louisbourg her rigging was sheathed in ice and the fore topsail so stiffly frozen it could not be furled.

Louisbourg harbor was blocked by ice-floes, so the fleet turned south to Halifax. There, in harbor, they saw the masts of Rear-Admiral Philip Durell's squadron which should, by this time, have been blockading the Gulf of St. Lawrence to keep out French supply ships.

Wolfe flew into a rage, storming at Saunders and the "incompetent" Durell, who claimed he had been delayed by the ice at Louisbourg and the fact that so many of his sailors were sick he could not man all of his ten ships.

It was May 5 before the blockaders left Halifax, and by then eighteen French ships had entered the St. Lawrence. Durell did manage to catch three stragglers in the gulf, but a further five slipped past him. It was a poor start to the naval side of the operation. Col. C. P. Stacey, the Canadian army historian of World War II, remarks in his military study of the campaign: "One cannot help feeling that if the French could get through the ice, Durell should have been able to do the same. Had he succeeded in doing so, Wolfe would probably have been saved a siege and a battle, and might have survived to die undramatically in bed."

It took another month to assemble the main expedition,

LE MAJOR ROBERT ROGER
Commandant en Chef les Troupes Indiennes au service des Américains

Major Robert Rogers. This French engraving describes him as "Commander in Chief of Indian troops in American service".

(Public Archives of Canada)

In fact Rogers' Rangers were mostly white American frontiersmen, like the group above. The man on the left wears winter campaign dress, the rest wear green uniform with buckskin additions.
(Drawing by Ronald Embleton)

collect the various units, regular and colonial, which were stationed in the colonies, and sort them out at Louisbourg.

Wolfe was to be hailed as "the soldier's friend", a general loved by his men, but his letters are marked by violent outbursts against the common soldier. Americans, Highlanders, Canadians, French — at times, he detested them all. He had a particular contempt for the American Rangers, calling them the "dirtiest, most contemptible cowardly dogs." They were fighters of a kind far beyond his experience — the British colonists' answer to the *coureurs de bois*. Major Robert Rogers, who raised seven companies of them, came from the frontiers of New Hampshire and had spent his youth smuggling goods between New England and New France, picking up an adequate knowledge of French in the process. He was a tough, unscrupulous woodsman with calm, clear eyes and an ugly nose. His ragged companies travelled by whaleboat or canoe, their smooth-bore guns loaded with buckshot or bullets, and fought like Indians, bringing back scalps.

They were "the worst soldiers in the world", according to the fastidious general, but he wanted more of them. The six Ranger companies arrived at Louisbourg well below strength and Wolfe suggested Amherst try to round up some recruits although, he added, the New Englanders obviously preferred the lazy life to any kind of service. Wolfe was to use these "dirtiest of dogs" in the dirtiest business of his campaign.

Even his sturdy British regulars were not to be trusted — "I know their discipline to be bad and their valour precarious. They are easily put to disorder and hard to recover out of it. They frequently kill their officers through fear and murder one another in confusion."

The regular redcoat — known since 1740 by the nickname Thomas Lobster — was a despised creature only a shade better off than a sailor. King's Regulations demanded he be five feet five inches tall, a Protestant, not ruptured or suffering from fits or other hidden disorders. He had enlisted (or been caught by a press-gang) to serve for three years. He had taken the King's Shilling, which had probably been dropped into his beer tankard by the recruiting sergeant when he was drunk. In addition the King had given him a bounty of four pounds, plus sixpence a day, a uniform, for which he repaid the King at twopence a day, and a steady diet of rock-hard ammunition loaf, cheese and rum.

For this, he would obey every order, trumpet blast or drum-tap, or be tied to a triangle of halberds and lashed with a cat-of-nine-tails. He expected to be cheated of his rations by his colonel and robbed by civilians, whom he robbed in return.

Shoehorned into the black, stinking lower decks of a transport, he would rot of scurvy, then be expected to stand rigidly on a battlefield and be ripped apart by musket balls or grape shot at a hundred yards' range. If he ran he might be hanged. If caught selling a piece of his ammunition loaf or stealing a chicken he could get up to the maximum of three thousand lashes. The woman who followed him through a campaign would also be whipped by the drummers if she got in the way. If he asked permission to marry her, he risked a hundred lashes for impertinence.

Life for the Lobster was the lash, the pox, and the threat of the gallows. Even battle could be a relief from the inhuman existence in camp. But the redcoats ferried ashore at Louisbourg were looking forward to a spell in camp after the hell of the ocean crossing. They cleaned themselves up for the parade-ground. Each man spread yellowish-white pipeclay on to the broad shoulder belt that supported his cartridge pouch. He washed his two shirts, two pairs of linen stockings, oiled to prevent sores, and spare pair of scarlet breeches and then stuffed them, with his spare leather neck stock, into his gray canvas haversack. He blacked and polished his buckled shoes, put on his long, flappy waistcoat, gray spatterdash gaiters up to mid-thigh, and the scarlet coat with regimental facings, which he had worn inside out on the voyage, so that it would stay relatively clean.

Most likely it had shrunk, for colonels of regiments spared themselves the expense of pre-shrinking the cheap material they bought to outfit their men. The leather stock fitted tightly round the neck, holding the soldier's well-greased head upright in its black tricorne hat. Once it was on, the Lobster could barely turn his head. He looked straight in front of him like a blinkered horse, and that was the way he fought.

The stock was supposed to deflect a bayonet thrust to the throat. The rest of his garb was designed to please his King and his officers and to make life as uncomfortable as possible. He could barely stoop without bursting trouser buttons and ripping his seat. And rats were liable to try to eat the grease on his hair.

The sight of the red columns marching and wheeling to the drag and paradiddle of the drums or dressed into line by the halberds of their sergeants, raised Wolfe's drooping spirits. He now wore a thick black mourning band on his arm, for he had just received a letter telling him that his father was dead.

He was saddened but not surprised. The general was seventy-five and had been ill when Wolfe sailed. He had not expected to see his father again. He covered his feelings by issuing a spate of orders.

Troops, when re-embarked, should be given as much fresh air as possible and allowed to eat on deck. They must have exercise and clean bedding. Each regiment would be supplied with fishing lines and hooks. Each man was to have a ration of ginger to purify his drinking water. Three thousand barrels of flour and biscuits were to be taken from the contractor's store at Louisbourg to replace provisions that had not arrived. Three regiments whose stores had been lost on the way from Philadelphia would draw tents from ordinance and make do with old camp kettles. One hundred invalids unfit to serve must be shipped home. General Amherst must send enough money to pay for a long siege (he didn't). Each company of seventy five men would be allowed to take along three women and each company of one hundred, four women. Women would be selected in the usual manner, by drawing lots.

This was a smaller proportion of women than that usually permitted to regiments on active service. Some would be wives, others camp-followers unblessed by clergy, but marriages were not to be taken very seriously. The women were expected to work. They washed, cleaned, moved equipment and served as nurses in field hospitals. They were marginally more respectable than the female sutlers who followed behind, selling food and comforts by day and themselves by night.

When his army was finally assembled, Wolfe found he had 8,600 troops instead of the 12,000 promised him, and 13,500 sailors. Although he complained to Pitt about the shortage, warning him that every (French)man in Canada would fight, he seemed pleased with the force at his command.

It was the best trained and equipped army North America had seen, supported by the biggest and best fleet. Some units had not been taught the latest drill maneuvers, but Wolfe cheerfully overlooked this.

"New exercises, new fiddlesticks", he told his officers. "If they are otherwise well disciplined and will fight, that's all I require of them."

Monckton's brigade contained four English foot regiments and the Fraser Highlanders. Townshend had three regiments and a battalion of Royal Americans; Murray had two, another battalion of Royal Americans and 100 artillerymen. In addition to these line regiments, Wolfe had an elite corps of grenadiers, picked from the Louisbourg garrison, three companies of light infantry and three companies of American Rangers, led by Major George Scott. The other Rangers, under Rogers, were now with Amherst.

It took six days for the expedition to clear Louisbourg harbor, because of fog and lack of wind and because of its size. There were twenty-two great ships of the line, five frigates, eighteen sloops and a long train of transports, supply ships, ordinance vessels, private American traders' vessels and fire-ships — 119 craft, not including Durell's ships, which were waiting in the St. Lawrence.

From the lofty Neptune, Saunders shepherded his armada past Lighthouse Point and out into the Atlantic. The ships came slowly, sails flapping in the fitful sunshine, then disappearing to drift and collide in sudden swirling fogs, grinding against chunks of floating ice; the bos'uns barking and cursing at the pigtailed wretches who clambered and hauled and struggled in the rigging.

The admiral grunted a command. All Yankee masters of hired civilian transports would obey naval orders promptly and precisely or his warships would fire on them. He added grimly that the cost of shot and powder so used would be charged against the hire of the offending ship.

At four in the drizzling morning of June 6, the last ship cleared harbor, the waiting warships set sail, and the fleet billowed northward. The redcoats on deck cheered hopefully and the officers in the sterncastles broached their private stocks of claret to drink toasts to "British colors on every French fort, port and garrison in North America!"

Wolfe joined in the toasting, then retired below to write his will. It began: "I desire that Miss Lowther's picture may be set in jewels to the amount of five hundred guineas and returned to her."

His other bequests to army friends added up to about five thousand pounds and were to cause his mother a great deal of trouble. For Wolfe did not have five thousand pounds. He was to die a general, but could never afford to live like one. He completed the will and signed it on June 8, the second day at sea.

A week later an officer suffering from scurvy was told by a surgeon to drink seawater. A bucket was thrown over the ship's side, hauled up, and found to contain water that tasted almost fresh.

The fleet had reached the St. Lawrence.

A crowd of anxious Canadians awaited Bougainville at Quebec. They lined the docks of Lower Town as he was rowed ashore from the fast frigate that had beaten the British blockade. Before he could climb the icy steps to the stone jetty he heard urgent shouts: "What news from France?"

The young Chevalier shrugged. His news was all bad. There would be little help from the King. And he had learned just before sailing that a huge British fleet was on its way. This set the town in an uproar. An attack had been expected, but not from the sea. The colony's fears were directed at the Lake Champlain route. Both Vaudreuil and Montcalm were in Montreal, preparing to defend that front. Bougainville took horse and rode to Montreal with the rest of his news.

The attitude of the French court had been summed up by Berryer, the minister for the colonies. "Eh, Monsieur", he shrugged. "When the house is on fire, one cannot occupy one's self with the stable."

To which Bougainville had replied "At least, Monsieur, nobody will say that you talk like a horse."

The Canadian "stable" would get no massive reinforcements, only 400 replacement troops, and no naval squadron — only four royal supply ships, to be followed by Joseph Cadet's private merchantmen.

The King's paper to Vaudreuil and Bigot complained about the enormous sums already spent on the colony and added: "His Majesty would be equally disposed to send the same help to the colony now, but the continuation of the war in Europe, the too-great risks of the sea and the necessity of concentrating His Majesty's naval forces does not permit of dispersing those forces at the present moment . . . "

So Canada would just have to sit tight and defend itself as best it could.

This response disappointed Vaudreuil, but was soon forgotten when he opened a second letter, addressed to him alone. In effect, it reversed the roles of governor and general. When Montcalm arrived in 1756 he had been ordered to obey Vaudreuil's orders in all military matters. He commanded only the regular troops from France, not the colonial marines, militia or Indians, who came directly under the Governor. He could advise, but must defer to Vaudreuil.

The letter Bougainville brought informed the Governor that Montcalm had been promoted to lieutenant-general — an actual rank which took precedence in military protocol over Vaudreuil's honorary lieutenant-generalship. In future he must consult Montcalm on all defense matters. He must not even show himself in the field at the head of his own colonial troops without asking Montcalm's permission.

As small compensation for this loss of authority, Vaudreuil was given the Grand Cross of St. Louis, a white enamel bauble, set with pearls and gold fleurs de lis. He was ordered to show the letter to Montcalm and explain the change of roles, but as the general continued to defer to him throughout the summer, it seems unlikely that he did so. A letter to Montcalm told him only that the governor had been recommended to consult with him on all operations (not administrative matters) and to act in concert with him.

So the suspicion and confusion in the French leadership flourished as danger approached. Bougainville's mission had profited only Bougainville. He got a colonelcy, the Cross of St. Louis and the esteem of Madame de Pompadour.

Back in Quebec, the governor blustered. "There is no ruse", he wrote to Berryer, "no resource, no means which my zeal does not suggest to lay snares for them and finally, when the exigency demands it, to fight them with an ardor, and even a fury, which exceeds the range of their ambitious designs . . . the burghers of this city have already put their furniture in places of safety. The old men, women and children hold themselves ready to leave town. My firmness is generally applauded. It has penetrated every heart and each man says aloud 'Canada, our native land, shall bury us under its ruins before we surrender to the English'." In the same ringing tones, he went on to extol the virtues of the contractor Cadet, whose zeal for the King's service was keeping the colony supplied. As he wrote, Cadet's convoy was entering Quebec Basin, having dodged Durell's ships with a few losses. The habitants cheered its arrival, although many of them knew they were welcoming back their own grain, which the zealous Cadet would now resell once more.

Montcalm marched the two hundred miles from Montreal, bringing with him most of the troops available in the colony. He left only Bourlamaque and his three battalions at Ticonderoga, while a detachment under the guerrilla leader St. Luc de la Corne were set to guard the St. Lawrence rapids at the entrance to Lake Ontario.

When he arrived at Quebec, exhausted by the journey, he called on Bigot to find out what had been done to prepare for an invasion from the sea. Nothing had been done.

Two years before, Montcalm had made tentative plans to stop a naval attack. He had chosen a gunsite on the heights of Cape Tourmente on the north bank of the river which would command the Traverse, the dangerous channel which all ships had to navigate on their way to Quebec. More batteries on the Isle of Orleans would probably sink any vessel that got through the Traverse and a fort on Point Levi, facing the Rock, would prevent any bombardment of the city itself.

None of these defenses was ever built. But there was only one suitable landing place near Quebec — the six miles of mudflats and broken cliff between the St. Charles River and Beauport, where Sir William Phips had made his assault.

Montcalm had planned to fortify this shoreline, and add a second line of redoubts on the St. Charles, across from the Lower Town. These plans, too, remained on paper or in the general's head, as he was off fighting to the south every summer. Despite his pleas to Vaudreuil and the officials in Paris the work was not even ordered.

He wrote in his journal "Unfortunately, indolence triumphed again."

With Bougainville's news of the approaching English fleet, indolence vanished for a time. Quebec boiled with hysterical activity. Montcalm's five regular battalions had scarcely arrived when swarms of militiamen descended on Quebec from farms and backwoods cabins. There were boys of twelve and ancients of eighty. At the Governor's call his "children", the Indian allies, loped in with scalping knives at the ready. Wolfe had not been far wrong when he predicted that every man in Canada would fight.

An almost continuous council of war went on in the Intendant's palace. Vaudreuil declaimed and boasted, Montcalm shouted and swore, while a turmoil of army officers, sea-captains, merchants, priests and town dignitaries elbowed, shoved and argued. Nobody appeared to be in charge. The life of the 150-year-old colony was at stake and all the estates of New France — property, Church and military — came noisily together.

Vaudreuil declared that the British could never maneuver their ships up the river. God and His elements would see to that. Most of the council agreed, and the Bishop ordained processions, prayers and pilgrimages to Notre Dame des Victoires in Low-

The de Salaberry House near Beauport, the stone farmhouse chosen by Montcalm as his siege headquarters.

(Public Archives of Canada)

er Town to make sure.

Despite the confusion, the Beauport fortifications were built with remarkable speed. Tents, huts and Indian wigwams blossomed around the stone farmhouse Montcalm had chosen as his siege headquarters. Three hundred sailors dug a line of trenches on the right bank of the St. Charles. A log boom was stretched across the river mouth and reinforced by two hulks sunk to their gunwales and mounted with ten cannon each. A pontoon bridge of small boats was strung across the river a mile upstream to provide a link between Beauport and the city. The narrow city gates were closed and barred, with the exception of the Palace Gate, and it was guarded by lines of wooden pickets.

Seven of the biggest merchantmen in Cadet's fleet were commandeered — with generous compensation to the owner — hacked down, and converted into fireships. The rest were sent upriver for safety, carrying reserve stocks of food. Their crews returned to man gun batteries in Lower Town and floating gun platforms like "Le Diable", an ugly hexagonal craft that carried twelve heavy cannon but drew only three or four feet of water. By early June, Vaudreuil was blissfully confident that Quebec could not be taken even if by some miracle the English found their way up the river. There were nearly 14,000 soldiers in the Beauport camps, with more than a thousand Indians. The garrison behind the walls of Quebec numbered about 2,000. A quarter of the colony's population was under arms.

Candiac, the home of the Montcalms in Provence. Here Montcalm's wife received his unhappy letters from Quebec.

(*Archives Nationales du Québec*)

Montcalm still cursed the incompetence around him but part of him was numb. Bougainville's last piece of bad news was that one of the general's daughters was dead. He did not know which one, and Montcalm was never to learn, but he suspected that it was "poor Mirète, who was like me and whom I loved very much."

In his quiet moments in his lodging on Rampart Street away from the jabbering Canadians, he soothed himself by writing of his contempt for the Governor and the ridiculousness of the situation:–

"Vehicles are lacking for the work on the fortifications, but not for carrying materials for making a casemate for Madame Péan (Bigot's mistress). No matter how tragic the end of all this may be, one cannot help laughing."

Chapter 7

The Traverse

Legend says a ghost ship laden with red-coated soldiers still appears through the fog on dark days at the mouth of the St. Lawrence. It creaks towards the shore at Pointe aux Anglais, on Egg Island, lurches on to the rocks and vanishes in the gloom, leaving in the air the faint cries of lost men.

Eight English ships were wrecked there, and 900 men drowned, when Rear-Admiral Sir Hovenden Walker's fleet was shattered due to the admiral's bad navigation. The year was 1711, and the fleet was on its way to attack Quebec.

The townspeople gave thanks for this second deliverance from the English and changed the name of the Lower Town church Our Lady of Victory (which commemorated Sir William Phips' defeat in 1690) to Our Lady of Victories.

From then on the myth grew that no hostile fleet could master the treacherous river. The governor encouraged this belief and so did the priests. It comforted the people and conferred much undeserved respect upon the Canadian river pilots who alone were supposed to know the mysterious currents and hidden shoals.

In fact, the pilots knew remarkably little about the river. No accurate charts were made until the English arrived. So little was known about the famous Traverse that the French made plans to block it with sunken ships, then found that it was simply too wide.

Major Mackellar, in a report based on his experience as a prisoner in Quebec, advised that the river should not be navigated without a Canadian pilot, but added "yet I am far from thinking it to be as difficult and dangerous as the French would have the world believe."

Montcalm believed what the pilots told him. Later he would call them "either liars or ignoramuses".

Admiral Durell, who was sent ahead to open up the channels to Saunders' fleet, used Canadian pilots, but did not trust

Captain James Cook, painted by N. Dance. The famous explorer played an important role in the naval siege of Quebec, although at this time his rank was only that of chief petty officer.
(From an engraving in the Public Archives of Canada)

them. He brought one with him from the Atlantic, Jean Denis de Vitré, who had been captured at sea and threatened with hanging unless he showed the way.

When Durell's 64-gun flagship Princess Amelia reached La Prairie Baie, the point at the start of the main river channel where pilots were taken aboard, he raised the French flag on his mainmast. There were whoops of joy from the villagers on shore, who thought this was the long-awaited French navy. Pilots plashed out in their canoes and were hauled aboard at gunpoint. The French lilies were lowered and replaced by the red cross of St. George.

The pilots were passed from ship to ship as the main fleet arrived. Each day they were shown the main yardarm and told they would dangle from it if the ship ran aground.

Meanwhile the conscientious James Cook, master of the Pembroke, surveyed the Traverse. For three days he rowed back and forth with a fleet of whaleboats, taking soundings, anchoring, weighing and tacking, against currents that reached seven knots on the flood tide and nine on the ebb. He dropped buoys and put marker flags on shoals to replace those removed by the French. Cook was thirty-one, the son of a Yorkshire farm laborer who had learned his trade as a deckhand on broad-beamed Whitby colliers in the coastal waters of the North Sea. His remarkable seamanship and private studies of mathematics and astronomy would later enable him to break through the navy's caste system and gain his own command. He would become the greatest British navigator of his day, rivalled only in world repute by the Frenchman who had dodged past him in the Gulf a few weeks before — the Chevalier de Bougainville. At the time of his survey of the Traverse, he was ship's master, or chief petty officer, of the Pembroke.

On June 11, the Pembroke's log records that Cook was "satisfied with being acquainted with ye Channel." He placed sounding boats at intervals along the shallows and the first ships of the line moved through. Wolfe left the three-decker Neptune, to push ahead in the light frigate Richmond. He arrived at the entrance to the Traverse on June 25 and the Richmond took her place behind the troop transport Goodwill, which was commanded by a loud and proud old mariner, Captain Thomas Killick.

The Canadian pilot assigned to the Goodwill showed little respect for the yardarm, Killick, or anybody else. He cursed the treacherous English for luring him out with a false flag. Canada would bury their army, he yelled, and the walls of Quebec would be festooned with their scalps.

Killick threatened to throw him overboard and declared he would pilot the ship himself. The colonel of the regiment aboard the Goodwill told him not to be a fool. As Capt. John Knox of the 43rd. describes the scene in his journal, Killick thundered: "Damme, I'll convince you that an Englishman can go where a Frenchman dare not show his nose!"

When the captain of the Richmond nervously demanded to know who was piloting the transport ahead of him, the skipper himself bellowed back through his trumpet; "It's old Killick. And that's enough!"

Knox joined the old man as he leaned over the bowrail, roaring orders to the helmsman, joking with the sailors in the guideboats below, and pointing out the various shades of blue and green water and the tiny ripples that indicated rock ledges and sandbanks.

Killick took his ship through, and when they reached clear water he put down his trumpet and said "Damme if there are not a thousand places in the Thames fifty times more hazardous than this." According to Knox, the Canadian pilot rolled his eyes in wonder.

This tale redounds to the credit of seadog Killick but plays down the real hazards of the Traverse and the feat of Cook, Saunders, Durell and others in working their clumsy vessels through the zigzag passage. The three-deckers, heavy with men and guns, drew twenty feet of water.

By the evening of June 26 most of the ships were safely through and anchored off the Isle of Orleans, opposite the Basin of Quebec. The river myth was shattered and a suddenly-humbled Vaudreuil wrote to Paris: "The enemy have passed through sixty ships of war where we dared not risk a vessel of a hundred tons."

The first troops to land were the despised American rangers — forty lean backwoodsmen in worn green caps and coats, led by young Lieutenant Meech, from Connecticut. They were rowed ashore at midnight on the 26th, landing near St. Laurent d'Orleans on the southern side of the Isle of Orleans. The night was soft-black and still; the only sounds were the lap of the tides and the creak of the boats.

They crept carefully through the thick woods that crowded to the water and mounted a slope, muskets in hand, knives and tomahawks dangling at their belts. They found a farmhouse in a clearing, cold and empty, without trace of food or livestock, and pushed on through the undergrowth until they heard voices and saw the flicker of an oil lamp. A group of men were digging a hole, about to bury a chest.

Without waiting for the order, a ranger jumped up and fired. The men swung round, seized guns and fired back before disappearing into the woods. One ranger was hit in the chest and killed. After the brief, blinding exchange of volleys the island fell silent again. Meech and his men returned to the farmhouse, where they spent the rest of the night. They heard nothing, but in morning they found the dead ranger nailed to the ground by a stake driven through his stomach. His body had been slashed, his hands nearly cut off and his scalp carved away.

The patrol advanced across the island. They found a pleasant countryside, with neat fields sown with wheat, barley and flax, and dotted with square stone farmhouses, some thatched, some with wooden roofs. A windmill spun lazily in the warm morning breeze and a stream trickled over a water-wheel. There was no sign of life. They returned to the fleet and reported that the island had been abandoned.

The bulk of the army landed and made camp on a plateau just below the village of St. Laurent. While the redcoats
stretched their legs and the artillerymen hauled their cannon off
the flatboats, Captain Knox strolled over to the white-spired village church.

After prudently removing any ornaments of value, the
curé had pinned a note to the door, addressed to The Worthy Officers of the British Army. It begged them in the name of God,
humanity, and their own well-known generosity to protect the
church and his own house next door. He added what Knox calls
"the frothy compliments peculiar to the French" and his regrets
that the English could no longer enjoy the radishes and asparagus
in his garden, which had now run to seed.

"A delightful country", says Knox, who was always impressed by scenery. "I am inclined to think that we are happily arrived at the place that, to all appearance, will be the centre of our
future operations." The island was indeed a pleasant place. Jacques
Cartier had named it the Isle of Bacchus because of the wild grapes
that grew there, then, remembering an explorer's grim duty to his
patrons, renamed it in honor of Charles, Duc d'Orleans.

For Wolfe, it was only a stepping stone. From its east-
erly tip, two miles from St. Laurent, he surveyed the defenses of
the city he had come to conquer.

One slow swing of his telescope convinced him that the
plans he had laid so carefully in Louisbourg must be scrapped. Mackellar's map and reports had prepared him for his first view of the
Rock ahead — stark, black and fearful, and above it an impressive
jumble of white towers and steeples straining upward in the flash-
ing sunlight. Stretching westward, upstream, as far as his telescope could see, were great, unassailable cliffs.

He had expected all this. He had not expected the boom
and sunken hulks blocking the St. Charles river below the rock, and
to the east the rows of tents, and piles of newly turned earth and
fresh-cut logs along the Beauport shore where he had planned to
land. He had intended to follow the Phips' route, fight "a smart
action" at the St. Charles, and take Quebec from the rear. Montcalm had forestalled him.

Two years earlier, after the Rochefort debacle, Wolfe
had laid down sound rules for amphibious operations — run into
the enemy port as soon as you appear before it; get the troops

ashore at once, and push on smartly; plan well beforehand, but be prepared to take a chance.

He had disregarded his first rule by landing on the Isle of Orleans — Mackellar had recommended this. He could not push ahead smartly to Beauport because it was too well defended. He could prepare for a long siege — which would give Amherst time to invade the colony from the south, but would also deprive James Wolfe of the glory. Or he could take a chance, according to his ultimate theory — "In war, something must be allowed to chance and fortune, seeing it is in its nature hazardous . . . the loss of 1,000 men is rather an advantage to a nation than otherwise, seeing that gallant attempts raise its reputation and make it respectable; whereas the contrary appearances sink the credit of a country, ruin the troops and create infinite uneasiness and discontent at home."

Wolfe said nothing to Mackellar, who was by his side. He closed his telescope and strode impatiently back to his new camp. He was unsure of himself, and his bladder ached.

On the way back he saw soldiers romping noisily through the trees, carrying stolen chickens and vegetables. They were annoyingly cheerful. He soothed his depression by drafting a general order, instructing officers to supervise all foraging expeditions and threatening severe punishment for "irregularities."

As he dictated the order, a sudden storm blew up from the northeast. Summer lightning crackled and torrential rain gushed down upon the soldiers, filling their newly-dug trenches and swamping them as they struggled to get their ridgepole tents up and to heave the ammunition boxes under cover. Violent winds tore through the trees and sent the ships heeling and tossing. The once-sparkling river surged and boiled. Transports were ripped from their moorings to crunch and tangle together; landing boats were capsized, smashed, or carried off downstream.

The storm ended as suddenly as it had begun. It was the first of many that would strike Quebec that violent summer. As Saunders disentangled his battered transports and issued them with spare anchors from the holds of his men-of-war, he reflected that he had been lucky with the weather on the voyage upriver. He must now seek a safer anchorage closer to the south shore, which was still held by the French. Watching from his house near the St. Charles, Montcalm was impressed by the seamanship of the British. He wrote: "It is quite probable that in similar conditions a

French fleet would have perished."

Next night, the French made their first move. Vaudreuil had great faith in an ancient weapon which still struck terror into men who sailed wooden ships. Fireships had helped to rout the Spanish Armada in the broad English Channel. Against a large fleet crowded into one narrow arm of a smooth river they must be devastating. At the cost of nearly a million livres — most of it profit to Cadet and Bigot — seven merchant ships had been prepared as a fiery sacrifice. Their gunports were sealed and their holds crammed with grapeshot — all ready to burst into life as the fire grew in intensity. Trains of powder led to tar-soaked channels cut in the decks; masts and rigging were coated with melted resin. They were fine examples of the incendiarist's art.

At ten o'clock on the moonless night of June 28 they were pushed off from the floating batteries below the Rock, to drift the six miles to Saunders' ships. They were manned by skeleton crews, nervously ready to jump for the boats towed astern as soon as the matches were applied.

An hour later, English sentries at the Point of Orleans saw dark shapes looming toward them. Then torches flared; they heard shouts in French, and with a great blast and glare the darkness was torn apart by curtains of fire. Le Louche, the young officer in charge of the fire-ships, had lit his powder-train too soon. Five other ships flared up as their crews jumped into their boats and pulled for their lives. Blazing wood and red-hot metal erupted skyward and sideways as the decks blew up and cannons and muskets exploded. The British sentries screamed and fled, pursued by showers of falling fragments and waves of sulphurous smoke. The captain of the remaining fire-ship, Dubois de la Milletiere, kept his nerve to the last. He steered for the British fleet as the booming, crackling hulks wallowed beside him. A blazing brand landed on his deck and his ship exploded under him. He and his crew of six were burned to death in their own holocaust.

They were the only casualties of the night. The nearest of Saunders' ships hurriedly raised anchor — the Centurion cut her cable — and drifted downstream, firing cannon to warn the ships below. They launched boatloads of sailors who rowed calmly up to the belching, spitting monsters, snagged them with grappling irons and towed them until they ran ashore, where they burned sullenly for the rest of the night.

Knox describes the "awful yet wonderful appearance" of the fire ships and seems to have enjoyed "the grandest fireworks . . . that can possibly be conceived."

Vaudreuil and Montcalm watched the display from across the river. The governor was furious, the general sardonic. He had written a mocking note in his journal that day about our "dear" fireships (referring to their cost) and had expected little from them.

The hulks were still smouldering the following afternoon when an advance party from Monckton's division established a foothold on the south bank of the St. Lawrence at the village of Beaumont, opposite the initial landing site at St. Laurent. Again the American rangers led the way, with a detachment from Wolfe's elite corps of light infantry. The village was deserted, but a small party of Canadians tried to ambush them from the woods beyond. The rangers killed seven and took five prisoners. After scalping the dead, they sent back word that the village was clear.

Monckton marched with ancestral dignity up the old pathway to the village church and nailed to its door the proclamation of His Excellency James Wolfe, Esq., Colonel of a Regiment of Infantry, Major-General and Commander-in-Chief of His Britannic Majesty's Forces in the River St. Lawrence.

It declared that the King had no desire to wage war on the Canadians. They would be permitted to stay in their homes and on their lands and to follow their religion, so long as they remained neutral in the fight between Britain and France.

"The unparalleled barbarities exerted by the French", Wolfe had written, "might justify the bitterest revenge in the army under my command. But Britons breathe higher sentiments of humanity and listen to the merciful dictates of the Christian religion . . . Yet should you refuse these terms and persist in opposition, then surely will the law of nations justify the waste of war as necessary to crush an ungenerous enemy; and then the miserable Canadians must in the winter have the mortification of seeing their very families for whom they have been exerting but a fruitless and indiscreet bravery, perish by the most dismal want and famine.

"In this great dilemma, let the wisdom of the people of Canada show itself. Britain stretches out a powerful, yet a merciful hand . . . France, unable to support Canada, deserts her cause at this important crisis . . . "

Wolfe showed a sound grasp of the differences between the Canadians and their French masters, but he had little hope of terrorizing them into neutrality. Vaudreuil, their Canadian leader, had ordered them to fight and was prepared to terrorize them if they refused. Their families would suffer in either case. So the great majority remained loyal, not to the King of France, but to Canada, and in most encounters they fought more effectively than the French regular troops.

The Abbé Casgrain comments: "What Wolfe said was only too true, but nevertheless not a Canadian spoke of surrender."

One of the biggest mistakes on the French side, according to the Chevalier de Johnstone, was their failure to fortify Point Levi, the high, elbow-like promontory that juts from the south shore opposite Quebec. Montcalm had planned to hold it with four thousand men, well dug in, but Vaudreuil vetoed this. His engineer, Pontleroy, told him the English could set up siege guns there which might hit Lower Town across a mile of water, but could not be elevated sufficiently to shoot up the cliff at the fortress and batteries on the heights. And while the English were setting up their guns they would be mowed down by fire from these lofty batteries. So a mere six hundred Canadian militiamen and Indians were left to guard the point.

Monckton marched four battalions along the river road from Beaumont and took the point in a day. As his men hacked and scraped at the stony ground to dig themselves in, they glanced anxiously up at the bristling guns of the Chateau St. Louis, high on its rock across the river. But they stayed silent. Next morning a floating battery lobbed balls and bombs at them, but there was still no sound from the fort. A French ship ventured out and fired a few shots before it was chased back by a broadside from the frigate Trent. From time to time the diggers had to drop their tools and seize their muskets as whooping bands of Abenakis and Ottawas rushed out of the woods, firing wildly, and ran back. Each morning, torn bodies would be found. The Indians took a dozen British scalps on the first day; the rangers collected nine from the Indians. The British regulars soon learned from the Americans how to carve heads and slash testicles, as the French regulars learned from the Canadians.

Murder and mutilation were the way of the land. Sgt. John Johnson of the 58th described Indian methods — "They throw their Tomma Hawk with great certainty for a considerable distance and seldom miss; no sooner have they delivered the Tomma Hawk out of their hand, but they spring up to him with their Scalping Knife; which is made in every respect like our Kitchen Carving Knives, and generally at the first approach rip him open, and sometimes take out his heart, but not always; it often happens that time won't permit to perpetrate that barbarous part of their inhuman cruelty — After all they cut round the top of the crown, to the Skull bone and raising up one Side of the Skin with the Knife, with a jerk they tear it off by the hair and the work is done; upon which they set up the Indian Whoop as a signal to their barbarous companions that the work is finished, as also a Shout of Triumph."

Occasionally as a dead Indian's head was being carved, his animal mask would fall off or his white warpaint rub off to reveal European features; for many Canadians fought as Indians, painting themselves reddish-brown and running naked in the woods. Wolfe issued stern orders against scalping white men, but savages and "Canadians disguised as savages" were excepted. By mid-August he was offering his men five guineas for each scalp brought in.

The fighting at Point Levi was watched daily by lines of townspeople on the Quebec ramparts. Beside the white puffs of musket fire and the smoky crash of cannon, English artillerymen and sailors could be seen heaving big guns ashore. These were the mighty siege weapons that would devastate Quebec. The iron 32 pound guns, ten feet long, weighed two and a half tons, while the gaping thirteen-inch naval mortars weighed a full four tons each. Montcalm planned to counterattack and drive the English back before their guns were in place but he was deceived by an English prisoner.

The prisoner said the Levi attack was only a feint; Wolfe's main force was about to descend upon Beauport. As this was what Montcalm had been expecting all along, he abandoned the Levi counterattack, called off a visit to the St. Louis battery on the heights, which had still to fire, and raced back to the Beauport lines. There was no English attack, but the defenders were so alarmed that a musket shot fired accidentally set them shooting blindly into the dark river.

By the time the guns of St. Louis did open up, Monckton's men were too well entrenched to be dislodged. Montcalm soon called off the cannonade to save powder and Wolfe took a leisurely walk along the south shore to select permanent sites for his siege guns. As the townspeople watched, these were wheeled along from Point Levi to sites more directly opposite Lower Town, near where today's ferries ply across the St. Lawrence between Levis and Quebec. Wolfe now had them at gunpoint.

Angry deputations banged on the Governor's door, demanding that he do something to save Quebec. Old men and boys gathered in excited knots in the street, shouting that if the white-coats wouldn't fight, they would. A police lieutenant and a merchant went to Beauport to ask Montcalm's permission for a citizen's force to cross the river. The general agreed with a shrug. These were Vaudreuil's beloved Canadians, seeking to make the attack that Montcalm had proposed and Vaudreuil vetoed. Let them try.

The citizens' army was a ludicrous mixture. Merchants in their best coats and breeches mingled with leathery old farmers in wool hats and the traditional fringed sash. Thirty schoolboys from a seminary formed their own picket. A hundred regulars from the La Salle and Languedoc regiments volunteered to join, and a few Indians went along for the pickings. About 1200 men and boys were finally assembled under Jean-Daniel Dumas, the Canadian colonial marine officer who had beaten Braddock. They tramped four miles upriver to Sillery, followed by tearful wives, mothers and daughters, embarked by night in small boats, and splashed across the river to loud cheers from the women. Somehow, the British heard none of this. They knew nothing of the citizens' army until the next morning, by which time that army had managed to defeat itself and flee in panic to its boats, leaving its dead behind.

Dumas had divided his ragged force into two columns. As they stumbled in inky darkness along the broken river bank, the leading column lost its bearings and halted. The second column found the first, mistook it for the enemy and opened fire. Both groups panicked, firing at each other, and tumbling back towards the boats. Dumas and the regulars tried to stem the rush and were succeeding when the schoolboys began to shoot and routed everybody. Two or three men were killed and the army took to the boats. By eight in the morning they were all back at Quebec, shaken and sick with humiliation. So ended what was called "the schoolchildren's feat."

Wolfe was now well established on the south shore and

on the Isle of Orleans, but had yet to make contact with Montcalm's real army. It sat there across the water, unmoving and unreachable. Montcalm had no intention of coming out to attack. Why should he? He lacked naval strength, and in any case time was on his side. So he must be outflanked. Wolfe had abandoned his original plan to attack the Beauport shore because Montcalm had beaten him to it. He toyed with the idea of by-passing the town and landing upriver, but this was too difficult at the moment. His gun batteries across from Quebec were not ready yet, and the French guns on the Rock were saving their powder to blast any ship that tried to slip below them. On July 3 he held a meeting with Saunders and it was agreed to try a landing above Quebec, but not until the siege guns were in operation. So, for the time being, there was only one direction in which Wolfe could go; and he was determined to go somewhere. Impatience gnawed constantly; there was so little time left.

On the evening of July 8 he landed on the north shore of the St. Lawrence, ten miles downriver from Quebec and separated from Montcalm's row of fortifications by the Montmorency River to the west and its dramatic gorge and cataract. He was rowed ashore with the first wave of grenadiers and light infantry, met only a scattering of sniper shots, climbed the cliffs and made camp above. When Townshend and Murray arrived an hour later with three thousand men they found only a long string of baggage in a field by the shore. Wolfe and his men had vanished, leaving no guide with orders for the main force, not even an officer to watch their bags.

Brigadier Townshend fumed. The purpose of an advance party, as he understood it, was to scout the land, warn of ambushes, and find a good path for him to lug his cannon up the heights. At daybreak he found one small, winding track and managed to haul up six 6-pounders. His men dug furiously and within three hours they had a footing on the clifftops and were laying a rough parapet of logs. Townshend stalked off in the morning sunshine to find Wolfe and complain.

The general was in no mood to listen to inferior officers. His journal records that one of them, presumably Townshend, was threatening to bring him before a Parliamentary inquiry for disregarding his feelings. So before Townshend could say anything, Wolfe told him that he had taken the devil of a time to get his brigade up the cliff. He then inspected Townshend's new camp and sneered that it looked like a fortress. Very secure for the brigadier, he added, but how would the men get out to advance and attack?

Townshend's rage boils over three pages of his journal. With an eye to future justification, he sketched his "fortress-like" breastworks. He decided (correctly) that Wolfe's camp had been built facing the wrong way, with its unprotected rear towards the woods where the Indians lurked. He bemoaned the loss of some of his cannon which Wolfe had taken away from him "to grace the park of artillery the General chose to ornament his quarters with." As he was moving his battalions to the new and, in his opinion, dangerous positions Wolfe had selected, he learned that the general was off to visit the rest of his army, leaving him in charge, but without orders. Wolfe had not said when he would be back; he hadn't even told his senior officer he was leaving.

"I ran down as fast as I could to the water side", Townshend huffs. "He received me in a very stately manner, not advancing five steps. 'Sir', says he, 'the Adjutant-General has my orders — permit me, Sir, to ask: Are your troops to encamp on their new ground, or not to do it until the enemy's battery begins to play?'"

With that, the general climbed into his boat, leaving Townshend glaring. He was rowed over to Saunders' flagship, where he infuriated the admiral by hinting that his sailors were gun-shy; they wouldn't sail close enough to the French floating batteries to protect the troops.

Captain Knox had caught a brief glimpse of Montmorency Falls from the Isle of Orleans, and had resolved to inspect them at close range when the opportunity arose. Knox was an insatiable tourist. After the landing on the north shore he saw his men safely encamped east of the Montmorency river and then took a stroll up to the edge of the gorge.

"I had very nigh paid dear for my inquisitiveness", he records. As he was admiring the view, a Frenchman took a shot at him from the other side. But the view was worth it. The river poured straight down nearly 250 feet in a narrow, white column, banked by rows of rocky brown precipice which widened out into a roaring amphitheatre of spume and mist. Far below, the spent waters flattened out on a broad gravel floor to dribble quietly into the St. Lawrence. Up where Knox stood, the lips of the gorge were closely fringed by forest, from which peeped the breastworks of both sides. As he discovered, they were just a gunshot apart.

On the other side stood another Scotsman, the future Chevalier de Johnstone. With his usual good fortune he had escaped from Louisbourg just before it fell and sailed to Quebec in a ship carrying English prisoners. Montcalm welcomed him, and Bigot kindly provided him with a new uniform, for he had left all but two shirts behind at Louisbourg. He became engineer and aide-de-camp to the Chevalier de Lévis, the French second-in-command, who defended the left flank at the Montmorency. So Johnstone had been the man who designed the redoubts now facing the English. And as he stood with de Lévis, watching them take their new positions, he was puzzled. The English *could* cross the river by the shallow water below the falls — but they would be crazy to try it, as this would put them directly under the French guns on the lip of the gorge. According to de Lévis there was no other way of crossing the Montmorency. He had followed the river to its source and there was no ford. Johnstone was unconvinced: there must be a ford, and Wolfe's spies must have told him about it; otherwise why would he put so many men in a useless position?

Johnstone asked among Canadians who knew the area — something the haughty de Lévis would not deign to do — and found a militia officer who had found a farmer who had waded across the Montmorency the night before with a sack of wheat on his back. The ford was three miles above the falls. De Lévis sent Captain Répentigny there with eleven hundred Canadians and four hundred Indians. The Indians swarmed across the river and crept up behind a large party of redcoats who were cutting logs in the woods, guarded by American rangers. Répentigny sent a messenger back to de Lévis, suggesting an attack. De Lévis passed the suggestion on to Vaudreuil's headquarters four miles away and the Governor held a council of war with Montcalm and Bigot. Only the Intendant voted for battle. Montcalm maintained that the English were harmless so long as they remained on the far side of the river. If driven away they would only cause trouble somewhere else. "Let them amuse themselves", he said. Meanwhile, the Indians decided for themselves. Without waiting for French orders, they opened fire, ran screaming out of the woods and took thirty-six ranger scalps. Répentigny complained that a great chance had been lost.

Montcalm now had the English across the Montmorency to his left and facing him across the St. Lawrence from the Isle of Orleans and the south shore at Point Levi. But they could not get at his army unless he chose to come out and fight. With visions of winter ahead and his lovely Candiac somewhere in the future, he was not fool enough for that. If he were to preserve the accursed colony he must save his forces for the main threat which, he still believed, would come from Amherst's army to the southwest. Amherst could cut the links between Quebec and Montreal and fall upon him from his rear.

Amherst was advancing, but more slowly than Montcalm feared or even Wolfe anticipated. He crept up Lake George towards Ticonderoga, stopping every few miles to build a new fort. He showed neither the brashness of Braddock or the cowardice of Abercromby; he acquired land like a real estate developer. Because the French had four armed vessels on the lakes, he paused to build a fleet of his own — a brigantine, a sloop and a large floating gun platform. The finding and felling of bent trees suitable for ribs, the hewing and planing of keels, keelsons, prows and sternposts; the laborious shaping of planks and hand-boring of nail holes, was to take all summer.

His orders from Pitt were to "make an irruption into Canada with the utmost vigor and despatch". From time to time he would order his brigadiers to make full speed ahead to help Wolfe at Quebec. Then he would detail a regiment to cut the tops off spruce trees to make spruce beer — a remedy for scurvy which the troops were free to buy at a halfpenny a quart. And he would build another log fort, assuring his army that it would give "plenty peace and quiet to His Majesty's subjects for ages to come." These forts would provide protection long after the protected had ceased to be His Majesty's subjects; some are still maintained by American states as tourist attractions. Their slow construction ensured that Canada would not be conquered that year and that Amherst would become the final victor after the impetuous young Wolfe had spent himself. He was a canny man, Jeffrey Amherst. He was later to refuse supreme command of the British forces opposing the American Revolution because his canniness told him the Americans would win. So he lived to reach comfortable retirement as a field marshal.

Chapter 8

Hot Stuff

At nine p.m. on July 12 a signal rocket flared into skies uneasy with the prospect of a summer storm, and the long bombardment of Quebec began. The six 32 pounders and five 13-inch mortars dragged from Point Levi roared out two salvoes, which fell short. The missiles splashed into the river and the French jeered from the heights. The gunners re-aligned their weapons with quadrant and plumb-bob and levered wedges into place. The first bombs crashed and shattered in flames on the wharves of Lower Town. The black mouths of the naval mortars gaped skyward. Swabbed, rammed and touched off at the lintel, they coughed their great projectiles up and outward, arcing 600 feet in the air, over the top-most ramparts and down to smash through the roofs of Upper Town. Besides solid shot and shells, the British were firing carcasses — paper cylinders filled with incendiary composition and buffered inside the barrel by pieces of sod. Ignited by the powder charge that fired them, they burned for four to eleven minutes — long enough to set fire to a building.

The engineer Pontleroy was wrong. The English *could* shoot up the cliff. As three hundred bombs and carcasses tore up the streets and blasted and burned stores and houses, townspeople rushed to the ramparts on the landward side, trundling carts and dragging bundles of food and bedding. There they waited till morning, when the gates would be opened, allowing them to take to the open country. The object of the bombardment, wrote the diarist of the *Journal du Siège de Québec* "was not so much to dismount the batteries as to frighten the people and make them abandon the town".

The Ursuline convent was hit several times. The nuns huddled in prayer before the Blessed Sacrament while volunteer firewatchers doused the flames around them. At daybreak, the Superior led a sad procession of nuns out to the General Hospital, well outside Quebec on the St. Charles River. The city was left to the two thousand Canadian troops of the garrison, a few volunteer

The British shelling, allied with fire, was fearfully effective. Notre Dame des Victoires (centre) and the surrounding area of Lower Town was especially hard hit, as this drawing made some months later by Richard Short makes clear.

(Archives Nationales du Québec)

firemen, and bands of looters who emerged between salvoes to steal what they could find in the deserted buildings. The shelling would go on, with short pauses, for two months. More cannon and mortars were brought up until Wolfe had twenty-nine pieces in place and the nights rocked to their thunder.

There was real thunder, too. For much of July, storms rumbled along the river, gushing sudden rains into the smoking gun pits and sizzling on the smouldering ruins of the town, while lightning leaped and darted and the bombs seared their traces across the water. On July 16, a high wind swept flames up to the Cathedral, and on the 22nd it was hit by a shell and burned to the ground, along with the centre of Upper Town. On August 8, a great fire raked Lower Town and engulfed the Church of Notre Dame des Victoires. By now more than 180 houses were gone. Half the town was in ruins. The nightly spectacle of the Rock spewing smoke and trailing rivulets of flame like an erupting volcano doubtless cheered the redcoats in their tents and depressed the French in the Beauport lines downstream. Yet its military value is questionable. If Wolfe had wanted to silence the Quebec batteries he should have

Townshend's cartoons of Wolfe obsessively inspecting the "Necessary Houses" provoked the General's wrath.
(McCord Museum)

aimed at them. If his object was to terrorize the inhabitants, he had achieved it on the first night. The systematic destruction that went on after that did not bring victory any closer. But the bombardment of a besieged town was a standard military tactic; so was the slaughter of civilians. As Col. Stacey points out, the twentieth century can scarcely afford to throw stones at Wolfe, "for his policy can be said to prefigure, in little, the area bombing policy of the RAF Bomber Command, applied against German cities in 1941-45."

Wolfe had told Amherst in a letter that if he were frustrated before Quebec he would damage the town and countryside as much as he could before retiring. So the demolition of Quebec and the burning of the countryside which followed may have been the result of Wolfe's fear of failure.

He spent the July days hurrying from one sector of his divided force to another. He visited Townshend at Montmorency to remind the men to keep their camps "sweet and clean" by burying filth and offal. New "Necessary Houses" must be erected at least every third day. Townshend's famous cartoons of the general inspecting these necessary houses were drawn about this time. They were such a success when passed around the brigade mess that one officer thought they might amuse Wolfe himself, and showed one to the general. He was not amused. He drew himself up, tightened the soft lips of the triangular profile Townshend sketched so well, and stared coldly at the artist.

"If we live", he told Townshend. "This shall be inquired into."

There were discipline problems outside the brigade mess, too. Over on the south shore, Wolfe found Monckton's men bored and ripe for mischief. They had been allowed to send to Pointe d'Orleans for one extra woman per company. Now there were too many women around. Petticoats and leather stays, hung out to dry, made the camp untidy. Female sutlers were ordered to stop selling extra rum to the men or they'd be battened down in the holds of the transports. One was whipped along the lines for keeping what the general called "a disorderly tent." Company commanders were ordered to arrest men guilty of constant swearing or of using indecent language "unbecoming gentlemen or soldiers."

For some redcoats, this final imposition was too much. Constant swearing was the Lobster's only release and he had no desire to ape the gentleman. If he was to be left with nothing to do because the general couldn't make up his mind, rained on, bitten by mosquitoes, liable to be scalped any night by fiendish savages and then denied his simple pleasures, damme, he might as well try his luck across the river with the mounseers and their fancy women. The first British deserters stole boats and slipped over to Quebec.

Canadians were deserting, too. The failure of the citizens' foray against Monckton and Montcalm's steady refusal to come out of his lair, disheartened the militia. Prisoners and deserters told the English that Vaudreuil had kept them in camp by threatening to turn the Indians loose on them if they returned to their villages. Wolfe then repeated his threat to lay waste their crops and burn their homes unless they accepted his offer of neutrality by August 10. So the Canadians were to be ruined if they stayed in camp and scalped if they didn't. Most of them stayed, and until the climactic battle they and the Indians did most of the fighting on the French side. As the Chevalier de Johnstone put it: "A Canadian in the woods is worth three disciplined soldiers, as a soldier in a plain is worth three Canadians."

While the unlucky habitants were being crushed in between, the leaders of both sides kept up a polite correspondence. Canoes flying white flags crossed the river unharmed, bearing notes between Wolfe and Vaudreuil. From time to time white flags would be waved across the Montmorency gorge, firing would cease, and arrangements be made for the exchange of prisoners. On July 4, Wolfe sent an aide over to the Governor with a dozen bottles of rum and a letter announcing his intention to attack Quebec on behalf of His Britannic Majesty. The Governor sent back a case of wine and the observation that he was surprised such an attempt should be made with so few troops. Later, Wolfe discussed his chances at a meeting with French envoys. A French officer told him; "We don't doubt that you will destroy the town but we are determined that you shall never set foot within its walls." The general replied; "I will be master of Quebec if I have to remain here until the end of November." As July wore on the exchanges grew less polite. Both sides complained of atrocities. But the worst of these were still to come.

On the night of July 18, the situation changed dramatically. Saunders completed his mastery of the St. Lawrence by slipping six ships under the guns on the Rock and upstream. One French shot hit the side of Captain John Rous's 50-gun Sutherland as she swung past on a racing flood tide. The rest went through her rigging. The frigates Diana and Squirrel followed, with two armed sloops and two transports. The Diana collided with a sloop and grounded on the south shore but the others got cleanly through without losing a man.

Next morning a rider from Quebec summoned Montcalm to the city to consider this setback. As he arrived on the heights, he found two bodies swinging from a double gibbet on the walls — sailors from the floating batteries, executed for their carelessness in letting the British get through. Across the river, he could see the crew of the Diana heaving her thirty-two guns overboard to lighten her, while his floating battery pounded away ineffectually. Two English ships, the Pembroke and Richmond, were boldly trying to tow the frigate free; and his guns couldn't hit them, any of them.

Montcalm was coldly realistic. The English had now done the impossible twice; they had brought big ships through the Traverse and now they had brought them past the Rock. So nothing impossible remained. If they landed somewhere upriver they would cut his supply lines to the rest of the colony. If they gained a foothold on the heights and attacked the city from the Plains of

Abraham, he knew he could not defend it. The walls on the west were too weak and the fortifications "ridiculous." Generations of inefficient engineers and corrupt contractors had seen to that. There was no ditch in front of the walls because the rocky ground would have to be blasted out and the blasting would bring down the walls. And for some reason Montcalm could never understand, no gunports had been pierced through the western walls, so none of the fifty-two cannon stationed there could fire directly at an advancing enemy. They all pointed along the walls, where the ditch should have been, to kill the attackers as they climbed. Montcalm still believed, and would believe to the end, that Wolfe's main attack would come at Beauport, but he could no longer afford to keep all his forces there. He sent Major Dumas with 600 men to keep an eye on the English from the heights above Quebec. Captain François Le Mercier, the artillerist, followed with his 18-pounders and mortars to set up the Samos battery near Sillery. More troops would be sent upriver as the British increased their strength there.

So Montcalm reacted efficiently to Saunders' feat, although he had maintained it couldn't be done. Wolfe, who never seems to have doubted that it could, went into a frenzy of indecision. His first thought was to land in force a few miles above Quebec. On July 20 he dashed off an order to Monckton, telling him to row part of his brigade upstream to the Sutherland, then land and dig in to await reinforcement. The order was written in such a hurry he dated it May 20 by mistake. Saunders sent a fleet of boats to the Montmorency camp to collect artillery for the assault and Townshend shipped nine companies of grenadiers to the Isle of Orleans to await further orders.

A few hours later the attack was postponed, then cancelled. Wolfe explained in a letter to Pitt that Monckton's landing could not have been reinforced before his men were attacked by the entire French army. Yet his aim throughout the siege was to draw out the entire French army and make them fight. And a mysterious entry in Wolfe's journal of July 19, the day after the Sutherland's successful passage, refers to the general's reconnaissance of the country immediately above Quebec and finds "that if we had ventured the stroke that was first intended we should infallibly have succeeded." The word "infallibly" was later scored out and "probably" inserted. The whole episode shows Wolfe at his worst, unable to decide and unwilling to explain himself. James Gibson, an American civilian with Wolfe's staff, wrote: "Within the space of five hours we received at the General's request, three different orders of consequence which were contradicted immediately after their reception . . . to the no small amazement of everybody who has taken the liberty of thinking . . . I am told he asks no one's opinion."

Even Monckton, the only brigadier who did not hate Wolfe, began to doubt him. Montcalm wrote: "All this becomes daily more obscure."

After cancelling the attack, Wolfe sent Carleton on a probing expedition twenty miles upstream to Pte. aux Trembles. His guide was the remarkable Captain Robert Stobo, who now surfaces again after five adventurous years. Stobo knew the structure and personalities of the Canadian colony better than Mackellar, who had been a prisoner in Quebec while he, as a hostage, roamed free most of the time. As he sailed past Sillery in Carleton's line of flat-boats, his old friend Le Mercier lobbed a few cannonballs at him from the Samos battery. Le Mercier had accepted Washington's surrender papers from him in the mud of Fort Necessity and after that Stobo had got to know and admire the artillery chief both as a soldier and a businessman. He had arrived from France as a penniless private and in twenty years made a million livres off government contracts, working in liaison with the Bigot-Cadet ring. And as the boats now proceeded upriver they were pursued along the north shore by Major Dumas, another old Stobo acquaintance from Fort Duquesne.

Stobo had been quite prominent in the social life of Quebec. He had some cash and excellent credit, and he travelled around the colony trading with the Indians, helped by his business contact Captain St. Luc de la Corne (who was now defending the Montreal rapids against Amherst). He wore a plumed hat, a red satin suit and shirts adorned with Rouen lace, and was well-received at the court of Canada's Pompadour, Madame Péan. Then came the defeat of Braddock and the capture of his papers, proving that Stobo was a spy. The atmosphere changed. He and his companion Van Braam appeared before Vaudreuil and six other officials in a trial that would become famous as a classic test of the duties of a hostage.

Prisoners-of-war were entitled to spy for their countries

if they got the chance; hostages promised to behave — yet Stobo declared that he had never given any such promise. The case was complicated by the fact that England and France were not technically at war when Stobo drew his map. So while soldiers on both sides were scalping prisoners and allowing their Indians to torture them or keep them as slaves, this legal point had to be decided nicely as between civilized nations. Bougainville wrestled with it in his journal — "What are hostages when the promises of which they are the pledge have been violated? It is true that England pretends that Major Washington did not have the right to promise to restore prisoners who belonged to that country, and that she refused to recognize the validity of the capitulation. In this case these hostages become no more than ordinary prisoners who are not, I believe, subject to any punishment for trying to serve their country."

Eventually Stobo was condemned by Vaudreuil to have his head cut off on a scaffold at Place d'Armes in Montreal, but according to Montcalm and Bougainville it had been arranged in advance that he would be reprieved by the King. He and Van Braam (who was acquitted) spent five months in comfortable confinement, with meals and girls sent in. Then they escaped. In their prison room was found a box containing three files, one punch, one iron crowbar, two chisels, one wedge and a set of tools for making keys. Apparently they had friends on the outside.

Although they were recaptured, Stobo escaped again and finally left Quebec in a stolen canoe, accompanied by Lt. Simon Stevens of Rogers' Rangers and seven other prisoners. They captured a French schooner and sailed it to Louisbourg, arriving there in the spring of 1759. Stobo was shipped back upriver to join Wolfe at the Isle of Orleans about July 4.

Now he led Carleton's advance party as its boats grounded at Pte. aux Trembles. About forty Indians fired on them, killing three, then vanished, leaving Stobo free to search the village. Some of the best families from Quebec had taken refuge there and it was hoped they would have useful documents. But only some pathetic letters were found, telling the English what they already knew — that Quebec was short of food. And there was no sign of the powder magazine that was said to be in the village. About 150 old men, women and children were rounded up and herded on to the flatboats with their cattle and sheep. The last boat pushed off just as Major Dumas rode up with his men. They fired a few

Wolfe's gallant conversation at dinner with lady prisoners no doubt inspired this unkind cartoon by Townshend. In it Wolfe instructs two ladies begging for mercy not to send any more written petitions — "But send me 50 pretty girls — and we shall see."

(McCord Museum)

shots at the departing boats, then returned to their post on the plains near Quebec, leaving the Indians to loot the houses left empty by the refugees.

The raid had been a failure, but the capture of lady prisoners gave Wolfe a chance to enjoy some civilized company. He entertained a group of them at dinner aboard the Sutherland. It was his evening off from the war and he was at his most gracious, making little jokes in French over the claret and signing his autograph for the visitors. He referred lightly to the fact that the French general wouldn't come out to fight him. Stobo was there in his bright, new uniform, listening to the ladies complain about their treatment by the farmers of Pte. aux Trembles, the goods that had been stolen from them, and the rigors of life in the country after the good times in Quebec. He knew some of them from his days at Bigot's court — particularly Madame Juchereau Duchesnay, mother of Reine Marie, the girl who had helped him get out of jail. Stobo talked a lot, as always. According to one prisoner he boasted of his connections in Quebec and produced a letter from an informer in the city.

After the dinner party a truce was arranged and the bombardment of Quebec suspended while Wolfe's artist aide, Captain Hervey Smyth, escorted the refugees to the Lower Town wharf. There the gentlemanly interlude ended. The port officials cursed Smyth for bringing them more mouths to feed, jeered at the well-bred ladies and packed them in farm carts, to be trundled back to Pte. aux Trembles. A few days later 250 more prisoners were sent back to Quebec — some of them had been entertained to dinner by Monckton. Vaudreuil sent Wolfe an angry note, accusing him of dumping prisoners on the starving town, and Wolfe replied that as his generosity was ungraciously received he would return no more prisoners under any conditions.

Meanwhile Montcalm learned from the refugees that Stobo was back; he morosely chalked up one more grievance against Vaudreuil, whom he suspected of engineering the spy's escape. "Who would believe", he wrote "that this man was free to the point of having escaped? It is he, they say, who conducted everything and he is in a condition to give a good account of the situation in our colony in every respect."

The navy continued to slide ships upstream past the Rock on favorable nights. Rear-Admiral Charles Holmes joined the growing upriver fleet and raised his flag aboard the Sutherland. The French decided to make one last attempt to destroy the fleet that remained anchored off Point Levi. They produced the "invention" that Baron Dieskau had boasted about in captivity in New York as an "infallible" way of destroying ships in a river. Mackellar had described it in a report on Quebec: "We found this Invention to be what they call (Radeux à Feu) fire rafts of which there is a Store provided. These are Loggs of Timber tyed together by the Ends so as to form a Chain and Coated over with the Strong Composition. They are to be set on Fire when the Ships are near and floated off from some of the Islands down the stream and clinging around the Ships Bows set them on Fire."

When it appeared, the invention was much more elaborate than that. It was nearly 700 feet long, a chain of rafts reinforced by dozens of small boats, barges and a few schooners, all linked together and stuffed with grenades, broken cannon and swivel guns loaded with grapeshot; even pistol barrels crammed with shot. It was more impressive than the fire ships, and this time there was no failure on the part of the crew. The officer in charge, de Courval, waited until the great floating firework was half a musket's range from the ships before lighting his slow-matches. The huge contraption roared up like a forest fire, spitting and banging, showering red sparks and flaming fragments. But Saunders, expecting something of the sort, had picket boats out in the basin, guarding his ships. The boatmen threw their grapples into the fiery wall and towed the monster ashore. Through the crackle of flame and crash of explosions, sailors on the threatened ships heard shouts of "All's well." The boatmen got a half pint of brandy each from the Stirling Castle's stores and one said, according to Knox: "Damme, Jack, didst thee ever take hell in tow before?"

Wolfe did not take the attempt so lightly. He sent a note to Quebec: "If the enemy presume to send down any more firecraft, they are to be made fast to two particular transports in which are all the Canadians and other prisoners, in order that they may perish by their own base inventions." His irritation is understandable, as a month had gone by since the first landing at the Isle of Orleans and he had yet to come to grips with the enemy. Now he thrashed about, looking for a crack in Montcalm's shell and leaving bait to draw him out of it. Having abandoned the briefly glowing prospect of a landing upriver he returned to the Montmorency. Again and again he studied the falls and the flats below. On one survey he cast his telescope over the Chevalier de Lévis' redoubts and into the lens came the elegant figure of the Chevalier himself, his telescope trained on Wolfe. The commanders eyed each other. No shots were fired; for, as Wellington was to remark when he had Napoleon in his sights at Waterloo, generals did not kill one another.

On July 26, Wolfe took Murray with 2,000 men up the east bank of the Montmorency, looking for the ford James Johnstone had discovered for the French three weeks before. They found it and camped for the night in the forest by the rippling shallows. As the troops wandered about from tent to tent, gambling and swapping boasts and stories, they did not know that 800 Indians under Captain Charles de Langlade were lying motionless, tomahawks in hand, less than a hundred yards away. They lay there for five hours while Langlade hurried to de Lévis' camp to announce another fine opportunity to slaughter the English. Again, de Lévis sent to Montcalm for permission to attack and none came. And again the Indians grew tired of waiting. At dawn they rose and swooped on Wolfe's regulars, killing or wounding 150, driving them and the general in headlong retreat to their camp. He roused Townshend's entire brigade and sent Murray back to counterattack at the ford. Although the Indians were driven back across the river, along with a detachment of Canadians who had come to support them, Murray lost a further forty-five men and came back in a hurry.

It was Wolfe's first defeat; worse, he had been beaten by a tribe of savages and a pack of Canadian dogs. It convinced him that he could not get at de Lévis from behind, but it strengthened his resolve to get at de Lévis somehow or other. He now decided on a plan that seems not only desperate but irrational. He would attack the French army head-on at one of its strongest points — the cliff on which de Lévis was encamped.

On the narrow beach below stood a redoubt and gun battery commanded at the time by James Johnstone. Wolfe proposed to land and capture it, and this, he believed, would bring de Lévis' force, followed by the rest of Montcalm's army, down to the water's edge for the "general engagement" he so ardently desired. What if Montcalm sat tight on his high ground and refused to wrestle in the mud below? In that case, Wolfe explained to Pitt later on, he would be able to survey the enemy camp from close range and decide where best to attack them. The brigadiers disliked the plan and so did the navy. Wolfe himself seemed to lack confidence in it. On the eve of the attack he notes the "dislike of Genl. Officers and others to this business — but nothing better proposed by them." So, for want of a better plan, the young master of amphibious warfare launched an amphibious disaster.

On the sunny morning of July 31 the 64-gun Centurion, famed as the ship in which Anson circumnavigated the world, surged majestically across the river from her anchorage near Point Levi, swept past the Beauport lines and dropped anchor near the mouth of the Montmorency. A red flag waved from the English camp at the gorge and forty 24-pound cannon hurled their shot across the gap to splinter the trees on the French side. Moments later the Centurion rolled to larboard as her first broadsides of 25 guns flashed and thundered at the cliffs. Two small shallow-draught transports, the Russell and the Three Sisters, headed for the shore and Johnstone's redoubt. As their bows scraped in the shallows, they dropped their hooks and the sterns swung slowly downstream, bringing their broadsides of fourteen guns apiece in line with Johnstone's small emplacement.

Wolfe stood, cane in hand, on the foredeck of the Russell. As she grounded, he cursed the navy. The admirable Master Surveyor Cook had miscalculated. His soundings had told Wolfe that the transports could ride the tide much further in. The second miscalculation was his own. He could now see that Johnstone's redoubt was much closer to the French trenches on the cliffs than it had appeared when viewed through his telescope from the British camp. Johnstone's guns thumped roundshot at the transports as every moment the tide receded, bedding them in silt. Wolfe remained on the prow, ignoring the fire. He later complained peevishly to Saunders that he was hit three times by splinters torn from the Russell's bulwarks and once had his cane knocked from his hand by a cannonball. This was the admiral's fault, he said, for not providing proper covering fire. He ordered his landing party of Louisbourg grenadiers to leave the transports, get into small boats and stay out of range. He stayed aboard, thinking, as his admirals and brigadiers continued to follow his now-impossible plan.

More than 300 boats filled with redcoats were now on the river, rowing back and forth along the six-mile Beauport front. The general alarm drummed along the shoreline as Montcalm turned out his white-coated regulars. He arrived at de Lévis' headquarters at two o'clock, bringing the battalions of Béarn, Guienne and Royal Roussillon. He had 12,000 men, the advantage of height and well-prepared positions, and the trusted de Lévis by his side. The men shouted *"Vive notre géneral!"* and, for the first time in months, he felt secure.

By mid-afternoon the heat was oppressive, the skies gray and heavy with the threat of a thunderstorm. Wolfe waved his stick and the attack began. Signal guns fired, flags waved along the river and the heavy flatboats, hauled by the aching arms of the bluejackets, creaked inshore. As the first wave of boats passed the stuck transports they hit a line of boulders just below the surface. Some wedged in and hung there, others lunged out of control as the oarsmen were knocked over by the impact, and swept downstream. Wolfe saw his spearhead blunted, his best assault troops floundering with muddy water between them and the shore and French shot spraying all around them. He shouted orders to delay the attack. By this time Townshend had brought his 2,000 men carefully down to the tidal flats below the falls and was

Townshend's famous portrait of Wolfe. The inscription reads "To Isaac Barre from his friend Geo. Townshend."

The capture of the French ships Prudent and Bienfaisant at the siege of Louisbourg.

(Royal Ontario Museum, Toronto)

The fortress of Louisbourg today.

(Nova Scotia Information Service)

The French tried and failed to destroy the British fleet besieging Quebec by sending fireships among them.
(Royal Ontario Museum, Toronto)

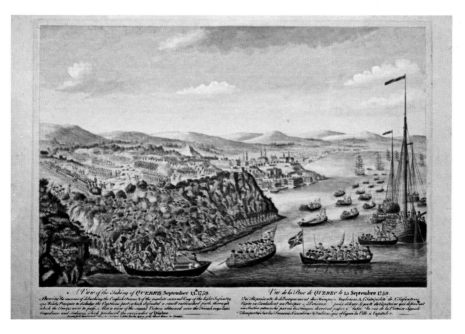

View of the taking of Quebec.

(Public Archives of Canada)

This is a detail of Francis Swaine's view of the battle on the Plains. Another detail of that painting appears on the cover of the book.

(Royal Ontario Museum, Toronto)

The attack at Montmorency. On the left the Centurion shells French positions on the cliff, while flatboats muster for the attack on the shore. In the background the city of Quebec is wreathed in smoke. From a contemporary drawing by Captain Hervey Smyth.

(Royal Ontario Museum, Toronto)

leading them steadily, gaiter-deep in water, towards the landing site. Hervey Smyth rowed over to halt them.

The invasion fleet lay sweating off shore for another hour while Captain James Chads, a skilled boatsman, probed and poked in the shallows to find a way through the line of boulders. Wolfe went with him in a ship's boat, oblivious as ever to the cannonade, intent only upon finding a tiny passage that might yet save the day. By five-thirty it was low tide and the boulders were no longer much of an obstacle, for the men could now wade ashore. He waved his cane once again.

The first boats to go in held thirteen companies of the Louisbourg Grenadiers, Wolfe's stormtroops, handpicked from the regular battalions that fought at Louisbourg the year before. They considered themselves Britain's best and made no secret of it.

Grenadiers were, by tradition, the tallest and finest of foot-soldiers — and those who were not naturally tall were made to appear so by the towering mitre-caps they wore. Originally they had been chosen to rush up to fortress walls and hurl hand-grenades — the most uncertain of weapons, and extremely danger-ous to the thrower — so they had to be steady, strong, and a little more intelligent than the ox-like troops of the line whose only job was to stand under fire and fire back when told to. At Quebec they did not carry grenades, but the grenadier spirit remained. They sang jingo songs like the one composed by Sgt. Ned Botwood of the 47th, who now stood, halberd in hand, yelling threats at the mounseers —

Come, each death-doing dog who dares venture his neck
Come follow the hero that goes to Quebec:
  Jump aboard the transports and loose every sail
Pay your debts at the tavern by giving leg-bail,
And ye that love fighting shall soon have enough:
  Wolfe commands us, my boys, we shall give them Hot Stuff!

When the 47th Regiment is dashing ashore,
While bullets are whistling and cannon do roar
  Says Montcalm "Those are Shirley's — I know the lapels"
"You lie", says Ned Botwood, "We belong to Lascelles'!'
Tho' our cloathing is changed, yet we scorn a powder-puff
  So at you, ye bitches, here's giving you Hot Stuff!

The grenadiers, like the 200 Royal Americans just be-hind them, had been in the boats for nearly eight hours. They were primed like their muskets, rammed tight with ardor and ready to ex-plode. For the past hour they had traded boasts and insults with the Royal Americans.

Captain David Ochterlony of the Americans shouted at Captain Wetterstroom, a German grenadier officer: "Though my men are not grenadiers, you'll see we shall be first at the redoubt!" The grenadiers howled and booed. Ochterlony urged his oarsmen on. He had fought a duel with Wetterstroom the day before and been slightly wounded. When the signal came, the grenadiers hurled themselves into waist-deep water, muskets held over their heads, splashing and cheering. They raced and skidded on the slippery mud flats, colliding and falling over one another in a wild, uncontrolled charge. The French hurriedly abandoned Johnstone's beach redoubt and took to the cliffs. The defenders above held their fire until they escaped. Then murderously accurate shots knifed down upon the unprotected grenadiers. The Canadian woodsmen, best marksmen in the land, were aiming from the edge of the cliff and making every bullet count.

Monckton's second wave — Amherst's and the Frasers — were now piling on to the beach. Wolfe strode through the tide which filled his boots, soaked his breeches and splashed the fine lace of his jabot, and stood watching the chaos around him and the carnage ahead. Instead of following their orders to form up in four sections and await the main landing and the arrival of Townshend's column, the grenadiers were behaving like undisciplined savages. The Canadian musketry was devilish, and Montcalm showed no sign of coming down to fight.

The skies darkened further and warm rain fell. The grenadiers' drummer rattled out the heady beat of their regimental march and the tormented vanguard made their own decision. They threw themselves at the cliff, scrabbling in the loose shale, slipping on the bare, muddy patches, clambering where they could over the roots of stunted hazels and cedars, fumbling and clawing upward. With muskets slung uselessly on their backs they were defenseless red-and-white targets for the marksmen above who calmly loaded, rammed, aimed, fired. Halfway up, the cliffs were broken by small ravines. Here the climbers struck the log fascines of Montcalm's outer defenses and came under cannon fire, the balls crashing down on them and grapeshot rending and tearing. The grenadiers had never been ordered to advance, but they had no thought of retreat. The Americans were just below, struggling and cursing as their officers urged them on. Only the dead and wounded rolled back down the cliff.

Suddenly a thundercloud burst overhead and the rain became a torrent. It blinded the French and soaked their powder. Johnstone, on the cliff-top, said he could not see halfway down. The grenadiers clung on until they realized that even if they reached the top they couldn't fire their muskets. They dropped back and the rain washed them down to the beach. Living, dead and wounded slithered back together in a cursing, moaning avalanche of horror.

The black storm, which Knox called "the dreadfullest that can be conceived", ended as suddenly as it had begun. The French peered down the now-steaming slopes and saw the English in full retreat. Already the Indians were moving down like ghouls upon the dead and dying.

David Ochterlony, shot through the lungs, lay gasping beside Johnstone's redoubt. Next to him, propped against a rock with both legs mangled, was his friend Lt. Henry Peyton. As the first Indians approached with their scalping knives, Peyton managed to fire his musket, killing one and driving the rest away. A Fraser sergeant offered to carry both men to the departing boats, but Ochterlony wanted to die where he was and Peyton decided to stay and guard him.

The battle was so obviously over that the French made no attempt to harass the evacuation. Several of Montcalm's officers walked around the beach, talking with the grenadiers and Highlanders as the wounded were carried to the boats and the two transport ships set afire. A private of the Guienne regiment saved Peyton and Ochterlony when they were again attacked by Indians. Peyton was pinned to the ground by a bayonet in his side, but he still managed to grab his attacker's scalping knife and stab him in the back with it. Ochterlony was half strangled and about to be scalped when the Frenchman wrestled the scalper away. A Captain Macdonald of the Frasers slung Peyton over his shoulder and carried him to the boats. French officers took Ochterlony to hospital in Quebec.

Townshend's column had just arrived at the beach when the drums began beating the retreat. The tide was rising and they had to hurry back across the flats before it got too deep. A detachment of Frasers was left to guard their rear, then follow them back east across the Montmorency. Wolfe stayed with the Frasers and marched back with them. These were the men he had fought at Culloden, now in the regiment he had helped to raise through their colonel, Simon, Master of Lovat. When they reached the water, he encountered again the stubbornness of the Highlander which had annoyed him so much in Scotland. The Frasers still fought as a clan, and retreated as a clan. They refused to cross the water until they were sure no surviving Fraser was left on the enemy shore. Townshend argued with them and Wolfe shouted commands, but they wouldn't budge until the last straggler arrived. By that time the water was over their kilts and the tide running strongly. Finally they did struggle across and Wolfe took no action against them for disobedience. They had salvaged their pride; he wished he had done the same.

He had lost 443 of his best men, including a colonel, eight captains, twenty-one lieutenants and three ensigns. The enemy had lost sixty all told. He had lost the confidence of his senior officers and blunted the "Hot Stuff" spirit of his men. Sergeant Ned Botwood lay dead below the cliff with his halberd beside him, still pointing upward.

Chapter 9

Wolfe in Despair

The leaders reacted to victory and defeat at Montmorency, each in his own predictable way. Col. Bourlamaque, on Lake Champlain, received two quite different letters by the same courier. A triumphant Vaudreuil informed him: "I have no more anxiety about Quebec." Montcalm wrote: "Our affair is undoubtedly only a small prelude to something more important, which we are now waiting for."

Wolfe retreated into his shell of gloom and pain. He was ill for a month. He blamed his grenadiers, calling them blockheads, he blamed Saunders and Cook, but finally he blamed himself. "I am sensible of my own errors in the course of the campaign; see clearly wherein I have been deficient; and think a little more or less blame to a man that must necessarily be ruined of little or no consequence . . . a man sees his error often too late to remedy." This admission came in a letter to Saunders, written at the end of August, after the admiral had persuaded him to delete parts of his report to Pitt that were too critical of the navy. By that time he saw that even if the Centurion's gunnery had been better and the two transports had not grounded too soon, the outcome would have been the same. "I take (the blame) entirely upon my own shoulders and expect to suffer for it", he added. "Accidents cannot be helped."

His brigadiers were not about to write off Montmorency as an accident. Townshend was still considering a parliamentary inquiry into Wolfe's behaviour and planning the speech he would make when he got home. Murray, who was never a cautious soldier, damned the Montmorency venture as stupid and foolhardy. A breach developed between Wolfe and the mild-mannered Monckton. By mid-August the general was writing to Monckton offering "hearty excuses" and begging his forgiveness for some unknown offense. Even the grave Carleton, the friend to whom he willed his papers, quarrelled with him. On the day of the defeat, Wolfe's aide

Captain Bell, wrote of "Col. Carlton's abominable Behaviour to ye General".

Wolfe's journal ends on August 16. He had the entries after that date destroyed before he went to his last battle. But Capt. Bell records that the burned pages "contained a careful account of the officers' ignoble conduct towards him in case of a Parliamentary inquiry."

Three days after Montmorency, the general turned his wrath upon the helpless habitants. He had given them until August 10 to obey his original church-door proclamation of June 27, or be burned out. Now he ignored his own deadline. As they continued to practice "the most unchristian barbarities against his troops . . . he could no longer refrain from chastising them as they deserved." The unpleasant Wolfe now emerged once more — the aide to "Hangman" Hawley after Culloden, the ravager of the Gaspé shore after Louisbourg. This time, however, he was not pacifying the countryside after a victory, he was vengefully destroying it after a defeat.

Like all Wolfe's plans, this had been considered beforehand — as revealed in his letter to Amherst promising destruction if he were frustrated before Quebec. Like most of them, it was put into effect suddenly and under the spur of impatience. He may have hoped that the smell of burning farms would bring Montcalm out to fight, but it was a slim hope, since he had sat tight while Wolfe destroyed the much more valuable city of Quebec. By this time he must have known — from Mackellar, Stobo and others — that Montcalm valued Canada and the Canadians no higher than Wolfe himself did. Even Vaudreuil, the Canadian patriot, would never risk losing what was left of Quebec, his birthplace, to save a few villagers. Under the law of his colony every man of military age was automatically a soldier in the militia. If he was hiding at home he was outside the law, and the Governor didn't greatly care whether Wolfe or the Indians got him first. Despite Vaudreuil's threats, militiamen were leaving camp by the hundreds to gather their crops and lay in stores for the winter. This local harvesting made little difference to the food situation in the camp, which was still being supplied from Three Rivers and Montreal; it was the habitant's own assurance of survival for himself and his family. If Wolfe knew this, as seems probable, then his scorched earth policy was primarily an act of revenge on the Canadian "hellhounds". In addition, it gave his troops an outlet for their own, growing rage.

Wolfe's men about to descend on Miramichi, a French settlement in the Gulf of St. Lawrence. The harsh orders were "to destroy the habitations and settlements". By Captain Hervey Smith.
(Royal Ontario Museum, Toronto)

The redcoats had not forgiven Montcalm for the Indian massacre of British prisoners at Fort William Henry two years before. The nightly scalping of sentries and the occasional torture of prisoners that continued throughout the summer brutalized Thomas Lobster. So did his contact with the American rangers, who would go out in small raiding parties and return with scalps dangling from their belts. Now the small parties became large punitive expeditions. Detachments of light infantry were sent out to the villages, then whole line regiments.

The first victims were the people of Baie St. Paul, forty miles downstream, where shots had been fired at British ships. Ranger captain Joseph Goreham was sent there with two hundred men to "destroy the habitations and settlements." The pillars of smoke from his work could be seen from Point Levi, and soon the flames spread back along the north shore to the Montmorency, and south and west of Quebec to the Etchemin River. Villages and farms were blazing for more than a hundred miles along the St. Lawrence. Major George Scott sailed fifty-two miles to Kamouraska and reported "burnt 998 good Buildings, two Sloops, two Schooners, ten Shalloops and several Bateaux and Small Craft, took 15 Prisoners (six of them Women and five Children) killed five of the Enemy . . . "

Thirty scalped bodies were left in the ruins of Ste. Anne de Beaupré. There the village priest, Robineau de Portneuf, had armed his flock to hold out against the destroyers as they advanced on the village. But the resistance failed; forced to surrender, the villagers came out one by one and were shot down and scalped. Father Portneuf was slashed to the ground with swords. After his scalp was removed his skull was smashed. Captain Alexander Montgomery had announced in advance that he would take no prisoners. His excuse for the scalping was that some of the villagers were dressed as Indians. So were some of the rangers in his command. But Montgomery was no ranger, woodsman or Indian-fighter. He was a regular in the 43rd Regiment, a brother officer of the reflective diarist, Captain Knox.

Townshend wrote to his wife: "It is war of the worst shape". Even the realistic Montcalm expressed shock: "Would anyone believe that a civilised nation could become so rabid as to mutilate dead bodies in cold blood? Such barbarity would have been abolished among the Indians if it had been possible to correct them. They were well paid for prisoners, but got very little for scalps." However little they were paid, the Indians continued to bring scalps to the French camp. By this time, according to the Canadian archivist, A. G. Doughty, there was little to be said in favor of either side regarding scalping. Wolfe, who threatened to hang any man found mistreating a woman, had a standing offer of five guineas per Indian scalp.

Amid the horrors, certain niceties were observed. On August 2, a French messenger brought Wolfe a letter from David Ochterlony, the American captain saved from scalping on the Montmorency beach. He was in the general hospital on the far side of Quebec, being tended by refugee Ursuline nuns. They were so good to him, he wrote, that he was moved to tears. He asked the general to reward the Guienne private who had rescued him.

Wolfe wrote to the nuns, promising to protect them when he took Quebec (he had already bombed their convent). He sent twenty pounds for the soldier, in care of Vaudreuil. The Governor proudly returned the money, declaring that the soldier had only done his duty in restraining the Indians. (He had already unleashed his Indians, without restraint, upon his own deserters.) As these polite letters were exchanged, Ochterlony died.

August flamed on, even hotter and stickier than July. Clouds of flies by day, and mosquitoes by night, fell on the fetid British camps. For men not on raiding missions, life was dreary and confined. The cows and sheep brought in from the burned parishes went to provide for the swelling numbers of sick and wounded in the field hospitals on the Isle of Orleans. The regular on duty got horsemeat when he was lucky, otherwise just bread and cheese. The sutlers' prices were exorbitant — Bristol beer 1s. 6d. a bottle, a pound of roll tobacco 1s. 10d., tea up to 2s. an ounce, which equalled a week's pay after deductions.

It was harder than ever to escape from camp on private foraging trips. The general threatened to court-martial anyone who left the lines "on any pretext whatsoever." Apart from that, foragers were likely to be scalped by the Indians. And with the countryside in flames there wasn't much left to forage, anyway. Quebec, even smoking and rocked by cannon fire, still looked attractive compared to the hot and stinking tents and trenches. Night after night, deserters slipped across the river in stolen canoes and secretly-constructed rafts. Townshend records the escape of a sergeant of the 35th who waded across the flats below Montmorency Falls in full view of English and French. The English shot at him, but he got away.

Many of the redcoats not in hospital were suffering from scurvy. They had the obvious symptoms in varying degrees — patches of discolored skin, swollen legs and rotten gums, a general feeling of lassitude and occasional dizzy spells. With them came peculiar side effects. Commodore Anson, who lost two hundred men to scurvy in a few months of his round-the-world voyage in the Centurion, described the disease as "surely the most singular and unaccountable of any that affects the human body". It produced "strange dejection of the spirits with shiverings, tremblings and a disposition to be seized with the most dreadful terrors on the slightest accident . . . whatever discouraged our people, or at any time damped their hopes, never failed to add new vigor to the distemper." It could cause fever, pleurisy, jaundice and violent rheumatic pains and could break open wounds long healed. Some of the victims ate and drank heartily and talked cheerfully so long as they were lying down. When they tried to stand up, they dropped dead.

These "dreadful terrors" could explain the behaviour of a British log-cutting party on the Montmorency who suddenly thought they saw Indians, panicked, and shot one another. Or the two sentries who fired at an imaginary enemy and were punished by having to stand by the latrines with women's caps on their heads. Scurvy aggravated fear, and the traditional cure — to be buried in the earth for a day with only your head above ground — was fearful, too. The disease is now so completely under control — thanks largely to Captain Cook's experiments with lemon juice on his famous voyages — that there are no current epidemics to study and we can only imagine its effects on men of the period. Undoubtedly Wolfe had scurvy, among his other ailments. And this may help to explain his erratic behaviour during August.

Each morning he emerged from his stone farmhouse at Montmorency looking pale and blotchy. He snapped and snarled at his aides and avoided his brigadiers, addressing them mainly by letter. His daily orders were clear enough, but he would not discuss his overall plan, if he had one. One of his few recorded remarks at this time was in answer to an officer who was talking about someone's constitution.

"Don't talk to me of constitution", he barked, blue eyes blazing. "If he has spirit, that is enough. Spirit will carry a man through anything."

In the dark, muggy nights of despair and recrimination Wolfe, on his farmhouse cot, may have felt that he had nothing left but his own spirit. His preoccupation with his bodily woes, the lonely self-importance of his first command, the certainty that glory or ruination must come within a few weeks, all led him to forget that he still had the best army ever seen in North America and one quarter of the best navy in the world.

On the morning of August 19, Hervey Smyth emerged from the general's door and announced that Wolfe had taken to his bed. The word swept through the Montmorency camp, across the river to the Isle of Orleans and Point Levi and far along the south shore — "The General is dying."

For the Lobsters, who still trusted and revered him for his steadiness under fire, this meant that the expedition was nearly over. For the brigadiers, it was time to look to their reputations back in London.

Wolfe probably believed that he was dying. The thought of death in battle or in bed was always with him. As he had told his mother, "a few years more or less are of little consequence to the common run of men. And therefore I need not lament that I am perhaps somewhat nearer to my end than others of my time."

Montcalm's defensive strategy was crumbling. Because of superior Canadian communications he learned on August 9 what Wolfe did not discover until two weeks later — that Amherst had at last taken Ticonderoga and that his second-in-command, Sir William Johnson, had forced the surrender of Fort Niagara. The English were now free to advance on Lake Champlain and Lake Ontario. Bourlamaque, outnumbered four to one, had blown up and abandoned Ticonderoga and moved back to the Ile aux Noix, the last strongpoint on the Champlain route. La Corne wrote that he could not hold his post at the head of Lake Ontario if the English came at it in force.

At a council of war in the de Salaberry house Montcalm reluctantly agreed with Vaudreuil that de Lévis would have to go to Montreal, taking seven hundred Canadians and a hundred regulars. When he got there, he would decide which front needed strengthening most. The men could ill be spared from Quebec, and neither could de Lévis — the one officer who could get along with both Montcalm and Vaudreuil and who kept them from each other's throats. With him went the last hope of a coordinated defense; the gap between French and Canadians became unbridgeable.

Bougainville was gone, too, tramping wearily back and forth along forty miles of riverbank west of Quebec, following the British ships that drifted up and down with the tide. He had twice beaten off a force of 1200 led by Brigadier Murray when it tried to land at Pte. aux Trembles, but had missed Murray when he sailed up to Deschambault, forty-five miles from Quebec. Murray landed safely there, and burned a large warehouse containing arms, ammunition and all the spare baggage belonging to Montcalm's

Louis Antoine, Comte de Bougainville, shown late in life when he had attained fame as an explorer. At Quebec he was in charge of the column wearily following the fleet up and down river. And on the crucial night of the attack he disappeared.

(Archives Nationales du Québec)

officers. This so alarmed Montcalm that he rode there himself with a detachment of grenadiers. If Murray entrenched himself, the supply lines would be cut and, his diarist wrote, "the colony was lost or next thing to it". But Murray withdrew. His orders were to "divide and distract" the enemy and, if possible, to draw them out to fight. But just as he was drawing them out, he was ordered back. Wolfe, on his sickbed, had decided that Murray's wanderings upriver were responsible for the stagnation of the siege. A midshipman had been sent to find him and call him back, but couldn't locate him. When Murray finally was reached he had been gone three weeks and had caused Montcalm more anxiety than all the rest of Wolfe's army. But for the second time, an upriver landing was called off.

Murray returned on August 25, bringing the cheering news of the capture of Niagara and Ticonderoga that he had obtained from French deserters. That day Knox wrote: "His Excellency General Wolfe is on the recovery, to the inconceivable joy of the whole Army." The jubilation in the British camp was accompa-

nied by a new optimism on the French side. Montcalm learned that
Amherst's armies were not advancing on either front. De Lévis had
reinforced La Corne at the rapids and Bourlamaque reported that
he was secure on the Ile aux Noix. He had four heavily armed ships
and the British had none. Amherst was shipbuilding.

On September 1, French sentries at Montmorency reported a stir in the British fortifications across the gorge. Heavy
guns were being trundled through the greenery, with much cursing and crashing of branches. That night a barn burned beside
Townshend's headquarters and other signal fires flamed in the
woods above the falls. The now familiar sounds of splashing boats
and the movement of heavily-burdened men came from the beach
below and more boats could be heard out in the river. The British
were evacuating the Montmorency camp and moving back across
the St. Lawrence. Vaudreuil wrote: "Everything proves that the
grand design of the English has failed."

The decision to move had been taken on August 31 at a
peculiar council of war. After two months of telling his brigadiers
what to do and seldom asking their opinions, Wolfe had passed the
buck. As he was ill and time was wasting away, he asked them to
meet and come up with a plan of attack. He gave them three suggestions to consider, all involving assaults on the Beauport camp
and all slightly different versions of the plan that had failed so completely on July 31. As Col. Stacey notes, a modern general who
asked his subordinates to make up his mind for him would be considered a very weak commander, but in 1759 the council-of-war
procedure was accepted. In addition, Wolfe was sick and may have
doubted his judgment, even his sanity.

As he must have expected, the brigadiers rejected all
suggestions of another Beauport attack. After consulting Admiral
Saunders they suggested an attack on the north shore above Quebec — "anywhere for an extent of four leagues (12 miles) from the
height of St. John (St. Jean Baptiste, now Les Ecureils) to Cap
Rouge River." Wolfe accepted the recommendation and prepared
to move upriver. Then he relapsed into his usual silence and would
not reveal when, where or even if the attack would be made. He
was still intent upon revenge on the Canadians. Instead of mass-
ing his forces for a final assault he sent 1600 men, including some
regulars and all of Major Scott's American Rangers, downstream to
burn more villages. They left on August 31 and did not get back

in time for the decisive battle.

On the night of the council of war Wolfe wrote in his last letter to his mother: "The Marquis of Montcalm is at the head of a great number of bad soldiers and I am at the head of a small number of good ones that wish for nothing so much as to fight him; but the wary old fellow avoids an action, doubtful of the behaviour of his army." Wolfe had about six thousand fit men left out of the 8,500 he had brought from Louisbourg; the rest were dead, had deserted, or lay groaning in the field hospitals.

Townshend was glad to leave "the cursed Montmorency camp" but he considered it a retreat. When he reached Point Levi he received a message from Amherst that his brother Roger had been killed at Ticonderoga. The blow came as he watched sad little groups of women and children brought into camp by the raiding parties, reminding him of his own family, and he was overwhelmed by melancholy and homesickness. He should never have returned to the army, he wrote Charlotte. If she had only pleaded with him not to go he would have stayed and would not now be "in a scene of Ambition, Confusion and Misery, and you oppress'd as I know you must be, with Terrours and affliction. I dare say poor Lady Townshend (his mother) too now starts at every knock at the Door."

"One month more," he assured her, "will put an end to our troubles." Townshend, the artist, never wrote with the clarity and precision of Wolfe, but his phrase "ambition, confusion and misery" is probably the best summary of the situation in the British command.

By September 7, Wolfe had mustered 3,000 men in transports, frigates and warships in the river near Cap Rouge and he and the brigadiers were installed in the Sutherland. The army's flatboats had been towed successfully upstream past the Quebec batteries while the men marched along the south shore. Col. Carleton, with the 2nd Royal Americans, was left to guard the hospital and stores at the Isle of Orleans and Col. Burton, with the 48th, was guarding the batteries at Point Levi. The bulk of the army was poised for a waterborne assault. But where?

Wolfe's first choice of a landing site was St. Augustin, twelve miles from Quebec. A feint attack would be made further upstream at Pte. aux Trembles. But a storm blew up from the north-east and for three days the redcoats crouched in the 'tween decks of the heaving transports as rain battered the tarpaulin-covered gratings over their heads. On September 9 it was still raining and 1500 men were landed on the south shore to stretch their legs and get some fresh air. The St. Augustin attack was postponed indefinitely.

Wolfe stared bleakly at his rain-spattered stern window as he wrote his final dispatch to London. It was addressed to Pitt's colleague the Earl of Holderness —

"On board the 'Sutherland' at anchor off Cap Rouge, Sept 9, 1759

"My Lord. If the Marquis of Montcalm had shut himself up in the town of Quebec it would have been long since in our possession because the defences are inconsiderable and our artillery very formidable; but he has a numerous body of armed men (I cannot call it an army) and the strongest country perhaps in the world to rest the defence of the town and colony upon . . .

"We are now here with about 3600 men, waiting an opportunity to attack them when and wherever they can best be got at. The weather has been extremely unfavourable for a day or two so that we have been inactive. I am so far recovered as to do business, but my constitution is entirely ruined, without the consolation of having done any considerable service to the State, or without any prospect of it."

The dismal letter gives no hint that, earlier that day, he had found his path of glory. He had seen a crack in the cliffs, practically on the doorstep of Quebec, but because of the rain had not been able to get a good look at it.

Next day, the 10th, dawned brilliant and sparkling clear. In the morning a boat arrived from Saunders' fleet below Quebec bringing a packet of dispatches, including reports from French deserters. Wolfe studied them, then led a procession of three boats downriver, landing at Goreham's Post No. 2 near the mouth of the Etchevin River, opposite Sillery. He took with him Monckton and Townshend, Admiral Holmes, Major Mackellar, Capt. Chads (the small-boat expert) and Capt. William Delaune. They wore ordinary grenadiers' greatcoats to hide their gold braid, but these flapped open and the French officer watching them through his telescope from Sillery reported "many officers in gay uniforms, one in particular in a blue surtout with much gold lace." They planted stakes in the ground and appeared to be laying out a camp site.

The importance of the moment was lost to the Frenchmen as it was lost to Wolfe's officers. Typically, he told them nothing. They saw him aim his glass at a rift in the tree-lined precipice on the other side which seemed to conceal a steep path. A few tents could be seen at the top and a log abbattis half way down the cliff.

This was the Anse au Foulon, the second cove upstream from Cape Diamond and just two miles from Quebec. Translated, its name was Fuller's Cove. Fuller's earth, used in treating linen, had been found there and was used in making cloth from the flax grown around Quebec. The St. Denis brook splashed down the fault in the rock and gurgled into the river. If Wolfe was excited by what he saw, he did not show it. He was stiffer, more formal than ever with his aristocratic subordinates. He did not tell them of his decision to land there or hint at the secret of the Foulon, if he even knew it. Mackellar or Stobo, his two senior experts on Quebec, could have pointed out the Foulon as a landing site. Yet Mackellar's report, written after the battle, bears all the earmarks of hindsight. He said the cove "seemed to promise a fair chance of success", but he got the name wrong, calling it the "Toulon". Stobo was not present. Three days before, Wolfe had sent him off to carry dispatches to Amherst — down the St. Lawrence by sloop, then overland across New England. The unknown author of Stobo's "Memoirs" claimed that his hero told Wolfe about the cove; others say that the garrulous Scot was a nuisance Wolfe was glad to get rid of. There is no documentary evidence to support either version: Wolfe destroyed the journal which doubtless gave the reason for his decision, and Stobo lost his letters to Amherst. He had to dump them overboard when captured at sea by a French privateer.

Any one of dozens of talkative French prisoners and deserters could have told Wolfe there was a path there which led to the soft side of Quebec. But the real secret of the Foulon lay in the nature of its defenders. That, more than its geography, made it the key to the citadel.

Chapter 10

The Back Door

The tide above Quebec rushes fiercely and can reach a speed of four knots on the ebb. For weeks it had hampered Wolfe's naval operations, restricting the times at which he could move his ships and setting them adrift when their anchors failed to catch on the smooth rock bottom. Now he was using it. While the big Sutherland tugged at her mooring off Cap Rouge the frigates and transports set just enough sail to give steerage and drifted up and down the fifteen miles between the Foulon area and St. Augustin.

Bougainville's flying column of 800 footsoldiers and 200 horsemen wore themselves out trying to keep pace along the shore. After several days of this they were no longer a flying column but a worn, bedraggled line of men who dropped to sleep the moment they were allowed to halt. Their leader no longer rode with them on every shuttle back and forth. Bougainville, master of the integral calculus, knew exactly when the tides turned and how long the ships would take to go from A to B. What he could not calculate was where and when they might suddenly land their troops. As he couldn't be everywhere he concentrated on the shoreline furthest from Quebec.

Montcalm had ordered him to keep moving slightly upstream of the enemy. Logic told the general that the landing must come either far upriver or at Beauport. He tried to read his opponent's mind. "I think," he wrote on September 2, "Wolfe will act like a player of *tope et tingue* who, having played to the left of the *tope*, plays to the right and then to the middle." He had played to Montcalm's left at Montmorency, to his right with Murray's landing at Deschambault. The middle would be Quebec or the Beauport shore near the St. Charles. An attack on the Rock itself was out of the question — "we need not believe the enemy had wings," he said. As for the two coves below the Heights of Abraham — Anse au Foulon and Anse des Meres — "100 men, well posted, could

Cap Rouge, where Wolfe's final attack began. From here the troops drifted downstream towards Quebec in flatboats like the one shown in the above sketch by Captain Hervey Smyth.
(Royal Ontario Museum, Toronto)

stop the whole army and give us time to wait for daylight and then march to the right of that sector." He had 100 men, well posted, at the Foulon, or thought he had. So despite the English naval maneuvers he still expected a landing at Beauport. He warned the weary Bougainville "M. Wolfe is just the man to double back."

The long worry of the siege was telling on Montcalm. "My health is going to pieces" he wrote. Yet it was still better than Wolfe's and he had shaken off the dejection of late August when he had written to Bourlamaque wondering which of the three of them (Bourlamaque, Bougainville and himself) would be defeated first. By September 11, he was giving the English "another month or something less, to stay here" and making plans for winter quarters.

Vaudreuil still believed the evacuation of the Montmorency camp marked the beginning of the end of Wolfe's campaign. English deserters told him (correctly) that Saunders was anxious to leave and that some of his smaller ships had already left the river. The ships above Quebec, he told de Lévis, "go up and down almost simultaneously, which indicates that they have no settled object." All Wolfe's brigadiers wanted to abandon the siege and go home, he was told; the general was determined to make one last attempt, but mainly for show. A few men would land, be repulsed, and withdraw. It would all be over in a week. He, Vaudreuil, would have conquered the mighty Wolfe. Perhaps then he could persuade his ministers to remove the irritating little French general and restore his undisputed command of the colony.

Colonel Ralph Burton, guardian of Point Levi, was the only officer to learn the details of Wolfe's final plan until the day it was put into operation. Wolfe sent him a note on the evening of the 10th, signing it "affectionately yours", for Burton was one of the few friends he had left.

"Tomorrow", Wolfe wrote, "the troops re-embark, the fleet sails up the river a little higher as if intending to land above the north shore, keeping a convenient distance for the boats and armed vessels to fall down to the Foulon; and we count (if no accident of weather or other prevents) to make a powerful effort at that spot about four in the morning of the 13th. If we succeed in the first business it may produce an action which may produce the total conquest of Canada; in all cases it is our duty to try the most likely way, whatever may be the event."

He mentions reports from deserters that the Beauport garrison were now eating bread made from new wheat, indicating that their regular supplies were used up, and adds that only the violent hand of their government and terror of the Indians was keeping the colony together. "The Canadians have no affection for their government, no tie so strong as their wives and children; they are a disjointed, discontented, dispirited peasantry, beat into cowardice by Cadet, Bigot, Montcalm and the savages." There was some truth in this, but it was overstated.

The troops got their orders the following day. They were to embark in flatboats gathered beside the Sutherland about nine on the evening of the 12th, taking with them only arms, ammunition and two days' food plus rum and water. As they would have to spend part of the night in the boats they would get an extra gill of rum. Tents and blankets would follow by ship. At the signal of two lanterns at the Sutherland's main top the boats would drop downstream. They were not told where they would land — a reasonable precaution, as men were still deserting to the enemy. Their final general order, addressed "To the Army" told them all they were required to know:

"The enemy's force is now divided; great scarcity of provisions is in their camp and universal discontent among the Canadians. The second officer in command (de Lévis) is gone to Montreal or St. John's, which gives reason to think that General Amherst is advancing into the colony. A vigorous blow struck by the army at this juncture may determine the fate of Canada. Our troops below are in readiness to join us; all the light artillery and tools are embarked at Point Levi and the troops will land where the French seem least to expect it.

"The first body that gets on shore is to march directly to the enemy and drive them from any little post they may occupy. The officers must be careful that succeeding bodies do not by any mistake fire upon those who go before them. The battalions must form on the upper ground with expedition, and be ready to charge whatever presents itself. When the artillery and troops are landed, a corps will be left to secure the landing place while the rest march on and endeavour to bring the French and Canadians to a battle. The officers and men will remember what their country expects of them and what a determined body of soldiers, inured to war, is capable of doing against five weak French battalions mixed with disordered peasantry. The soldiers must be attentive and obedient to their officers and the officers resolute in the execution of their duty."

The men cheered as the order was read out. This was the stuff to give the Lobster. It was inspirational, if only partly true. There *was* discontent among the Canadians, but it was by no means universal. There *was* reason to think Amherst was advancing, although Wolfe now knew that he wasn't. Montcalm's five regular battalions had been weakened, true, but including Canadians and Indians he had between eleven and fifteen thousand men — more than twice the attacking force. But the total effect of Wolfe's words was dramatic. Its reminder of what England expected from her men would be echoed by Nelson at Trafalgar, 46 years later.

"The men were ready", wrote Quartermaster Sergeant John Johnson,"...nay, how could it be otherwise, being at the heels of gentlemen whose whole thirst, equal with their general, was for glory? We had seen them tried and always found them sterling. We knew that they would stand by us to the last extremity."

Johnson, then with the 58th at Point Levi, could not know that at that moment the principal gentlemen were gathered in the wardroom of the Sutherland composing an angry letter to their general:

"Sir, As we do not think ourselves sufficiently informed of the several parts which may fall to our share in the execution of the descent you intend tomorrow, We must beg leave to request from you as distinct orders as the nature of the thing will admit of, particularly as to the place or places we are to attack. This circumstance, perhaps very decisive, we cannot learn from the publick orders, neither may it be in the power of the Naval Officer who lands the troops to instruct us — As we should be very sorry, no less for the publick than for our own sakes, to commit any mistakes, We are persuaded that you will see the necessity of this application, which can proceed from nothing but a desire to execute your orders with the utmost punctuality.

> We are, Sir
> Your most obedt. hble. Servts.
> Robt. Monckton
> Geo. Townshend
> Jas. Murray"

Wolfe received the letter as he fretted in his cabin a few hours before the attack and scrawled a quick, sarcastic reply by lantern light, addressed to Monckton:

"My reason for desiring the honour of your company with me to Goreham's post yesterday (actually two days before) was to shew you, as well as the distance wou'd permit, the situation of the Enemy & the place where I mean't they shoud be attack'd; as you are charged with that duty I shoud be glad to give you all further light & assistance in my powere — the Place is called the *Foulon* distant upon two miles or two miles & a half from Quebec where you remarked an encampment of 12 or 13 Tents & an Abbatis below it — you mention'd today that you had perceived a breastwork there, which made me imagine you as well acquainted with the Place as the nature of things will admit of, I took Capt. Chads with me also & desir'd the Admiral's attendance, that as the former is charg'd by Mr. Saunders with conducting of the boats, he might make himself as much a Master of his part as possible; and as several of the Ships of war are to fall down with the troops, Mr. Holmes wou'd be able to station them properly after he had seen the Place . . . Capt. Chads will begin to land the men a little of this side of the naked Rock which you must remember to have seen, within which (to the east-ward) the enemy is posted.

"It is not a usual thing to point out in the publick orders the direct spot of an attack, nor for any inferior officers not charg'd with a particular duty to ask instructions upon that point. I had the honour to inform you today that it is my duty to attack the French Army, to the best of my knowledge & abilities I have fix'd upon that spot where we can act with most force and are most likely to succeed, if I am mistaken I am sorry for it & must be answerable to His Majesty and the Publick for the consequences."

Townshend got a short note: — "Brigadier-General Monckton is charged with the first landing and attack at the Foulon, if he succeeds you will be pleased to give directions that the Troops afloat be set on shoar with the utmost expedition; as they are under your command; and when the 3,600 men now in the fleet are landed, I have no manner of doubt but that we are able to fight & to beat the French Army; in which I know you will give your best assistance."

The letters were dated 8.30 p.m. — half an hour before the troops began climbing into the boats. They reached the two brigadiers in time to fuel a smouldering rage that would burn all night. They had been put in their place. So had Murray; he got no reply.

Admiral Holmes was equally annoyed. He had been given the job of supervising the landing. It was the most hazardous task he had ever undertaken and he knew he would get most of the blame if, as he expected, it went wrong. He had no illusions about the Foulon — "the distance of the landing place, the impetuosity of the tide; the darkness of the night; and the great chance of exactly hitting the very spot intended without discovery or alarm; made the whole extremely difficult." Holmes wrote this five days after he had managed to hit the spot. He was still bitter. He said the Foulon landing had been proposed to Wolfe a month before, when the cove was still unguarded — "He now laid hold of it when it was highly improbable that he should succeed."

Either Wolfe was desperate, or he knew much more about the Foulon than Holmes or the brigadiers, all of whom disapproved of it as a landing site. A week earlier, one of Montcalm's five regular battalions — the Guienne — had been camped on the heights above the cove. After spending one day there, September 5, the Guienne was ordered back to Beauport. Why? Most English accounts say Montcalm sent it to the heights and Vaudreuil brought it back. On the eve of the British attack Montcalm sent it back again, but Vaudreuil stepped in once more, saying "We'll see about that tomorrow." French versions give Vaudreuil's story, written after defeat: "I was counting heavily upon the Guienne battalion; I thought it was still on the heights of Quebec, but M. de Montcalm had recalled it the same day (the 12th) at nightfall, without informing me."

Montcalm's aide, Johnstone, says the Guienne was ordered back to the heights but did not go because of an administrative mix-up caused by the adjutant-general, Montreuil. Mackellar learned later from some Guienne soldiers that they had expected to move back on the 12th, but Montcalm kept them at Beauport because an English deserter told him that camp was about to be attacked.

At all events, the Guienne was not on the heights when it was most needed. There was only Vergor, who had replaced the French Captain St. Martin a few days before, and thirty men instead of the 100 Montcalm reckoned could hold off an army.

The back door to Quebec stood open. Did Wolfe know this? Was this the "intelligence" he received on the morning of the 10th which, Townshend believed, caused him to change his plans? Probably he did know about Vergor and the Guienne's move back to Beauport, but he could not have known of the order to move the battalion once again to the heights, or he would hardly have risked landing directly below. Unless, of course, he knew that the order would be countermanded. And this would mean that Quebec was betrayed from within, not merely by spies or deserters, but by a conspiracy of highly-placed traitors.

Historians Doughty and Parmelee hint that Vergor was in contact with Wolfe — "Of treachery, in connection with the post on the heights of Quebec, there is reason to suspect Vergor." Murray's biographer, Maj.-General R. H. Mahon, goes further. He says Bigot and Cadet arranged for the Foulon to be unguarded and the English boats to pass unharmed, lured Bougainville away from his post, and told Wolfe where to land. Stacey calls this a work of fiction: "There is plenty of evidence that Bigot and Cadet were rogues, but none at all that they were traitors."

As the darkness deepened on the evening of the 12th, other events took place which showed that with or without a conspiracy to betray Quebec, Wolfe's gamble was not as desperate as it looked.

Just after nine, the first redcoats scrambled over the bulwarks of their transports and down into the flatboats and ships' longboats rocking gently alongside. There would be 1800 in the first wave, led by twenty-four volunteers under Captain Delaune. They filled thirty-five boats and the little schooner impudently named "Terror of France". The transports Ann and Elizabeth, Laurel, Adventure and Ward were to follow them after half an hour, bringing ammunition, tents and supplies. One hour after the first wave left the Sutherland, Townshend was to bring his men downriver in the frigates Lowestoft, Squirrel and Seahorse, to be landed by the now-empty boats. On the way, his convoy would pick up the sloop Hunter, which was anchored off Goreham's Post No. 2 with a lantern in her shrouds, acting as a marker for the oarsmen. When Townshend's force was ashore, the boats would cross the river to ferry over the rest of the army — Burton's from Point Levi and Carleton's from Point of Orleans — who would be waiting opposite the Foulon. Admiral Holmes was to supervise naval operations from the Lowestoft, while Captain Chads directed the actual landing of the boats. All army officers were ordered to obey Chads without question.

As the men in the boats sipped their rum and water and settled down to await the signal to go, a flash and rumble from downriver told them that the nightly shelling of Quebec had begun.

Wolfe, in his cabin, had settled his worldly affairs. He had written his last letters to the brigadiers and entrusted his will and Miss Lowther's picture to Jack Jervis. Now he was dressing for battle.

His servant François had laid out on his bunk the new scarlet coat with its blue lining, white facings and gold trim, a snowy fresh shirt with lace jabot and cuffs, warm waistcoat, and serviceable white breeches and stockings. His boots stood on the floor, brilliantly polished, and the belt for the small hanger sword he seldom wore was pipe-clayed to perfection. François helped him dress, fitted the queue that held back his dark-red hair, and straightened his lapels. Wolfe inspected his face in a small mirror, noting the blotches and the lines of pain around the too-bright eyes. He tightened his thin lips. Spirit! if a man had spirit, he could conquer all. Solemnly he held out his left arm and the servant tied around it the black band he wore in memory of his father. He shrugged on a heavy gray greatcoat, grasped his stick, and strode out on deck.

As the sun went down Montcalm was inspecting a new gun position on the Beauport cliffs. In the brief twilight that followed he saw signs of movement in Saunders' big ships over by the south shore. Men were aloft in the shrouds and along the yards; a few sails were unfurled and one or two ships were looming closer as the light failed. This was not particularly sinister. Every few nights the English tried to slip more ships upriver. Yet every night the siege drew nearer to its climax. As the English guns began their usual nightly bombardment of the city the general turned back towards the de Salaberry manor. An excited officer hurried up behind him, shouting. De Poulariez, who had replaced de Lévis as commander of the left flank, reported that barges were approaching the mudflats near the Montmorency.

A direct attack on Beauport! That was the warning of the latest British deserter; that was what Montcalm had long expected. Wolfe was doubling back. Trumpets brayed the alarm and along the six-mile front Canadians and regulars were routed from their tents to man the trenches. Montcalm sent an aide to Vaudreuil's house by the St. Charles to tell the governor something was afoot and to inquire — the general did not hide his sarcasm — if he would feel it appropriate to come over and offer his advice. Montcalm, with Poulariez and Johnstone galloping in his wake, rode along the cliff towards the danger spot. As they neared the Montmorency, British ships' guns opened up on the shoreline behind them. Between rounds, they could hear boats being rowed noisily in the river.

But by two o'clock in the morning, no attack had developed. Montcalm sent Poulariez back to his headquarters and rode back to the de Salaberry house. He dismounted and spent the next few hours walking by the shore with Johnstone.

As Johnstone remembered their conversation, the general had dismissed the noisy English boats and was worrying about a convoy of French supply barges, due to arrive that night from Cap Rouge. "I tremble lest they be taken", he said. "We have only a few days' provisions left." Cadet's organization had continued to bring supplies down by boat even after the British fleet moved up past Quebec, but this was becoming increasingly dangerous. Cadet had sent a note to Bougainville asking him to send the barges that night, when the tide would bring them down under cover of darkness. If they were delayed even one day it would be too risky and he would have to send carts to bring the supplies by land; and he was very short of carts.

What Montcalm knew, but did not tell Johnstone, was that Cadet was short of carts because so many were being used in the construction of Mme. Péan's bomb shelter. And while the defenders of Quebec were down to two ounces of bad bread per day, Bigot and Cadet were still using grain to fatten chickens for their tables. The plundering went on as the city was destroyed. Montcalm promised himself that the plunderers would be made to pay if he ever got back to France to tell his story. He had told the Minister of War in a letter — "it seems as if they were all hastening to make their fortunes before the loss of the colony, which many of them perhaps desire as a veil for their conduct."

This was a hint that the Bigot ring might be capable of treason in addition to their other crimes. But only a hint. If Montcalm had any evidence of treason, he kept it to himself; and he did not usually keep things to himself.

Upriver, Cadet's supply barges lay beached on the foreshore at Cap Rouge. Four caulkers sent from Quebec had worked on them for several days, smearing hot pitch from smoky cauldrons into their leaky seams, but for some reason they did not sail. The caulking may not have been finished or the cargoes not loaded in time. Or Bougainville may not have received the message to send them on the night of the 12th or not at all. For, on that crucial night, Bougainville vanished.

Rumor placed him twenty miles up the St. Lawrence at Jacques-Cartier on a gallant mission connected with his cousin's wife, a certain Madame de Vienne, whom Mahon describes as "a lady of notoriety and charm". She had left Quebec two days before with several cartloads of possessions to take refuge at Jacques-Cartier, and Bougainville had written a note to one of his officers there, asking him to take good care of her. There is no proof that young Bougainville took the night off to take care of her himself — only 200-year-old scandal. But he must have done *something* that night. For when the British boats cast off from the Sutherland at two a.m. and several frigates raised anchor to make a diversionary move upstream, his tired leaderless men simply stayed put. No attempt was made to follow the British either upstream or down. If some highly-placed traitor had decided to lure Bougainville from his post, Mme. de Vienne was as succulent bait as any. Certainly, he was fatally late in arriving at the battle in the morning. He was to become a great figure in French history, but this was not his day. As he said himself, he was only an apprentice soldier.

Wolfe's boats swept quietly down, increasing speed as the oarsmen pulled and the tide increased from three to four knots. Captain Chads lined his bow up on the faint mast light of the Hunter which glinted ahead, vanishing and reappearing as the mist swirled over the river.

Captain Smith of the Hunter heard them coming and manned his guns, just in case. He, alone among the British forces, knew that a French convoy was expected that night. Three hours before, two French deserters, attracted by his light, had paddled out to his ship in a canoe and told him this, in exchange for favorable treatment. He had not had time to send a message up to the Sutherland. No boat, rowing against the tide, could have made it before the invasion fleet set off. So he waited, ready to relay his important information if the approaching boats were British, or sink them if they turned out to be French. As Wolfe's boat passed, Smith had no time to give details, but his message got through. Wolfe now had the password — provision boats.

After the Hunter, Chads set course for the north shore and the Foulon. As his boat approached the black cape past Sillery, the first shout came from the river bank: *"Qui vive?"*

Captain Simon Fraser of Balmain, one of the few French-speakers aboard, had been ordered to do the talking: *"La France! Et vive le Roi!"*

"A quel régiment?"

"De la Reine". That was a mistake. The Régiment de la Reine was with Bourlamaque on Lake Champlain. But the sentry was sufficiently impressed. He could not demand a password, for none had been arranged. He ran along the shore, shouting to the next post: *"Laissez les passer. Ils sont nos gens avec les provisions."*

The boats glided on, under the looming wooded cliffs that hid the Samos battery. A second sentry scrambled through the birches and willows down to the water's edge and challenged; *"Qui vive?"*

"Gens avec les provisions. Tais-toi! Nous serons entendus!"

As the sentry knew, they might easily be overheard by the British. He waved them on. Minutes later they rounded the last headland and swept into the Foulon cove. There was no sentry on shore, but the current was pulling more strongly. The sailors rowed hard against it but could not hold the overladen craft. One by one they were swept past the notch in the cliffside and on under a steep wall of rock. Wolfe saw his chosen path slipping past him. Chads' boat finally hit gravel and Delaune and his twenty-four volunteers jumped for the beach. Wolfe stepped ashore with cautious dignity. They had missed the cove by 500 yards, but there could be no turning back now.

Above them soared a black mass of rock 175 feet high. Hollow fear of failure clutched at Wolfe. After all those weeks of indecision, the surveys, the plans drawn up and then rejected, he had arrived at what appeared to be the worst landing site of all. Then the strange calm that came over him when an enemy was at hand reasserted itself. According to Quartermaster-Sergeant Johnson he said mildly to Hervey Smyth and Barré: "I don't think we can by any possible means get up there, but we must use our best endeavour."

The boats, spaced at twenty-foot intervals, were piling

up behind him. Wolfe consulted with the vanguard leader, Colonel Howe, then ordered Delaune to climb.

The cliff was a reminder of the Montmorency disaster, although much higher. The rock face had a thin covering of loose shale and soft soil, soggy from the summer rains. As soon as a boot dug into it, it gave way. But there were tree stumps and stunted maples, birches and mountain ash trees to provide handholds. And, this time, there was no raking musketfire from above.

Delaune and his men hauled themselves up in the darkness, branch by branch. Colonel Howe followed them, his sword dangling and catching in the foliage. As they disappeared upward, two companies of light infantry scrambled behind, and were in turn swallowed up by the dark.

It was just after four o'clock, with an hour to go before the first glimmerings of daylight appeared. The journey from the Sutherland had taken two hours, and not a shot had been fired. Now there was only the creak and splash and crunch of more flatboats arriving, a low mutter of voices and from above the crackle and slither of climbers who lost their footing. Wolfe waited on the beach. The men were ordered to stay in their boats and keep quiet.

Then, at last, the challenge from above rang out. *"Qui vive?"* A moment's pause, then a musket shot, followed by a volley, screams and more shooting, the oaths of struggling men and the sounds of bodies smashing through the brush.

The general stood, clutching his stick, waiting for the sounds of victory. And they came — a throaty chorus of huzzahs. He waved the stick and the redcoats swarmed ashore and attacked the climb, muskets in hand, swearing cheerfully. There was no further need for silence. They tangled their belts in the trees and bramble bushes, they fumbled and dropped their weapons, but they rose in an irresistible mass. Wolfe climbed, too. Although still weak from the surgeon's blood-letting, he waved away helping arms. The thin arms strained urgently from branch to branch, the lace ruffles caught and tore. Wolfe heaved and gasped his way upward.

Vergor's post had been taken in minutes. The sentry's challenge had been answered in French by Captain Donald MacDonald of the Frasers, a Jacobite who had served with the French army. He offered the limp story that he had been sent to relieve Vergor. That delayed the sentry's shout of alarm just long enough to allow the first climbers to creep up and surround the little camp. Most

General Wolfe climbing the Heights of Abraham. The artist, R. Caton Woodville, has added daylight and dignity to the scramble up the cliff.   (Public Archives of Canada)

of the thirty Canadians were asleep in their tents. About half were taken prisoner and the rest ran away. Vergor, still in his nightshirt, rushed from his tent and was brought down by a bullet in the ankle.

As Wolfe reached the top, Howe's men had found the path down to the Foulon and were clearing away the log defenses that blocked it. It was a good path, though steep. Before dawn British troops were marching up two abreast. And as watery daylight spread up from the sea, Wolfe saw the rolling fields of Maître Abraham lying empty before him, and beyond them the walls and spires of Quebec.

Chapter 11

The Inevitable Hour

The Samos battery pounded Townshend's ships and flatboats as they headed for the Foulon to land the second wave. His men had just climbed down into the boats when four 23 pounders and a 13 inch mortar opened up at short range. The boats were pulled around to shelter behind the heavy hulls of the frigates but not before several were hit. Knox reported eight men wounded in his boat. The sides of the Lowestoft and Squirrel were battered for half an hour. Then, as they rounded the point into the cove, the cannonade stopped. The French gunners had heard a detachment of redcoats approaching through the woods and had rammed spikes into the touchholes of their cannon and run. When Townshend reached the beachhead, all the sounds of battle had ceased.

Montcalm heard the firing as he walked with Johnstone five miles away, but was not unduly alarmed. Perhaps the British had captured the supply convoy, perhaps they were staging another small diversion. He sent a messenger to Vaudreuil's camp to inquire what was happening above the town, but did not consider rushing reinforcements there. He was sure Bougainville could handle any diversionary attack. Johnstone was not so sure. To him, Bougainville was an amateur. For all his bravery and brains, he had never studied the basic textbooks of war or fought in a formal European battle.

The two men waited until dawn showed them Saunders' fleet riding peacefully at anchor. Only rippling waters and the cries of seabirds broke the silence of the Beauport shore. The English were not going to attack. Montcalm dismissed the troops who had manned the trenches for most of the night and they rolled thankfully into their tents. The general and his aide had mounted their horses and were riding slowly back to the de Salaberry house when a messenger galloped to meet them, shouting that the English had landed.

One of Vergor's men, so shaken that he was barely coherent, had run all the way from the Foulon with the incredible story that Wolfe's men had climbed the heights. At first nobody believed him. Montcalm's secretary Montbeillard dismissed the man as crazy with fear and decided to go to bed. Montcalm rode towards the St. Charles to look for himself. But still he was not alarmed. On the way, he and Johnstone stopped at the de Salaberry house for a cup of tea.

Vaudreuil was still at his desk, writing letters. He had declined Montcalm's chilly invitation to visit Montmorency during the night and watch some mysterious English operation. Apparently nothing had come of that. Now he had a note from the Chevalier de Bernetz, who was commanding the city while de Ramezay was in hospital, telling him there had been a landing at the Foulon. The note, timed 5.45 a.m., gave a garbled version of events there taken from the survivor of Vergor's party who had shouted warnings on his terror-stricken way to Montcalm's camp. Bernetz added his own assumption that, since the firing had ceased, the English must have been pushed back. However, he proposed the Guienne battalion be moved to the heights at top speed.

Nothing was to be done at top speed. Vaudreuil continued to write letters. He composed a polite but confusing note to Bougainville:

"I have received, Monsieur, the letter you did me the honour to write with the deposition of the prisoner or deserter attached. I have passed it all to M. le Marquis de Montcalm. It seems quite certain that the enemy has made a landing at the Anse au Foulon. We have put a large force in motion. We hear a little shooting. M. le Marquis de Montcalm has just left with 100 men of the Government of Three Rivers as a reinforcement. As soon as I know for certain what is going on I shall inform you. I am anxious to have news of you and to know whether the enemy has made any attempt on your side.

"I have the honour to wish you good day.

"At a quarter to seven

"Your messenger will see M. de Montcalm in passing and will be able to give you news of him.

"Vaudreuil."

"The enemy's forces seem considerable. I do not doubt that you will be attentive to his movements and follow them. I rely on you for this.

"V."

By the time the messenger left, Wolfe had been ashore for three hours. Bougainville was at least fifteen miles away and had no firm orders to return to Quebec. The Guienne had at last been ordered to the heights but was still five miles away at Beauport, along with the rest of the regulars. The defenders were suffering from what a diarist on Montcalm's staff called "a mixture of misfortune and disorganization".

Montcalm reached the St. Charles and saw a thin row of redcoats on the rim of the slopes across the river. "This is serious", he muttered, and sent Johnstone back to Beauport to order all the regulars to the heights. He did not realize just how serious until he had ridden through the city and had a clear view of the plains beyond. There he saw line upon line of silent soldiers — not a detachment or a landing party but an army, drawn up in line of battle. Montcalm said nothing. Major Malartic, who had now joined him, said he had never seen the general so melancholy — "it seemed as though he felt his fate upon him."

Wolfe had picked his ground at leisure for the first set-piece battle in North America. As his battalions arrived up the Foulon path he marched them eastward along the clifftop, then north across the open fields straddling the Sillery road, about one thousand yards from the walls of Quebec. They marched to the tap and rattle of the drumsticks, heads held forward by the leather stocks, Brown Bess muskets at the slope. Then came the shouted order "Take Care!", a drum tap and "Wheel into Line!" and, company by company, they turned through a quarter-circle and halted. "Dress!" "Close Step!" the sergeants bellowed, and the line took shape.

Subalterns and sergeants moved along the ranks, checking each man's weapon and ammunition — sufficient powder, ball and paper for twenty-four rounds. The cartridges drawn from the magazines on the transports had been opened, checked and made up again; now they were examined once more for damp sustained in the landing. Each consisted of a ball wrapped in paper with 4½ drams of black powder. The Brown Bess was lighter than the French musket — eleven pounds two ounces, with a barrel three and a half feet long and an effective range of 75 yards. It had a .753

inch bore and its iron ball weighed one and a third ounces. Now the subalterns and sergeants inspected each muzzle, lock, pan and ramrod, and each soldier had to produce his turnkey and picker. Once everything had been inspected, orders were barked out. "Handle Cartridge"; he pulled a cartridge from the pouch and bit it open with his powder-blackened teeth. "Prime"; he poured a little powder into the pan and the rest down the barrel. "Load"; this time he put two balls, with wadding, down the barrel. The first volley would be vital. The charges were rammed home, the ramrods replaced in their loops under the musket barrels, and bayonets fixed. There was plenty of time.

The regimental standard bearers stood out in front, their silk colors rustling against their corded staves. One ensign carried the King's Color with the crosses of St. George and St. Andrew and the other the regimental standard bearing the device of its colonel. Only the Royal Americans carried the King's cipher, GR II. The drum beats mounted their excitement as more units arrived, joined now by the savage skirl of the Fraser pipes playing "Lovat's March" as Simon led his clansmen out to join the redcoats who had dragged his father to the scaffold, destroyed his salmon weirs and ravaged his family's castle and lands. The Fraser bonnets lacked the Jacobite white cockades they had worn at Culloden and their kilts and plaids bore a new pattern prescribed by the English, since the old setts which showed a man's rank by the number of colors and stripes were outlawed and forgotten. Lovat may have wondered why he, a Highland gentleman with a classical education from St. Andrews University and a gourmet's taste for food and wine, should be fated to fight for the loutish German king. But fighting was the only trade left open to the Frasers. They had their kilts, now belted high above the knee, and their basket-hilted claymores. When they charged they would fling aside the English musket, flourish the great sword and shriek the old cries in their own tongue.

The British front line stretched for nearly half a mile. It was only two ranks deep — the first "thin red line". The Louisbourg grenadiers had been restored from their disgrace at Montmorency to the honored place on the right. They were distinguished from the rest by their clerical-looking red mitre-caps, bearing the white horse of Hanover and the motto *"Nec Aspera Terrent"*. Next to them stood Bragg's 28th battalion; Kennedy's 43rd and Lascelles' 47th were in the centre and the Frasers and Anstruther's 58th on the

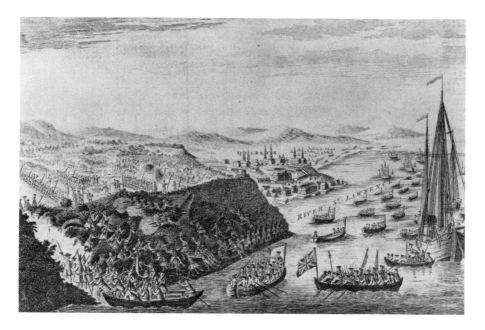

An anonymous British engraving of the battle misleadingly shows the landing of the troops and the battle taking place at the same time. In the background the French tents and fortifications on the Beauport shore are clearly visible.   (Royal Ontario Museum, Toronto)

left. Monckton commanded the right and Murray the left. Otway's 35th guarded the right flank from Canadians and Indians in the woods along the clifftops by the St. Lawrence. Amherst's 15th, with two battalions of Royal Americans, formed the second line, under Townshend, and Webb's 48th, under Col. Burton, was held in reserve.

According to Townshend's official dispatch, Wolfe had 4,441 men in the field.

The plateau was fairly level, covered by grass and cornfields and studded with clumps of bushes. But it was less than a mile wide and heavily wooded to the north of the Ste. Foy road where it ended at the cliffs over the St. Charles. As the British front line formed up, the only interruption came from these woods where bands of Indians and Canadian sharpshooters fired from behind the birches and maples. Col. Howe's light infantry advanced into the woods with their bayonets and the snipers disappeared for the time being. To counter this menace to his left flank, Wolfe sent Townshend's division to form a line facing the road at right angles to his front.

A misty rain fell on the scarlet ranks as Wolfe waited,

Captain Hervey Smyth, the official artist on the spot, showed everything going on at the same time. Even the Quebec guns and the British south shore guns continue their artillery duel.
(Royal Ontario Museum, Toronto)

confident at last that Montcalm would come out. "There they stand", said Montcalm bitterly, "where they have no right to be." After thirteen weeks, he had been outmaneuvered. He had clung to his natural stronghold and the well-made Beauport defenses, letting the Canadians and Indians frighten and weaken the English, until the natural defenses, one by one, had given way before English seapower. He had been forced to send the invaluable de Lévis to block the apparently greater threat from Amherst's army. He had sent Bougainville with three thousand men to stop an upriver landing and Bougainville had failed — where *was* Bougainville, anyway? — and now he would have to fight a formal engagement. The fleets in the upper and lower river cut off supplies from Montreal or France, and the army on the plains blocked the cart tracks to the rest of the colony. He could not defend Quebec from its walls because he knew, and the British must know, too, that those walls would not withstand a full-scale attack. There were dozens of cannon in the city and a hundred more down on the St. Charles and along the Beauport shore, but even if he had the time to bring them to the western walls and the horses to drag them, there were no embrasures through which to fire them. The idiocy of the engineers, the corruption of the contractors and the obstinacy of the Canadians had brought the general to the brink of defeat. But not over it. He took the last fatal step himself.

Wolfe had no way of retreat. If Montcalm had ignored his enemy's chosen battlefield, wasted his flanks by guerrilla attacks from the woods and waited until Bougainville arrived to take him from the rear, Quebec might have been saved. But now the beat of his own drums, the forward surge of his white-coats and the wild desperation of the Canadians began to overwhelm the general's judgement.

The Guienne battalion beat its way at forced-march pace up Palace Hill and was cheered by old men, women and children peering from the ramparts to the north. As its banners fluttered past the walls of the St. John bastion, the St. Ursula bastion and out by the St. Louis gate on to the plains, other battalions were thudding across the pontoon bridge below, heading toward the town. The regulars broke step on command as they tramped over the swaying boards, bayonets glinting, tricornes set squarely on their powdered wigs. The Canadian militia surged over in disorderly bands, some wearing bits of uniform, most in their habitant sashes and wool caps, knives lashed to the barrels of their hunting guns. The Indians came at a trot, naked and terrifying in blue and white warpaint. The clamor mounted as the soldiers of the old France and the woodsmen, farmers and savages of the new, swept through the shattered streets and on to battle. Over the drumming and trumpeting came the cries of women who had seen husbands or sons in the militia ranks, the answering shouts of the men and the birdlike whoops of the Indians. Priests called out blessings and prayers as their poor flock went by in pitiful pageantry.

Montcalm sat on his black horse outside the gate and watched his army emerge. The stiff-necked regulars stole sideward glances at him as they marched past; the militia stared openly and some shouted greetings. They were ready to fight. He knew his regulars would still be ready if he made them stand and wait all day, but the Canadians were impatient and would lose heart. So he decided to attack while their spirits were high, and before the English had time to dig in. He would not wait for Bougainville, for the extra cannon he had ordered from the Quebec garrison, or even for the last of his men to arrive from Beauport. Nor would

Montcalm on the Plains . . . . "waving his sword as if to excite us to do our duty."
(*Copyright Rolph-Clark-Stone Ltd. — Public Archives of Canada*)

he wait for Vaudreuil to arrive and interfere with his plans or claim the glory if he won. In his moment of decision Montcalm's mood flickered between gloom and a kind of exaltation, but he could still find room for jealousy. He remained to the end a warmer, more human man than Wolfe. As he rode along his lines, a small, round figure in his green and gold coat, the Cross of St. Louis shining above his cuirass, Joseph Trahan, an eighteen-year-old militiaman, thought how fine he looked, "waving his sword as if to excite us to do our duty."

The battalions of Béarn and Guienne formed twin columns in the centre of the Buttes-à-Neveu, a slight ridge beyond the walls. The Languedoc and La Sarre formed up in line to the right, flanked by colonial troops from Quebec and Montreal; on the left were the Royal Rouissillon, more Montrealers, and a unit from Three Rivers. The "great number of bad soldiers" which Wolfe had expected, had come down to about 4,500 men on the field; and Wolfe now had roughly the same number. Nevertheless, Montcalm was determined to attack. He consulted his senior officers and there was some discussion whether the battalions should advance in line or in column, but general agreement that advance they must. Brigadier Senezergues was given command of the right wing and Lt. Col. Fontbonne, the left. Montcalm had little confidence in either of them. He sorely missed de Lévis and Bourlamaque.

"We cannot avoid action", he told Montbeillard. "The enemy is entrenching; he already has two pieces of cannon. If we give him time to establish himself we shall never be able to attack him with the sort of troops we have." One of the English guns was now firing — the carriage of the second had broken — and four French guns, dragged out from the city, replied. "Is it possible", Montcalm asked irritably, "that Bougainville doesn't hear all that noise?" Montbeillard mentioned that the French were still very thin on the ground — a hint that perhaps the general should wait for Bougainville — but Montcalm wheeled his horse and moved back along his lines.

The Chevalier de Johnstone arrived on the battlefield in a fury. He had summoned the army from Beauport on Montcalm's orders, but at the cost of long arguments with both French and Canadian staff officers. Colonel Poulariez had made him repeat the order before Senezergues and Vaudreuil's aide-de-camp Lotbinière, who said the governor had ordered the men to stay where they were. Brigadier Senezergues wanted Johnstone, a lieutenant, to take responsibility for moving the army. Johnstone refused. Vaudreuil would claim afterwards that he, personally, had ordered every available man to the heights, leaving only a few guards at the Beauport batteries and the pontoon bridge — yet 1,500 men from two Montreal battalions never got beyond the St. Charles river. Johnstone, the Scotsman, was caught in the jealous interplay between French and Canadians. Although he spoke like a Frenchman, he did not think like one, and he never understood the pettiness of the authoritarian rulers of New France. He had fought for the divine right of kings; now he was defending the grand ambitions of little men.

On the heights, he found more confusion. Montcalm had demanded twenty-five cannon from the Quebec batteries but Bernetz, the acting garrison commander, had refused to release them because he still expected an assault on Lower Town. Only Vaudreuil could overrule him and Vaudreuil was still writing letters. The actual garrison commander, de Ramezay, had been roused from his hospital bed and was creaking slowly back to his post on a horse-drawn cart. So Montcalm had only four guns when the cannonade began.

It was the ritual opening to a formal engagement. Without it, the Duke of Cumberland said, a battle would be a dance without music. The artillerists had sighted the guns with carpenter's squares, handspikes and wedges to adjust the elevation while the gunners stood by with smouldering linstocks. At just over three hundred yards their aim was accurate enough. The English ranged across the field like a red-and-white hedge. One spray of grape — a canvas bag filled with iron balls — could halve a company in close formation. With ranks only two and three deep the losses were smaller but the terror no less for the man who saw the deadly hail coming towards him or a solid ball bounce before him. The redcoats stood like prisoners facing a firing-squad. They could hear the gunners yelling the French equivalent of their own gunners' refrain — "Sponge — powder, ram load...ram, ready and fire!"... then the slam of iron, the sizzle of flying shot. And then came the sergeant's gruff order to close up, to fill the holes torn in the ranks. After long minutes of this, Wolfe passed the order for the men to lie down. By now the field was gray with smoke and they could no longer see the shots coming.

The English gunners had now repaired their second cannon and were lobbing six-pound rounds into the packed French centre where the Guienne and Béarn columns stood, hemmed in by hawthorn and cranberry bushes. Major Dumas' Canadians and Indians had returned to the British left flank and were sniping furiously from behind bushes and through the tall stalks of the neighbouring cornfields. Howe's light infantry were besieged by Canadians in a group of farm buildings along the Ste. Foy road. These were taken and retaken, then set afire. Billows of black smoke hid the fighting from the men on the plains but the crackle of muskets, screams, and the whoops of Indians could be heard. Out on the flanks Townshend's battalions were steadily losing men to the snipers. But the battle proper had yet to begin. Another ritual had to be performed.

It was a general's duty to flaunt himself before his men. Montcalm rode steadily past his whitecoats, nodding encouragement. Wolfe strode disdainfully through the cannonade, pausing to joke with his officers. He was almost supernaturally calm, gracious and even gentle. A captain fell, shot through the lungs, and Wolfe knelt beside him, cradled his head in his arms, and promised him he would be promoted when he recovered. It was no idle promise. He dispatched an aide to Monckton, ordering that the promotion go through if he were to be killed before he could sign the papers. Then he dusted down his white breeches, straightened his coat and stalked over to Townshend's flank, where the shooting came from. His distinctive figure, gleaming in scarlet and gold, was a tempting target for the Canadian marksmen, who had none of the regular's inhibitions about shooting generals. A bullet caught him in the right wrist, tearing the tendons. Wolfe wrapped his lace handkerchief around it and walked on, carrying his stick in his left hand, magnificently courting death. "I shall never forget his look", a redcoat wrote. "He was surveying the enemy with a countenance radiant and joyful beyond description."

As he passed Kennedy's battalion in the centre of the line, a stray ball struck him just below the navel. The wound may not have been serious but no ordinary man walks with a bullet in his stomach. Wolfe walked on, and at that moment he was no ordinary man. In a shaft of sunshine through the lifting smoke he saw that the French lines were about to move forward. His luck and his surgeon's efforts had given him time to bring them to battle. A little more time, and he would have his victory and his glory. The inevitable hour was at hand. He walked steadily back towards the cliffs over the St. Lawrence and stood on a hillock between Bragg's 28th and the Louisbourg Grenadiers on the right wing.

Montcalm rode across his front line for the last time. "Êtes vous preparés, mes enfants?" he shouted and the whitecoats cheered "Vive notre géneral! Vive le roi!" He looked sad and very tired.

The drummers stood at the ready, left heel in the hollow of the right foot, left knee bent to balance the side-drum, elbows up, and the buttons of the sticks level with the ears.

Montcalm waved his sword. A warning tap, then the drums rolled along the line, beating the *pas de charge*, an ominous, impetuous metre — ta rum-dum, ta rum-dum, ta rum-a-dum, rum-a-dum, rum-dum! The ensigns threw out the fly of their colors and the army moved, slowly at first on the uneven ground through bushes and sudden hollows, then increasing speed as the front ranks struck a slope, the rear pressed forward and the drums beat faster. Ta rum-dum, ta rum-dum! The deep roar of cheering men swept across the plains. Saunders' ship captains heard it from the river below and logged the time — ten o'clock.

The French broke into a run — "much too fast", Malartic thought — and the solid front line began to shake loose. The centre

A rather fanciful version of the commencement of the battle . . . Note the enemy snipers on the British right flank.

(Royal Ontario Museum, Toronto)

columns were too far ahead of the left; the Canadians, barefoot, or in light deerskin moccasins, loped freely while the French regulars trotted stiffly in their buckled shoes and gaiters.

The English were back on their feet now, standing stiffly with arms presented as the white line bore down on them. Two hundred yards, 150, 130 — the French came to an untidy halt; their front rank raised their muskets and fired an uneven volley. Redcoats groaned and fell and the ranks closed again as the survivors shuffled sideways over their bodies. "Dress! Close up! Hold your fire!" The sergeants shook their halberds and the men obeyed. The Lobster knew how to stand and wait. It was the first thing he learned.

The French line shook in confusion. The Canadians knelt to fire and lay down to reload, ramming their muzzles while lying on their sides. The regulars loaded like the British, standing up. Montcalm had mixed Canadians in with his line battalions and now he saw that the mixture didn't work. The regulars stumbled over the Canadians on the ground, cursed them, and tried to kick them out of the way. The Canadians ran across the line, looking for cover to shoot from, for that was how they fought. Malartic, shouting orders in the centre, saw the orderly ranks of the Guienne and Bé-

The Battle of the Plains of Abraham. A 1919 engraving.

(Public Archives of Canada)

arn battalions break up. Now the French second line fired over and through the first and the confusion grew worse. The two English cannon plowed furrows through the scrambling columns as the French moved forward again.

They were not running this time, but surging ahead, walking and trotting in a white and blue mass, their muskets pointing straight ahead. Seventy yards, sixty, fifty and the front line fired again.

Quartermaster Sergeant Johnson stood on the British left, watching grimly for the movement of a British musket. None came. Wolfe had ordered that no shot be fired until the French were forty yards away. More redcoats were blasted to the ground. Again the lines closed up. The survivors, sick with fear, saw muzzles aimed at them as the French came through the smoke.

Forty yards. Wolfe shouted an order from his hillock on the right and his drummers tapped it along the line. "Give fire!"

The Lobster had waited ageless, dizzying minutes for the cry. Now he could count the buttons on the white coats before him. He had time, too much time, to choose a target. His Brown Bess nuzzled his cheek and cuddled his shoulder; then, with a great kick,

The British charge. "Egad, sir, they give way everywhere."

(Public Archives of Canada)

spat its two iron balls that short forty yards. Platoon after platoon fired their volleys in such rapid succession that they sounded to the French like a single cannon shot. Following his drill, the Lobster re-loaded powder and ball, rammed, marched forward ten paces to clear his own musket-smoke, aimed and fired again. The second volley was fired in less than a minute. He re-loaded again and pointed his bayonet to repel a charge.

None came. The smoke swirled aloft to reveal a shattered French line — a bleeding, heaving pile of broken dead and struggling wounded. Those still standing gazed in helpless horror, waiting for the next volley. In that stunned moment, Wolfe signalled a charge. English drums rattled along from right to centre. On the left the Fraser pipes shrieked. The Lobster dropped the cartridge he was about to tear open with his teeth and cheered as he rushed the barrier of corpses with his bayonet. The Frasers drew their broadswords and howled for the crags of Lovat.

The French right broke first, then the sprawling mass in the centre. The left held out longest, supported by the steady

The Death of Wolfe — Benjamin West's famous but inaccurate 1771 painting.
(The National Gallery of Canada, Ottawa)

fire of Canadians lying flat on the ground. Then the La Sarre and Languedoc battalions followed the Royal Roussillon, the Guienne and the Béarn, victors of Oswego, Fort William Henry and Ticonderoga, into headlong rout.

The first British cheer was heard in the ships below at 10.15. Fifteen minutes had passed since the French advance began.

Wolfe led the charge of the Louisbourg Grenadiers. His left hand was pressed to his wounded stomach and his right wrist dangled uselessly, but he was shouting with the rest. He had gone only a few yards when a sniper's bullet smashed into his chest. He dropped to his knees, still upright, and two officers and a soldier caught him before he could topple over. Blood foamed from his mouth but he gasped a request that they hold him up so that the army would not see him fall. Four men carried him about a hundred

West's successful painting produced at least one imitation, "most respectfully submitted". The caption is as dubious as the drawing: "We have overcome all Opposition!" — exclaimed the Messengers — "I'm satisfied" — said the Dying Hero, and Expired in the Moment of Victory.

(Public Archives of Canada)

yards to the rear and laid him down. One of the grenadier officers, Lt. Henry Browne, called for a surgeon. Wolfe, already only semiconscious, murmured "It is needless. It is all over with me". Grenadier James Henderson opened his waistcoat and found his shirt soaked in blood. "Don't grieve for me", the general breathed. "I shall be happy in a few minutes, but tell me, how goes the battle?"

He drifted into unconsciousness without hearing Henderson's answer. A surgeon's mate came running over and tried to stop the bleeding. He told Browne and the others what they knew already, that the end was near. As the men waited, there came a great outburst of British cheering, the loudest yet, as the French centre columns gave way. Through the smoke, the men at Wolfe's side could see the whitecoats in full flight. "They run!" one shouted. "See how they run!"

Wolfe stirred and his eyes opened. "Who run?" he asked vaguely. "The enemy", an officer said. "Egad, sir, they give way everywhere!"

The pale blue eyes brightened. Painfully but distinctly Wolfe gave his last order: "Go, one of you, my lads, to Colonel

The Death of Wolfe by Edward Penny conforms to the facts more than West's grander version.
(Royal Ontario Museum, Toronto)

Burton. Tell him to march Webb's regiment with all speed down to Charles's River to cut off the retreat of the fugitives from the bridge."

He turned on his side, breathing "Now, God be praised, I will die in peace", and in a few minutes he was gone. He had won his victory, attained his glory and left his successor a clear order that would complete the conquest of Canada that day. But the order was not carried out and the conquest was to be delayed for another year.

Chapter 12

"More Important Matters"

As Wolfe's body was carried down the Foulon path to the frigate Lowestoft, his army fell apart. Monckton was badly wounded in the chest and taken away, unconscious. In theory, Townshend was now in command but it was more than an hour before a messenger reached him to tell him this. By that time Wolfe's disciplined redcoats had become a rabble.

In the meantime, Murray tried to take command; he had heard that Wolfe, Monckton and Townshend were all dead. Instead of chasing the fleeing whitecoats, he decided to quench any sparks of resistance remaining on the field. Gleefully his men picked over the piles of victims, robbing the dead and stabbing the wounded.

The Frasers did chase the French, howling after them with their claymores and lopping off heads and limbs. They chased them as far as the woods on the northern edge of the plateau and there they met a fierce hail of fire from Major Dumas' Canadian snipers. As most of them had thrown away their muskets and could not swing their great swords in the trees, they were stopped with heavy losses. The Canadians held off four times their number until Anstruther's and the 2nd Royal Americans finally drove them over the brink of the plateau and down towards the St. Charles. By then most of the French regulars had reached the city walls and were streaming down to the pontoon bridge and the safety of a big fortification called the hornwork on the Beauport side. They were beaten and panic-stricken, but they still had their colors. Not one regimental standard was captured by the British. So the honor of the whitecoat regiments and the lives of most of their members were saved by the despised Canadians and by the failure of Wolfe's officers to carry out his last order. Colonel Burton did not receive it; it may never have been sent.

Montcalm, fatally wounded, enters the city after the battle.

(*Public Archives of Canada*)

The French, too, were leaderless. Senezergues and Fontbonne were dying. Montcalm, shot in the thigh and groin, was swept back towards the city by the tide of fleeing men. Montbeillard saw him enter the St. Louis gate, still on his black charger, but supported in the saddle by three men. Like Wolfe, he tried to conceal his wounds. Inside the gate, a woman saw him and screamed, "Oh, my God, my God, the Marquis is killed!"

"It's nothing", he said. "Do not distress yourself for me, my good friends." He was helped down the little streets to the house of a surgeon, Dr. Arnoux, while the remains of his army surged past him.

As the first refugees reached the pontoon bridge they met Governor Vaudreuil, heading for the battle. It had taken him four hours to cover the two miles from his headquarters to the St. Charles and he had kept with him some of the best units in the Canadian militia. He never explained what he was doing for those four hours. He arrived in time to claim credit for the rally of Dumas' Canadians who covered the retreat, although he did not go within half a mile of them. The defeat, he said, was the fault of "M. le

Marquis, who unfortunately made his attack before I had joined him."

The Chevalier de Johnstone, still on horseback, halted on the edge of the plateau as the Canadians were hacked and blasted down. They clung on with incredible stubbornness and ardor, he reported. They were driven down the slope, inch by inch, and few survived. As he tried to pick his own way down, Johnstone blundered into a small ravine and found himself face to face with a group of the Frasers he had fought beside at Culloden, and a squad of Amherst's redcoats. They turned their muskets on him. His horse was hit four times but did not fall. Bullets tore his coat and the pommel of his saddle as he galloped downhill, over the dead and the crawling wounded. His horse collapsed under him as he reached the hornwork.

Inside the log fort there he found a frightened group of regular officers arguing among themselves and with Vaudreuil. Two veteran captains of the Béarn regiment were pleading with the governor to surrender Canada before the English captured the hornwork and killed them all. "Nothing will save us", one shouted, "unless you surrender the whole colony at once." Others demanded that the pontoon bridge be cut, although part of their army was still on the Quebec side of the river and wounded men were still limping across. Johnstone learned that soldiers with axes were already chopping at the ropes that held the bridge of boats together. He and the commander of the hornwork, Hugon, ran back to the bridge and chased the axemen away. When they returned to the hornwork, Bigot had arrived and was closeted in a room with Vaudreuil.

Using the remnants of his authority as Montcalm's aide, Johnstone pushed his way in. The Intendant was seated at a table with pen in hand and Johnstone suspected that he was drafting a surrender document. Vaudreuil told him to get out. Johnstone stamped from the hornwork in a fury. But as he walked home to the Beauport camp, he cooled down and depression hit him. He was, he recalled, "heavy at heart over the loss of my dear friend, M. de Montcalm, broken in spirit and lost in reflection concerning the changes which Providence had brought about within the space of three or four hours."

It was Culloden all over again. Once more, it seemed, he was to become a man without a country.

At 11.45, an hour and a half after Wolfe's death, Townshend learned that he was in command. The scene on the plains was chaotic. Whole battalions were moving around without direction, colliding with one another and firing at random. Looting parties ranged all over the battlefield. All the while snipers were firing from the woods, killing more men than had fallen before the French muskets in the battle. And two French cannon were still in action, stopping half-hearted attempts to storm the city walls. Townshend sent aides off to halt the pursuit of the French, and began to re-form the British line. He had restored some form of order when a troop of blue-coated horsemen appeared behind him. They were the vanguard of Bougainville's three thousand men, arriving at last from upriver.

It had taken Vaudreuil's messenger more than an hour to find Bougainville and give him the governor's vague note, telling of the landing at the Foulon. He received it some time after eight o'clock on the road between Cap Rouge and St. Augustin some twelve to fifteen miles away. Although he claims to have set off immediately for Quebec, collecting men from the various outposts along the way, it was noon before he neared the battlefield. By that time he knew that Montcalm had attacked and lost. But he did not know the confused, leaderless state of the British, or he might have pushed ahead and rolled them off the heights. All he saw was one battalion, which Townshend had managed to turn around to face him as he approached from Sillery, and evidence of a large force behind them. As he paused to work out the odds in his mathematical mind, Townshend mustered a second battalion and brought into action two captured French guns which managed to spit out a few erratic shots, despite the fact that the gunners had brought the wrong ammunition. It was enough for Bougainville. He wheeled around and headed inland towards Lorette. "All the enemy's forces turned on me", he explained to Bourlamaque.

Townshend let him go. It was not his business, he told Pitt, "to risk the fruits of so glorious a day and to abandon so commanding a situation to give a fresh enemy battle upon his own terms and in the midst of woods and swamps."

So he allowed the rest of the French army to escape. And he did not try to take Quebec. He ordered his redcoats to dig in where they were, on the plains. They were tired after a night in the boats, a climb and a battle. It would have taken great leadership to spur them on to another attack that day. "Wolfe, one suspects, might have done it", Stacey observes. "Townshend could not, or at any rate, did not".

All afternoon, the men dug trenches and hacked down trees and bushes to fortify them. The houses on the Sillery and Ste. Foy roads were occupied and their windows boarded up. Sentry posts were established along the cliffs. The password was "Wolfe" and the reply "England." Sailors rolled big naval guns ashore at the Foulon and strained at the ropes to haul them up the slope while engineers widened the path ahead. Burial parties labored to get the dead underground before the Indians got at them. "All along the battlefield of the plains", a nun wrote, "still reeking of blood and covered with the slain, the victors were opening the turf to hide from view the hideous effects of war." A sailor picking over French bodies for loot was impressed by the fearsome work of the Highlanders' broadswords. The bullet and the bayonet, he thought, provided by comparison a decent death. Turning over an officer's body to get at his silver-mounted sword, he found the head hanging by a strip of skin. The neck had been chopped through with one stroke. As he looted, a firing-squad shot a Royal American deserter caught fighting on the French side.

In the midst of this activity, Townshend sat down to compose his first general order for the next day. In his first hours of command, a sobering change had come over him. He felt the weight of responsibility and he knew he would be blamed for not following up Wolfe's victory. Wolfe's plan had worked — he had triumphed over his brigadiers. He was victorious, dead and unassailable; and the haughty Townshend was condemned to live on in his shadow. The new commander composed a reluctant tribute: "The remaining general officers . . . wish that the person who lately commanded them had survived so glorious a day and had this day been able to give the troops their just encomiums."

It was not enough, either for the troops or for the hero-worshipping public back home. Townshend was to be damned for not mentioning Wolfe by name in his reports, damned for almost everything he did after the hero's death. There would be a raging public debate and a duel. Townshend, who had produced the best picture of Wolfe ever painted, would use his wicked pen once more to sketch The Irish Venus Mourning General Wolfe — a mysterious sequence of nude female figures posturing at Wolfe's gravestone which seemed to indicate he had girlfriends other than Katherine Lowther. Wolfe fascinated him. In his later years he began to champion the man he once detested. In another man this could be attributed to shame or remorse. But Townshend was too cynical and arrogant for shame or remorse. He simply changed his mind.

Montcalm was sinking slowly. His surgeon gave him twelve hours to live and he had no complaints. At least, he said, he would not see the English occupy Quebec. But he was not allowed to die in peace. In mid-afternoon a messenger arrived from Vaudreuil with a note asking the general's advice. No doubt the governor wanted this with an eye to the inevitable inquest on the lost battle, but he was also genuinely confused and bewildered. Johnstone said he was asking advice from everybody he met.

Painfully, Montcalm dictated a reply to his aide, Captain Marcel. The governor had three alternatives, he said. He could revitalize the army and counter-attack; he could avoid the British and retreat by an inland route to Jacques-Cartier; or he could surrender the colony. He, Montcalm, would not suggest which course to take.

As the messenger galloped with the reply across the pontoon bridge to the hornwork, he saw the regular battalions marching behind their banners back to the Beauport camp. They had recovered from their panic. Inside the hornwork, too, the confusion was dying down. Vaudreuil was holding a council of war.

Only one man favored a fresh attack on the British. Bigot, the civilian, the scoundrel who had swindled the King and possibly betrayed him, spoke up for heroism. As he expected, all the gold-braided officers were against him. They had had their fill of heroism, had seen their leaders mortally wounded and their men become frantic fugitives. Retreat, they said, and save the army. Bigot shrugged. He had made his gesture and it would improve his record when the inquest came. Vaudreuil noted that the officers of France were "indisposed for battle". The council of war decided to abandon Quebec. The army would march at nine o'clock that night, leaving guns, ammunition and food supplies behind. The

Quebec garrison and the civilian refugees must not know they were to be deserted. De Ramezay, the garrison commander, would be left to hold on as best he could. He would be given draft articles of surrender to use when his food ran out or when the British stormed the walls. Vaudreuil sent these papers to Montcalm, asking him to pass them on to de Ramezay. He added: "I cannot tell you how pained I am to hear of your wounds; I hope that you will soon recover and assure you that no one is more anxious for you than myself as I have been so attached to you . . . " He had already sent a courier to de Lévis at Montreal, asking him to join him at Jacques Cartier and take Montcalm's place at the head of the army. The Governor was recovering his poise.

Night crept in, cold and dark. The siege guns across the river thundered as usual, streaking their projectiles at the city. On the heights, yawning British sentries forced themselves to stay awake by remembering the sight of scalped bodies. At the General Hospital down by the St. Charles, the nuns were trying to care for more than a thousand sick and wounded who crowded every inch of floor space. Mother St. Ignace reported: "We were surrounded by the dead and dying, who were brought in by the hundreds and many of whom were closely connected with us, but we had to lay aside our grief and seek for space in which to put them." A guard of British redcoats was placed around the hospital and an officer — Mother St. Ignace says he was Townshend — came to reassure the nuns that they would not be harmed.

Promptly at nine the whitecoats straggled out of their tents at Beauport and took to the road in the dark. "It was not a retreat", said Johnstone, "but a horrid, abominable flight, a thousand times worse than that in the morning upon the Heights of Abraham." They hurried along in little groups, as if the British were after them. Bigot, Cadet and their henchmen took with them cartloads of belongings and their precious account books with their fabulous stories of fraud. The swindlers rode with the governor at the head of the column. "They flew through the air like a cannonball", said a farmer. By six in the morning they had reached the village of Lorette and by five the following afternoon they were safely at Point-aux-Trembles, protected by Bougainville's fresh troops, and heading for Jacques-Cartier.

They had left their tents standing, and their stocks of food unguarded. These supplies, which could have fed the six thousand hungry people left in Quebec, were looted by the Indians before daybreak. The British did not discover they were gone until the early hours of the morning when a rearguard of 130 men blew up a powder magazine, set fire to a floating battery and cut the pontoon bridge. Nor did de Ramezay. When he realized that he had been deserted, he hurried to Montcalm and asked him what he should do.

The dying general had other thoughts on his mind. He was back in Candiac with Angélique. In his last letter he had told her: "The moment I see you once more will be the happiest of my life . . . I believe I love you more than ever." Now he could only dream of the reunion that would never come. He told de Ramezay: "I have no longer either advice or orders to give you. I have much more important matters to attend to than your ruined garrison and this wretched country. My time is short, so please leave me. I hope you get out of your difficulties."

Yet when the dejected commandant had left, taking the draft surrender papers, Montcalm thought again of his army. He dictated a letter to the British commander: "Obliged to yield Quebec to your arms, I have the honour to beg Your Excellency's kindness for our sick and wounded . . . the humanity of the English sets my mind at peace concerning the fate of the French prisoners and the Canadian. Feel towards them as they have caused me to feel. Do not let them perceive that they have changed masters. Be their protector as I have been their father."

The ailing Bishop of Quebec, Mgr. de Pontbriand, shuffled in and prepared him for death. The bishop and Captain Marcel waited with him through the night as he sank lower. Towards the end he talked again of Candiac, asking Marcel to visit his family. Then again of the army: he was glad de Lévis had taken over so that it was in good hands. He died at daybreak, just twenty-four hours after Wolfe appeared on the heights.

That evening, as the cannon shells fell on the city, Montcalm was carried through the broken streets to the chapel of the Ursulines. De Ramezay and his garrison officers walked behind, and townspeople joined the procession as it went along. The chapel was in near-darkness, lit only by wax tapers around the bier and the occasional flashes of shell-fire glinting through the torn roof. The curé of Quebec, Abbé Resche, intoned the *Libera* over the rough

The French answer to West's Death of Wolfe. This Death of Montcalm was painted with a great deal of imagination by Louis-Joseph Watteau.

(The National Gallery of Canada, Ottawa)

plank box which the caretaker, Bonhomme Michel, had nailed together that morning. Then it was lowered into a shell hole in the floor which had been widened to make a grave. At this, the Ursuline chronicle records "the sobs and tears broke out afresh, for it seemed as though New France were descending into the grave with the remains of her general."

As he left the chapel, de Ramezay may have agreed with the chronicler that New France was finished. Quebec had been in uproar all day, since it was discovered that the tents standing so bravely at Beauport were empty and the food gone. "Despondency was complete", de Ramezay wrote, "discouragement extreme and universal. Murmurs and complaints against the army that abandoned us rose to a general outcry." The Mayor and the leading citizens signed a petition demanding surrender. They refused to serve any longer as militia officers because, they said, the British would either shoot them as civilians under arms or ship them to France as prisoners of war. They estimated that all the food in the city would be gone in four days. Bigot had sent a mere fifty barrels of flour before abandoning Beauport. At a council of war, de Ramezay's officers voted thirteen to one for surrender. The British were mounting 24 pound naval guns on the plains and sighting them on the city walls. Still, de Ramezay hung on. He was a Canadian, son of a governor of Montreal, with thirty-nine years of service in the colonial marines. He had long endured the sneers of the overbearing French; now they had run away, and he despised them.

De Lévis stormed into Jacques-Cartier and took command of the beaten army. He was now a general of France and would spare no one's feelings. He damned Vaudreuil for retreating and all but called him a coward. He cursed the battalion officers as weaklings. And he ordered a march back to Quebec. A battle had been lost, but not the colony. The army was more or less intact, although its morale was gone and the Canadians and Indians were slinking off. The only way to pull it together was to march on the enemy. Stragglers and Canadian militiamen would rejoin it along the way. When it reached the plains, a decision would be made whether to attack the British or to slip men and supplies into Quebec to resist the siege. If the worst came, Quebec would be evacuated and destroyed, leaving the British no shelter for the winter.

De Lévis arrived on September 17, four days after the battle of the plains, and by the morning of the 18th he had the army on the march. The soldiers perked up, the officers recovered their dignity and the Governor, swallowing the new general's rebuke, regained his perennial optimism. "I was much charmed", he wrote, "to find M. de Lévis disposed to march with the army towards Quebec." Bigot rounded up a food convoy from secret stores which he alone could find. Bougainville moved forward once more from Cap Rouge. He sent one hundred horsemen ahead with bags of biscuits on their saddles to skirt around Quebec and deliver them to the garrison via the Beauport shore and the St. Charles. By the evening of the 18th, the French were back at St. Augustin, well on their way to Quebec, with drums tapping and flags flying. They were stopped in their tracks by the news that Quebec had surrendered.

Townshend had spent three days on the plains, digging entrenchments, and had lost thirty-six men, killed by cannon fire from the
city walls. These losses were high, considering that only fifty-
eight British had been killed in the actual battle. The weather had
turned chilly and Saunders was more anxious than ever to get
away. Townshend had made up his mind to be home before winter,
come what may. "The command of an army is as disagreeable as
any other", he wrote Charlotte. "Men are as mean here as in any
other profession...do not think, my dear life, that any command
tempts me to stay."

At noon on the 17th, he made his move. Eight great ships
of the line moved across the Basin towards Lower Town. Their rows
of black muzzles gaped at the defenders. A column of troops marched
along the meadows by the St. Charles, heading for the Palace Gate.
The garrison drums beat the general alarm, but the militia officers
refused to answer it. At three p.m. de Ramezay raised the white
flag.

That evening Bougainville's cavalry trotted into Quebec
with their bags of biscuits and promises that help was on the way.
But it was too late. De Ramezay no longer trusted the French army
and he had already given his word to the British. The town major,
Joannès, was his reluctant negotiator. He had hacked down the
white flag when it was first raised, and beaten with his sword two
men who tried to pull it back up. His dealings with Townshend in
the general's tent on the plains were drawn-out and acrimonious
as he tried to delay surrender as long as possible. But the terms
finally agreed upon were generous. The garrison would march out
with their arms and baggage, drums beating and slow-matches
burning, taking two cannon with twelve rounds for each piece.
They would be put on the first available ships and sent to the nearest port in France. Citizens' property rights would be respected,
"the free exercise of Roman religion" guaranteed, the bishop and
clergy protected; and soldiers would be sent to guard the churches
and convents.

On the morning of the 18th, Townshend and Saunders
formally signed the surrender, and that evening fifty artillerymen
entered the St. Louis Gate pulling a gun-carriage bearing the Brit-

ish colors. The Louisbourg Grenadiers took post on the gates, while naval Captain Hugh Palliser landed in Lower Town with a detachment of sailors. Townshend marched with his staff and two companies of grenadiers to the Chateau St. Louis, Champlain's fortress on the rock.

A line of French troops was drawn up before the ruined walls and wrecked gun batteries. The commandant stepped forward to hand Townshend the keys to the fort. The whitecoats turned smartly to file away and grenadiers took their place. From the river below came the crash of a victory salvo by the guns of the fleet. It rocked even the three-decker Royal William, in whose stateroom lay the embalmed body of James Wolfe, awaiting the voyage home.

Chapter 13

The Second Battle

The Rev. Eli Dawson, chaplain to HMS Stirling Castle, stood over Montcalm's grave in the Ursuline chapel and rolled out his victory sermon to the conquerors: "Ye Mountains of Abraham, decorated with his Trophies, tell how vainly ye opposed him when he mounted your lofty Heights with the strength and swiftness of an Eagle! Stand fixed forever upon your rocky base and speak his Name and Glory to all future Generations! Ye Streams of Lawrence and propitious Gales! Speed the glad Tidings to his beloved Country! Ye Heralds of Fame, already upon the Wing, stretch your Flight and swell your Trumpets with the Glory of a Military Exploit through distant Worlds!"

It took the heralds of fame four weeks by fast frigate to reach Portsmouth and set England aflame with triumph. Townshend's victory message reached Pitt on the night of October 16, just as the printers of the Public Advertiser were setting in type Wolfe's gloomy dispatch of September 2, with its account of the defeat at Montmorency and the stalemate that followed. Pitt wrote through the night, scrawling delighted messages to the King and his favorites, boasting of the success of his war policy. As the news spread, a hundred bonfires flared, guns boomed in the parks, and Londoners reeled their way through the alehouses and gin-cellars, drinking on the house and roaring a new patriotic song: —

"Hearts of Oak are our ships;
jolly tars are our men.
We always are ready.
Steady, boys, steady!
We'll fight and conquer
again and again"

"All was rapture and riot; all was triumph and exaltation", Tobias Smollett wrote. Wolfe was "exalted even to a ridiculous degree of hyperbole."

Pitt outdid everyone in hyperbole. His speech to the Commons ransacked the history and legend of Rome and Greece, vainly seeking a parallel to Wolfe's achievement. Walpole called it the worst harangue of Pitt's career. Thomas Gray, whose Elegy had inspired the hero, called it "a studied and puerile declaration.... In the course of it, he wiped his eyes with one handkerchief and (Alderman) Beckford ... cried, too, and wiped with two handkerchiefs at once, which was very moving..."

Wolfe's praises were pounded from every pulpit in New England, linked in most cases with the defeat of popery and the prospect of safety from the savages unleashed by the French. One preacher saw further ahead. The Rev. Jonathan Mayhew, of West Church, Boston, foretold that the British colonies "with the continued blessing of Heaven ... will become in another century or two, a mighty empire." He added carefully "I do not mean an independent one", but, as Parkman says, he had read the meaning of Wolfe's victory.

On November 17, the Royal William anchored off Spithead. A black funeral barge, escorted by twelve boats, brought Wolfe's body into Portsmouth harbor. Bells tolled, guns fired in slow salute, one per minute, and the entire garrison lined the shore as the general was returned to the port he had called a hellish sink of vice. Behind the troops the "diabolical citizens of Portsmouth" stood in silent respect. The body lay in state for three days at the Wolfe home at Blackheath, then was buried in the family vault at the parish church of St. Alfege, Greenwich.

Katherine Lowther did not go to the funeral; she stayed in a castle in the north of England, sheltering from the sudden surge of well-wishers anxious to console the dead hero's fiancée. She avoided Wolfe's mother, declaring in a letter to one of Mrs. Wolfe's companions — "I feel we are the last people in the world who ought to meet." She added: "I knew not my picture was to be set but I beg, Madam, you will tell Mrs. Wolfe, I entreat her to take her own time about giving the necessary directions. I can't, as a mark of his affections, refuse it; otherwise I would willingly spare myself the pain of seeing a picture given under far different hopes and expectations." The miniature, which Captain Tom Bell had brought home along with Wolfe's will, was set in diamonds as directed and given to Katherine the following spring. She wore it on a pearl necklace, but under a black velvet cover. Six years later she married and became the Duchess of Bolton. She burned Wolfe's letters and gave away the miniature.

Mrs. Wolfe had now lost both her sons and her husband. She was nearly sixty, bent with rheumatism — a sad and angry old woman. She took little notice of the flowery tributes to her son, or of Pitt's plan to build an expensive white marble memorial to him in Westminster Abbey. With Yorkshire stubbornness, she insisted that the nation first pay what it owed him. Wolfe, thinking that he had inherited his father's small fortune, had made bequests totalling nearly seven thousand pounds. In fact, his father had left everything to his widow, who needed the money. Wolfe himself had practically nothing to leave.

Mrs. Wolfe first asked Pitt for a pension "to enable me to fulfil the generous and kind intentions of my most dear lost son to his friends, and to enable me to live like the relict of General Wolfe and General Wolfe's mother". Pitt referred her to the Duke of Newcastle (the same Duke who had spread the tale that Wolfe was mad) and the pension was refused. Next she claimed that the War Office owed her son ten pounds a day in extra pay during the time he was acting Major-General, Commander-in-Chief, which would have added about £2,500 to his estate. This was refused on the ground that he was always subordinate to Amherst and only a local, acting unpaid commander-in-chief in the St. Lawrence. She then claimed two pounds a day as major-general. This was turned down because Wolfe was held to be a major-general only in America; when he died he reverted to colonel, and would be paid as a colonel for the entire campaign. So while sculptors chiselled the inscription "To the Memory of James Wolfe, Major-General and Commander-in-Chief" on the Westminster memorial paid for by a grateful King and Parliament, the bureaucracy chiselled away his pay. Mrs. Wolfe pursued her claims until her death in 1764, and Wolfe's bequests were settled from her own estate. The War Minister who refused to pay up was Charles Townshend, then busily defending the reputation of his brother, George.

George Townshend was accused of rushing home to steal Wolfe's glory, but in fact he took his time. On the eve of the general's funeral he was still at sea with Saunders. As the returning fleet reached the English Channel, the admiral learned that the French fleet was loose in the Bay of Biscay, being pursued by Admiral Sir Edward Hawke. Although his ships were foul inside and out and his crews tired, Saunders turned to follow Hawke. Townshend stayed aboard, refusing an offer of transportation to England in one of the troopships. In a raging storm Hawke's twenty battleships defeated twenty-one French men-of-war in the dangerous waters of Quiberon Bay. It was a stunning victory, the decisive sea-battle of the war, and it deprived France of the ships needed to save Canada. French seapower was finished for the next fifteen years. It was another tremendous achievement in 1759 "the year of miracles" when, as Macaulay wrote, "men woke up to ask each other what new victory there was that morning."

Although Saunders and Townshend arrived too late for the Battle of Quiberon Bay they received credit for trying. On January 23, 1760, they were summoned to Westminster to receive the thanks of Parliament. Townshend was much in demand by portrait-painters wanting to immortalize the "second hero of Quebec". But stories of his disagreements with the first hero had already filtered through the coffee-houses. Wolfe's loyal aides, Smyth and Bell, had been in England for several weeks, talking.

Townshend's published accounts of the battle were unenthusiastic in their praise of Wolfe and not sufficiently mournful about his death. The same could be said of Saunders' dispatches, Monckton's and certainly Murray's, but Townshend was an easier man to detest. He had personal enemies such as the Duke of Cumberland, who disliked all Townshends and brother Charles in particular. They waited several months until the brigadiers' letter of September 12 came to light, then launched an anonymous pamphlet in the form of an open letter to Townshend. Its twenty-four pages of ornate venom accused him of everything from cowardice and desertion to flattery, vanity and ingratitude. It started out quite mildly by blaming him for ignoring his wounded superior Monckton when he accepted de Ramezay's surrender, and proceeded to charge him with deserting his post, calling off the pursuit of the beaten French and failing to attack Bougainville. It ended with the demand that he go back to Quebec or resign from the army.

It told him: "You received into your protection the capital of an empire larger than half the Roman conquests; and though you had formally entered your protest against attacking the place,

you alone enjoyed the honours of its being taken . . . Your appetite
for glory being now fully satisfied, you descended from the heights
of Abraham . . . and prudently quitted a scene where danger would
probably be too busy." The Townshend forces replied with another
anonymous letter by "An Officer", which is generally attributed to
Charles. It credited George with the idea of attacking at the Foulon
and suggested that the writer of the first letter had been driven
insane by "rancorous malice."

"So impotent is his incoherent malignancy" it went on,
"that he is guilty of strange wanderings from the honourable subject he would fain stigmatize; but outrageous envy commonly de-
feats that very end which it had proposed to itself."

Both letters wandered very strangely from the subject
and lost their arguments in thickets of verbiage. But the affair had
gone beyond words. Townshend looked for someone to challenge
to a duel and settled on Cumberland's closest henchman, the Earl of
Albemarle. The earl, who had been described by Wolfe as "one of
those showy men who are to be seen in palaces and courts", lacked
the brains to write such a letter, but that didn't matter. By choosing
him, Townshend demonstrated that he believed Cumberland was
behind the libel. However, he picked as his second the gossipy Earl
of Buckinghamshire, so long before the duel was to take place all
London knew about it and the King ordered it stopped.

Dawn came to Marylebone Fields and found Albemarle
and his second waiting with swords and pistols. Townshend arrived
late and apologized. "Men of spirit don't want apologies", said the
'showy man'. "Come, let us begin what we came for." At that
moment the captain of the guard at St. James's arrived and sent the
would-be duellists home. Townshend spent the remainder of 1760
in the country, pretending to be bored with the whole subject of
Quebec, while in the coffee houses and drawing rooms his enemies
sniggered over the humiliating end to his affair of honor. He had
been late for his own duel, which showed very bad manners. He
told his brother Charles he sometimes wished he had stayed in
Canada.

The new military governor of Quebec, Brigadier-General James
Murray, leaned comfortably over his brandy glass, spread a letter

Further evidence of the damage caused by British shells is given by these two views of the Bishop's Palace and the ruins of Mountain Street, which connects Upper and Lower Town. Both drawings were done on the spot by Richard Short.

(Archives Nationales du Québec, and Royal Ontario Museum, Toronto)

out on his dinner table and read it to his guests. "Quebec has indeed fallen", it said, "but we have excellent means of retaking it this winter — the cold, the Canadians and the Indians."

Murray's fierce little eyes glinted and a French officer across the table shifted uncomfortably. The letter had been written by one of de Lévis' staff and intercepted by the British. It reflected the French guest's own hopes, although he, as a member of de Ramezay's garrison, was about to be shipped back to France and would not see the city recaptured.

Murray gave a rueful grin and the tension was broken. He could understand the French optimism. Quebec was a ruin. More than five hundred houses were gone. Lower Town was a maze of roofless walls, Mountain Street a rubble-strewn path with the gaunt remains of the Bishop's palace clinging to its slope.

In Upper Town, the Cathedral was a black shell, the Jesuit College pockmarked by cannon shot and the Jesuit and Recollets churches torn and roofless. The skulls and bones of long-dead friars, blasted from their graves, lay scattered among the broken stones.

When Townshend sailed home and Monckton went to recuperate in New York, Murray was left with seven thousand men, only five thousand of whom were fit. Before moving into the city they had demolished all the fortifications they had so recently built on the plains. Gunports were pierced through the western walls. The bases at the Isle of Orleans and Point Levi were evacuated and the siege guns dismantled and floated across the river. Every available man was put to work clearing the streets. But the defenses were still weak. Murray understood why Montcalm had chosen to fight outside the walls. When his turn came to defend Quebec, he would do the same.

He had lost mastery of the river: when Saunders' fleet left in mid-October, the French slipped several vessels up past Quebec, to join the frigates they had kept far upstream where Saunders couldn't get at them. Murray had only the sloops Racehorse and Porcupine, with three armed transports. When naval operations began again in the spring he would be out-gunned. Yet the jut-jawed brigadier was by no means dismayed. Lust for glory burned in him, too, and was all the fiercer for the extravagant praise of Wolfe. For he was one of "the windy Murrays", a family of savage wit and enormous stubbornness.

His brother Patrick, Lord Elibank, had once beaten the

great Dr. Johnson in an exchange of insults. When Johnson, in his dictionary of the English language, defined oats as "a grain which, in England, is generally given to horses, but in Scotland supports the people", Elibank retorted: "And where will you find such men, and such horses?" Another brother, Alexander, was a political agitator who insulted the King's ministers and incited a riot in London. Ordered to kneel before the Bar of the House of Commons and apologize, he refused to kneel except to God, and was committed to Newgate Gaol for contempt. When he got out, crowds carried him through the streets under the banner "Murray and Liberty".

Burdened with this family background — and the suspicion that the Murrays were secret Jacobites — James had a hard struggle for promotion in the King's army. He ran away from home to serve as a private in Holland and reached the rank of sergeant before his family found him and refurbished him properly as an officer. When he became a general he could claim to have held every rank except drummer. As one of his officers, Lt. Malcolm Fraser, said, he had every military virtue except prudence.

The French officers liked him. Malartic was "unable to speak too well of him". And the Canadians accepted him. By midwinter nearly six thousand had come in from the countryside to Quebec, handed over their arms and sworn allegiance to the English King. Knox said they seemed more bitter towards Vaudreuil than the English. The women wanted to see the Governor scalped.

Knox admired the ladies of Quebec for their cheerfulness and good manners. Evidently they were well-mannered enough not to notice the horsey smell that clung to him. He was living in a small stable with a manger at one end and a hayloft above. The more cynical Lt. Alexander Campbell wondered why the ladies took so much trouble to teach the officers French, and suspected that they wanted to hear themselves flattered and courted in their own language.

While the officers flirted decorously in the few remaining warm drawing-rooms, men were freezing to death on the glassy streets and in the wind-pierced ruins that served as barracks. By December, the rubble was wreathed in snow, the temperature had plummeted to zero and the ferocity of a Quebec winter was upon them. Work parties marched out daily to cut logs and drag them back on sleighs, returning with frost-bitten feet and fingers. Sentries died at their posts and vanished in the drifting snow. The red-

Brigadier-General James Murray, military governor of Quebec after Wolfe's victory.
(Archives Nationales du Québec)

coats now wore any clothing they could find — habitant shirts, white French uniforms, and scraps of fur. After an ice-storm in January, the kilted Frasers reached their guard posts in Lower Town by sliding down Mountain Street on bare behinds. Such sights upset the nuns, who began knitting long woollen drawers for the Highlanders.

There was no fresh food; only tough, salt pork. Scurvy swept through the garrison. One hundred and fifty men were dead by Christmas; the toll would reach seven hundred by spring and a thousand by the end of April. Hundreds of bodies lay unburied, frozen to the iron-hard ground. Rum helped many a man survive. It also brought drunken rampages through the streets, looting and robbery, followed next day by floggings.

Women who sold rum without permission were stripped to the waist and whipped through the streets. Several men were shot or hanged for robbery. In one case, two were condemned, but Murray ruled that only one need die. They threw dice to decide. Knox reports that the winner showed no outward satisfaction. The loser, who was executed immediately, "behaved quite un-daunted, though with great decency." Men caught trying to desert

"A Perspective View of the Town and Fortifications of Montreal in Canada." It was to Montreal that Vaudreuil and de Lévis brought their defeated forces in 1759 to plan their counter-attack in spring.

(Public Archives of Canada)

were given a thousand lashes. The tap of the drum and screams of the victim tore the grim silence of the frozen town.

In September, Vaudreuil had retreated to Montreal with de Lévis and most of the army. There was much to be done before winter set in. Letters had to be written, explaining the loss of Quebec, and ships found to sneak them out of the St. Lawrence past the British guns and the rapidly-forming ice.

The Governor began by blaming the surrender squarely on poor de Ramezay. He refused to touch the surrender documents, leaving the garrison commander to forward them to Paris himself. There must be no hint that the governor, before his abrupt departure, had authorized the commander to raise the white flag and drafted surrender terms. Then there was the lost battle of the plains, which must be blamed entirely upon Montcalm. As de Lévis observed, a defeated general was always to blame. Vaudreuil might have added that a dead one was even more to blame.

The letter Bougainville had brought from Paris the previous spring put Montcalm in supreme command of military affairs in the colony. Although Vaudreuil seems to have concealed this news from the general while he was alive, he now made much of it. "The letter", he told the Minister of Marine and Colonies, "flattered his self-love to such a degree that, far from seeking conciliation, he did nothing but try to persuade the public that his authority surpassed mine. From the moment of M. de Montcalm's arrival in the colony down to that of his death, he did not cease to sacrifice everything to his boundless ambition. He sowed dissension among the troops, tolerated the most indecent talk against the government, attached to himself the most disreputable persons, used means to corrupt the most virtuous and, when he could not succeed, became their cruel enemy. He wanted to be Governor-General. He privately flattered with favors and promises of patronage every officer of the colony troops who adopted his ideas. He spared no pains to gain over the people of whatever calling, and persuade them of his attachment; while, either by himself, or by means of the troops of the line, he made them bear the most frightful yoke. He defamed honest people, encouraged insubordination and closed his eyes to rapine of his soldiers."

In another letter, Vaudreuil declared that Montcalm was killed while trying to escape from the battlefield. As a literary knife-wielder he surpassed even the author of the open letter to Townshend. Of course, he had motives other than personal spite, as is shown in a letter to the Minister of War. Montcalm, he wrote, had perpetrated "a stroke so black" it was barely conceivable. Shortly before he was killed he had compiled lists of allegations of corruption against Vaudreuil's government, and given them for safe keeping to a certain Father Roubaud at St. Francis. The Governor hastened to warn the minister of this, in case the papers reached Paris. "I am sure" he added "that the King will receive no impression from them without acquainting himself of their truth or falsity." The papers were never found. Father Roubaud renounced his faith and went over to the British side without exploding his bombshell. Still, Vaudreuil worried that the general might somehow pursue him from beyond the grave. He tried to get hold of Montcalm's personal papers, which had been willed to de Lévis, but de Lévis refused to hand them over.

Intent upon his feud with the dead, Vaudreuil failed to notice that his colony's financial system was crumbling under him. The machinery of corruption was running wild; Bigot had lost control of it and Paris had cut off the supply of real money.

Even in normal times there was little gold or silver currency in Canada. Business was transacted in cards stamped with the royal arms issued by authority of the French court, and in notes issued by Bigot on ordinary writing paper. The paper notes could be cashed, if desired, once a year. Each October, the holder could present them to Bigot, who would obtain a draft for their value on the royal treasury. Every year the French court complained about the size of these drafts and suspected the Intendant of swindling, but every year they were paid — until 1759. M. Querdisien-Tremais, an investigator sent out from Paris, reported on September 22 that it was extremely difficult to get any information about Bigot's financial system. "The greatest disorder exists", he wrote. "Every kind of officer from the highest to the lowest engages in trade and the greed for gain is insatiable." But even before this was written, it seems that the court had decided not to honor Bigot's drafts, and Bigot knew it.

Early in October, a crier made a hasty trip through the streets of Montreal, ringing his bell and shouting that anyone who wanted his paper money cashed had three days, instead of the normal whole month, to present them at the intendant's office. People living outside the town didn't hear of the proclamation until the three days were up. Crowds of note-holders surrounded Bigot's house, jeering and cursing, to be assured that they had not missed the boat because there was, in fact, no boat. The British controlled the St. Lawrence, so the drafts could not be sent to France. This was not strictly true, as a ship carrying Vaudreuil's letters slipped past Quebec after Saunders' fleet left, but it was the best excuse Bigot could find. He did not want the drafts to reach France because they were exorbitant, and would not be paid in any case.

By mid-October the paper notes were changing hands at a fifth of their face value. The government's credit had collapsed and de Lévis had to borrow gold and silver coins from his officers to pay for army supplies. What the army could not pay for, it stole. Officers took cattle, poultry and vegetables from the habitants, giving them worthless paper notes or nothing at all. Cadet continued to charge the King for supplying full rations to thirteen thousand phantom troops, but did not deliver enough to feed even the seven thousand who were still present.

Bigot professed to be shocked by the theft and corruption around him "All the world is ill", he wrote. Then he took Madame Péan out on their usual nightly round of dancing and gambling. For despite its staggering problems, Montreal was a gay town. The ladies wore their best gowns, and the senior officers and swindlers strutted in velvets and brocades; the heady atmosphere of Little Versailles survived that final winter. De Lévis was the lion of the social season, presiding over the festivities with his new mistress, Madame Penisseault. He had acquired her after a complex exchange of partners among the rogues of La Friponne. When Bigot took over Madame Péan from her pliable husband, Major Péan, the major found consolation in the wife of his partner Penisseault. De Lévis moved in, and the obliging major moved on once more, to make new friends and business connections. De Lévis was not personally corrupt, but got along well with the swindlers. "One must be on good terms with everyone", he said jovially.

The Chevalier de Johnstone avoided the social circle, or was frozen out of it. He found Montreal dismal after the excitement of Quebec. He now despised the French officers, who behaved more like merchants than military men, and spent much of their time trading with the enemy. Although food was scarce, large shipments were smuggled to the British at Quebec in exchange for wine and brandy. Johnstone wondered at the endurance of the Canadians who, he wrote, were being "devoured by rapacious vultures." He detested Vaudreuil more than ever; for the governor had refused to allow him to return to France on the last ship and was holding up his promotion to captain. He was now the oldest lieutenant in Canada, and had come to feel very much a stranger in the service of France.

Everyone had his own scheme to retake Quebec, including "women, priests and ignoramuses", but Johnstone had little hope for any of these plans. The Bishop hoped that the Jesuits inside Quebec would start a religious uprising, or at least provide spies. Others proposed to storm the walls with ladders. To prove how neatly and easily it could be done, they staged a practice demonstration against a Montreal church wall. Some of the ladders slipped on the ice or were knocked over in the fury of the mock attack, while others simply collapsed. When the wounded were carried off with broken arms, legs and heads, the ladder idea was abandoned for good.

April came at last. Warm rain reduced the snowbanks in

the streets of Montreal. In the river the ice cracked, split and rumbled loose; gray water gushed free, and slowly the St. Lawrence shook itself awake. The French leaders watched impatiently. "The melting of the ice", Malartic wrote, "does not correspond to the eagerness of our troops to start."

De Lévis had mustered about seven thousand men, half of them regulars. He had the frigates Atalante and Pomone, ten transports, a supply ship and a schooner laden with all the artillery and stores Cadet could round up — some of them had been bought or stolen from Quebec and smuggled upstream. He had the blessings of Bishop Pontbriand and his priests, who had spent the winter months urging their flock to prepare for the great crusade. But he knew that without support from France the expedition would fail. Captain Le Mercier, the artillerist and La Friponne profiteer, was in Paris, pleading for ten thousand troops to save Canada, but the result of his efforts would not be known for several weeks.

On April 15, the river channel was open at Montreal and the small fleet followed the ice downstream. At Lachenaie it was joined by the barges of the La Salle battalion and at Verchères by the Guienne. Three hundred Indians followed in their canoes and La Rochebeaucour's horsemen paced along the river road. The seasons were on the side of the French. It would be two weeks before the spring thaw reached Quebec and released Murray's frigates from the ice. As the expedition moved on its chilly way, the river villages offered cheers and prayers, but showed great reluctance to surrender their young men, most of whom had deserted from the militia the previous fall and sworn allegiance to the English. Vaudreuil issued a proclamation releasing them from this foreign oath, but Murray was later to argue that this violated the law of nations. A Captain Nadeau was forced to join De Lévis on pain of death, and later hanged by Murray for breach of faith. As always, the Canadians were caught in the middle. By this time, as Professor G. M. Wrong points out, the French soldier cared nothing for Canada, and the Canadian soldier cared little for France.

Vaudreuil and Bigot stayed behind in Montreal. The Governor sent de Lévis a letter of encouragement —" Madame de Vaudreuil is continually in prayer. Madame neither thinks nor speaks of anyone but you ..."

The army reached St. Augustin on April 26, three days

after an ice bridge there had fallen into the river. Big chunks ground past the ships and ice walled the river bank. Bone-chilled men dragged the barges over the ice to the shore for protection. De Lévis decided to leave the river and march the rest of the way through mud and rotting ice to Quebec. As the men were landing from the transports, the first spring storm stuck. Fierce winds and lashing rain churned up the ice, smashing and overturning boats. "It was a frightful night", said de Levis, "so dark that but for the flashes of lightning we should have been forced to stop." One boat, heavy with cannon, sank and several artillerymen were drowned. A survivor flailed his way onto an ice-floe, which was swept down-river into the darkness.

Early next morning a lookout on the sloop Racehorse, clamped in the ice at Quebec's Lower Town dock, heard the man's cries and rescued him. He was revived and carried up the hill to Murray's headquarters where the general, roused from bed, heard his story and realized that the French were much nearer than he had thought. By daybreak, half the garrison troops, with ten guns, were marching out by the St. Louis gate and back on to the Plains of Abraham.

"What a remarkable and visible instance of fortune favoring the English", Johnstone wrote. "Had it not been for this unaccountable accident to the artilleryman ... M. de Lévis would have captured all the English advanced posts."

Murray had known all winter that an attack must come. He had examined the defenses of Quebec and decided, like Montcalm, that he must fight outside the walls. Like Montcalm, he lined his troops up on the Buttes à Neveu. He had far fewer men than de Lévis — about 3,600 against 7,000 — but a stronger position and twenty-two cannon. And he had pride and an overwhelming ambition to outshine Wolfe in history. He had told Pitt "our little army was in the habit of beating the enemy." So he proceeded to make exactly the same mistake that Montcalm had made seven months before and for similar reasons. He saw de Lévis appear before him and begin to dig trenches. This, he thought was his "lucky minute." He abandoned his strong position and charged.

Once again the drums throbbed and the red line advanced, but not with the parade-ground precision of Wolfe's battle. Now the plains were deep in a treacherous mixture of snow, ice and slush. The precious cannon mired down, the men fell and

De Levis exhorting his troops at the battle of Ste. Foy, the attempt to re-take Quebec that almost succeeded.   *(Public Archives of Canada)*

dropped their muskets in the wet. De Lévis' advance guard prudently fell back, luring the English onward, beyond the plains and into knee-deep snow, about half a mile beyond the first battlefield. They were now in the wooded swamps where Bougainville had stood last time — the ground Townshend refused to venture upon in good weather. Once more the deadly Canadian snipers opened fire from behind trees. Murray's cannon fell silent. They could find no suitable targets, and much of their ammunition had been lost when the man-handled carts fell into snowdrifts.

Three well-placed French guns now raked the redcoat lines. The Lobsters stood for over an hour, although more than a thousand were killed and wounded. Then the left flank crumbled and Murray's army fled just as Montcalm's had fled. They rushed back through the St. Louis gate, leaving their cannon to be captured and their wounded to be scalped. It was a bloodier battle than Wolfe's and it proved that history could repeat itself very rapidly without teaching impetuous generals anything.

Even the loyal Quartermaster Sergeant Johnson complained of his general's "mad, enthusiastic zeal." He wrote apologetically "We are too few and weak to stand an assault, and we were in almost as deep a distress as we could be ... half-starved, scorbutic skeletons."

The British under Murray are driven back from Ste. Foy to the city. History repeated itself.
(Royal Ontario Museum, Toronto)

"Our army pursued them hotly," the Chevalier de Johnstone wrote, "and if the cry had not been raised among our forces to stop, it would probably have happened that we should have entered the city of Quebec with them, not being at any distance from the gates." Like the English, the French failed to follow up their victory. So ended what is called the Battle of Ste. Foy, but was actually the second battle of Quebec.

A wave of optimism rippled up the St. Lawrence. "The jubilation here is unparalleled," Bougainville reported from the Ile aux Noix. Vaudreuil was "unable to express the keenness" of his joy, but sent triumphant letters all over the colony. He assumed that de Lévis would be in Quebec before they were delivered, so he did not bother to send him any more gunpowder. Bigot hurriedly wrote to the general, offering him the use of the best bedroom in his intendant's palace in Quebec. The Intendant insisted that he himself would make do with a bed in a small room when he arrived.

In London, the news caused annoyance rather than shock. After the bonfires of the previous October, Quebec had been forgotten. Wolfe had conquered Canada and that was that. Horace Walpole commented: "America was like a book one has read and done with; but here we are on a sudden, reading our book backwards."

The backward reading continued. De Lévis was redigging the trenches on the plains which had been dug by Townshend and filled in by Murray. Murray was dragging guns up to the walls, as Montcalm had tried to do. To the great distress of Sgt. Johnson, even the officers were ordered to help with this task — "None but those who were present on the spot can imagine the grief of heart the soldiers felt to see their officers yoked in harness, dragging up cannon from the Lower Town; to see gentlemen who were set over them by His Majesty to command and keep them to their duty, working at the batteries with the barrow, pickaxe and spade." The sight of officers doing manual labor would encourage the troops of two centuries later, but in 1760, unless Sgt. Johnson was a reactionary old liar, it brought morale to zero. The men took to the rum again; in response Murray staved in the sutlers' barrels and hanged a drunken looter. Yet within a couple of weeks he had one hundred and fifty cannon in place, spewing ball and grape at the whitecoats on the plains.

De Lévis was still landing his cannon at the Foulon and using horses and men to drag them up the path that Wolfe had widened. Each gun cost the King 1,800 livres and sometimes double that, because Cadet liked to issue his bills twice over. The munitionaire had moved his operations to the battlefront and now strutted around carrying a general's baton. He was treated as the equal of his friend de Lévis. He lost a little respect when some of his guns proved to be of inferior quality by blowing up. They were not ready for a full-scale bombardment of Quebec until May 11, and by that time it was too late.

Both sides had known from the start of the siege that the outcome depended on support from France or Britain. The flag of the first ship up the river would determine the winner.

At eleven on the chill, blustery morning of May 9, French watchers above the Foulon and the English defenders on Cape Diamond saw a vessel round the point of the Isle of Orleans.

For a minute Malartic thought she was French. There

was a shout of *"Vive le roi!"* Then the British flag broke from her maintop and the English on the walls went wild. She was the frigate Lowestoft, veteran of many wars, and now she fired a twenty-one gun salute as the redcoats, Murray among them, cheered and cheered from the ramparts. A week later the battleship Vanguard and the frigate Diana arrived and, with the Lowestoft, advanced above the Foulon and scattered de Lévis' fleet. Two large British squadrons followed, and the French gave up the siege.

On his retreat to Montreal, de Lévis wrote a bitter letter to Paris. He claimed that "one single frigate" from France would have given him Quebec and saved Canada for another year.

At that moment one single frigate was on her way to Quebec escorting a convoy of twenty Cadet supply ships. She was the 30-gun Machault, sold to the King by Cadet. Problems in finding a crew delayed her departure from Bordeaux and by the time she reached the St. Lawrence, the river was thick with British ships. They trapped her in the Bay of Chaleur and seized Cadet's convoy. It carried good brandy and wines, and a great deal of rotting horsemeat.

The promised succour from France had been small, late, and mostly corrupt.

Chapter 14

The
Captains Depart

Robert Stobo reported to General Amherst's headquarters at Albany, New York, on June 5, 1760 and was sworn in as a captain of Amherst's own regiment, the 15th Foot. He had spent an eventful nine months since leaving Wolfe at Quebec the previous summer. His sloop had been taken by a French privateer and Stobo had thrown overboard his uniform and the dispatches he was carrying from Wolfe to Amherst. He was freed and managed to reach Boston, where the Governor of Massachusetts loaned him seven pounds and four shillings to speed him on his way. He finally reached Amherst on Lake Champlain late in 1759, about the time the general decided to abandon his operations for the winter.

After that, Stobo went home to Virginia, to receive a hero's welcome and a thousand pounds, plus back pay for his years in captivity. This was not enough: he wanted a captaincy in the British army (he was still only a colonial officer) and he wanted it free, without having to pay the going rate of £2,400. So he sailed for London to see Pitt, carrying letters of recommendation from Amherst and Monckton. Again his ship was seized by a Frenchman and again he had to dump his papers. He ransomed himself for £125, reached London, and within a month was on his way back to America with Pitt's endorsement in his pocket. (Stobo seems to have been unusually unlucky in his choice of ships, but he picked only two of the 812 captured by the French in one year).

At his Albany swearing-in he found Amherst laying cautious plans for the final conquest of Canada. This time, every loophole of escape was to be denied to the French. There would be a three-pronged attack on Montreal, using the three traditional routes. Murray would leave Quebec and sail up the St. Lawrence; Brigadier William Haviland would advance along Lake Champlain; and Amherst himself would lead the main army from Lake Ontario through the St. Lawrence rapids and down to Montreal. Somehow, these movements must be coordinated across hundreds of miles of wilderness so that the three arrived before Montreal at the same time. Stobo, carrying dispatches once more, was sent from Albany to join the 15th Foot at Quebec. He sailed by schooner from Louisbourg and arrived at Quebec without incident. He found that the eager Murray had left the city without waiting for final orders from Amherst. He caught up with him sixty miles upstream.

Murray's 2,400 troops were advancing comfortably in thirty-two warships and transports, accompanied by nine floating batteries and a trail of barges. They stopped every few miles to exchange shots with bands of Canadians on shore. They also landed detachments to disarm villagers, demand oaths of neutrality, and trade their army salt pork for fresh eggs and butter. Captain Knox, ever the happy tourist, was delighted by the scenery — "I think nothing could equal the beauties of our navigation this morning; the meandering course of the narrow channel; the awfulness and solemnity of the dark forests with which these islands are covered; the fragrance of the spontaneous fruits, shrubs and flowers; the verdure of the water by the reflection of the neighboring woods; the wild chirping notes of the feathered inhabitants; the masts and sails of the ships appearing as if among the trees, both ahead and astern, formed altogether a charming diversity."

Next day the charm was obscured by smoke as the army burned a hostile settlement near Sorel. "I pray God this example may suffice", Murray wrote, "for my nature revolts when this becomes a necessary part of my duty." He blamed the Canadian resistance upon the clergy and told a priest who was brought before him: "The clergy are the source of all the mischiefs that have befallen the poor Canadians, whom they keep in ignorance and excite to wickedness and their own ruin. No doubt you have heard that I hanged a captain of militia (Nadeau); that I have a priest and some Jesuits aboard a ship of war to be transmitted to Great Britain. Beware of the snare they have fallen into; *preach the Gospel*, which alone is your province."

Murray's fleet anchored off the island of Ste. Thérèse, just short of Montreal, and he waited impatiently for the other armies to arrive. Haviland appeared a few days later, having routed Bougainville from the Ile aux Noix. He had planted cannon on both sides of the river and bombarded the island for six days. Major Rogers' American rangers had broken through the French booms which blocked the river channels and brought guns up behind the fort. Surrounded and short of food, Bougainville left forty sick and wounded men to fire the fort's cannon for as long as they could, while he and the rest of his 1,700 men took to the stifling forests and swamps.

The Chevalier de Johnstone, who was with him, found this retreat the worst yet — "I was so overcome with fatigue and so totally exhausted, not being able but with great pain to trail my legs, that I thought a thousand times of lying down to finish my days." Then he remembered the slow business of dying at the stake while Indians hacked off pieces of charring flesh, and found new strength. He may also have remembered the sight, many years ago, of a Scots rebel in London in the process of being disembowelled, watching his own entrails being burned after he had been half-hanged, and just before his final beheading. Whether the Indians got him or the English, Johnstone's prospects were grim. He stood in the river for an hour, only his head above water, recovering from the tortures of the heat and the flies, then followed Bougainville to Montreal. It was the only sanctuary left, the last French stronghold north of Louisiana.

Amherst took his time, as ever. His ten thousand men sailed quietly along Lake Ontario, the boats threading their way through the pleasant Thousand Islands, which stand in the green water like clumps of potted plants. They were escorted by seven hundred Indians, in the charge of the British expert in handling natives, Sir William Johnson, captor of Baron Dieskau. Tribes from far and wide were deserting the French and joining the scalp-rich cause of the English king, even though this meant fighting beside the Iroquois who had eaten their fathers and brothers.

Near present-day Ogdensburg, New York, Amherst found three hundred men guarding the entrance to the St. Lawrence rapids. Although he could have sailed past them, he paused to conduct a three-day siege, then gracefully accepted their surrender. His Indians watched the formalities, sharpening their knives for the anticipated massacre of prisoners. The Mohawks were particularly eager, remembering the Mohawk scalps they had found hanging in French huts a few miles back. But lines of redcoat bayonets held them back. They were only permitted to dig up the graves of the freshly-dead and scalp the corpses. Five hundred of them stamped home in a fury.

Sir Jeffrey Amherst was painted in the traditional suit of armour by Sir Joshua Reynolds. In the background British boats career down Reynolds' version of the Lachine rapids, while Amherst's helmet rests on a map of his objective, Montreal.

(Public Archives of Canada)

The Lachine rapids took the tremendous waters of the Great Lakes, and thrust them, churning and protesting, through narrow rocky channels down to the stillness of the river. They have since been bypassed by the man-made channels and large locks of the St. Lawrence Seaway, but when Amherst tackled them, they roared mightily against him. He had two snow brigs and hundreds of boats. His Indians and captured Canadian pilots could handle only a fraction of this fleet. He lost sixty-four boats, smashed to bits in the foaming Cedar and Cascades rapids. Eighty-four men were drowned and seventeen cargoes of cannon and shot lay on the bottom. La Corne, the guerrilla leader, watched the destruction from the shore, but did not attack. The rest of the army got through and landed at Lachine; by September 6 they were camped before the walls of Montreal.

Murray was now on the other end of Montreal Island, advancing upon the town. Farmers were rushing out to welcome his men with apparent delight. They offered horses and saddles for the officers and pails of milk to the men, apologizing that they had nothing stronger. Despite Vaudreuil's threats of instant execution, the Canadian militiamen were deserting in their hundreds. Malartic looked from Montreal over to Longeuil on the south shore and saw villagers hurrying to the crossroads to take the neutrality oath before Haviland's officers. The town was now surrounded by 17,000 men; its garrison had dwindled to about 2,500 and its walls could not withstand bombardment for more than a few hours. They had been built to keep out bands of Indians, not an army of 17,000 men.

Behind those walls, the dignitaries of Old and New France met for their last councils of war. Bigot opened the first meeting with a review of affairs in the colony. His words were grave but he was affable as ever, an ugly man whom everyone liked. The Montrealers, he reported, had refused to take up arms and were trundling their possessions away. The country people had joined the English or melted away into the bush. The Indians had gone, too. The only course was surrender, in the hope that Britain would hand the colony back to those best fitted to govern it, as soon as the rulers of Europe had made peace among themselves. Vaudreuil listened to the Intendant's statement, which contained nothing he did not already know, and went through a pantomime of being convinced by it. Then he produced a fifty-five article surrender document that he had already prepared. He, too, was sure that it was only a temporary surrender. The English did not really want Canada. They had handed it back (for $240,000) in 1632 and they were realistic enough to know that they could never rule it according to their customs. In the meantime, property rights and religion must be preserved. So long as these were not tampered with, the English would remain trespassers, not conquerors.

The French officers envisaged a different kind of surrender. They cared nothing for Canada, its religion, property rights or thieving leaders. They were prepared, indeed thankful, to leave what one of them called "that miserable bad place". All they wanted was to preserve the semblance of military honor; to march out with their arms and banners, as de Ramezay's garrison at Quebec had done. The regular officers had their careers to think of. If they laid down their arms they would be put on the inactive list, at half pay, until the end of the European war. De Lévis did not mention this financial detail in his long pleas for the preservation of honor, and probably only Bigot, among the Canadian establishment, was sharp enough to perceive it.

In the end, Bougainville, the apprentice soldier, was sent to Amherst's tent with surrender proposals protecting property and military honor, in that order. He found the British general amenable to most of the civil requests but determined to squelch the French army, for they had made free and terrible use of Indians.

Indians revolted Amherst. He used them, but hanged them the moment they got out of line. He could not understand — or forgive — the French tolerance of their frightful customs. Britons had been tortured, mutilated, scalped and eaten, until even his ox-like redcoats were sickened. They knew Vaudreuil kept records of scalps bought and paid for and, according to Horace Walpole, they would have scalped the Governor on the spot if they had caught him. As for Montcalm, he could not be forgiven for the Indian massacre of his prisoners at Fort William Henry. Murray's men remembered seeing the scalp-locks of their comrades waving from the bushes after de Lévis won the second battle of Quebec. Their allies, the American Rangers, took scalps as a matter of course, and even Wolfe had permitted the scalping of Indians and disguised Canadians. But not Amherst. He fought his battles slowly and righteously and he expected others to do the same. He would now punish de Lévis and the ghost of Montcalm.

He sent Bougainville back with word that the Canadians would be allowed to keep their land and religion, but that all troops in Canada must lay down their arms and not serve again during the present war. He was resolved, he said, "for the infamous part the troops of France had acted in exciting the savages to perpetrate the most horrid and unheard-of barbarities in the whole progress of the war, and for other open treacheries as well as flagrant breaches of faith, to manifest to the world, by this capitulation, his detestation of such ungenerous practices and disapprobation of their conduct."

De Lévis fumed and pleaded with Vaudreuil not to accept such terms but the Governor had no time left for the glory of French arms. It had plagued him for years in the person of Montcalm and had failed to save his beloved Canada; it could go to hell on half pay while he salvaged what he could. The general then made a proposal that would stand him and his officers in good stead later on: he would transport what was left of his army to St.

Helen's island, in the river, and hold out to the death. It was a suicidal idea and Vaudreuil vetoed it, as de Lévis knew he would; but the gesture had been made. The record in Paris would show that the army had been prepared to fight on, but the Governor gave in.

At six o'clock on the morning of September 8, Vaudreuil sent word that he accepted the British terms and later in the day he signed the capitulation. He signed away half a continent — not just the small part of Canada still in French hands, but all the lands and waters to the west that Champlain had dreamed of and that the great explorers had seen but never settled. He signed away the vision of New France along with the squalid reality of Montreal.

De Lévis did not attend the ceremony. He was busy burning the colors of his regiments, depriving the English generals of the trophies which meant more than an empire to a military man.

Next day a column of redcoats entered Montreal through the Recollets gate, and wheeled into line on the square of the Place d'Armes. The French trooped into the square without flags, drumming or trumpeting, sullenly dropped their muskets and marched away to a camp assigned to them on the ramparts. They now numbered barely two thousand, since hundreds more had deserted.

The British flag replaced the lilies of France on Citadel Hill. Major Isaac Barré took a fast ship for England to tell the King and his ministers that the war in North America was over. He carried Amherst's official dispatch to Pitt and also a letter to a friend that revealed the general's private satisfaction — "I entered this inhabited country with all the savages and I have not hurt the head of a peasant, his wife or his child, not a house burnt, or a disorder committed."

Order was maintained during the occupation of Montreal. A redcoat found looting was hanged immediately. The Iroquois were sent home with thanks and presents — four lace hats, 119 pounds of wampum, 242 pounds of silver trinkets, 600 cords of birchbark and 44 anchors of brandy. Amherst was glad to see them go and the Canadians, who had feared a massacre, were immensely relieved. The refugees who had packed Montreal went back to their farms and the town began to settle down. According to the surrender terms, the French troops and all officials who wanted to go would be shipped to France within fifteen days. During these days, relations between the armies were correct, but bitter. During the

The French surrender at Montreal, 1760.

(Public Archives of Canada)

two sieges of Quebec, the opposing commanders had exchanged gifts of wine, spirits and delicacies for their tables — de Lévis had even sent spruce beer, *sapinette*, for Murray's men. Now they refused to meet. Vaudreuil gave a dinner party for Amherst and no French officers showed up. Malartic had to get special permission from de Lévis to visit Murray, with whom he had often dined at Quebec.

Stobo got a long hard look at Vaudreuil, who had sentenced him to death, as he marched with his company in a victory parade. The Governor was on a stand beside Amherst and the captain had no opportunity to approach him, to compare notes about the ups and downs of life.

James Johnstone was an outlaw once more but, as ever, he had useful friends. Before the surrender at Montreal he had met a Colonel Young of the Royal Americans who had been taken prisoner by de Lévis at Quebec that spring, but, having rank and money, had found comfortable lodgings in a Montreal merchant's home. Young turned out to be a cousin of Johnstone's brother-in-law, Lord Rollo, a man of influence. With de Lévis' permission, Johnstone discarded his uniform. He took the name of Chevalier de Montagne as well as a room next to Col. Young. After the surrender, one of Amherst's aides, Lieutenant Mills, came to dinner. Young addressed Johnstone as M. de Montagne, Johnstone spoke only French, and all was going well until one of the merchant's young daughters came in and persisted in calling him Mr. Johnstone. Mills looked puzzled. Johnstone, with one eye on the back door as an escape route, decided to confess.

Lt. Mills was sympathetic, particularly when Col. Young told him that Johnstone was a relation. He suggested that Johnstone keep his Jacobite history secret until Amherst left Montreal — there was no telling how the general might react to the discovery of a Scots rebel who had also fought with the French and their Indians — and wait until General Murray took command. Murray was a Scot and a generous man, if erratic. Mills undertook to sound him out and warn Johnstone if he appeared in danger of being hanged, drawn and quartered.

"I was in terrible alarm for some days", Johnstone wrote. "Someone came and knocked rudely upon my door towards seven o'clock one morning. Having opened it, I was astounded to see a huge young man in English uniform standing there. He asked me if I was James Johnstone and I said yes . . . I was certain he had come to arrest me. He told me he was a near relation, of the same name as myself, the son of Lady Girthead . . . . "

The huge young man, artillery captain James Johnstone, announced that Murray had known of the renegade for a long time. If he stayed out of the way, he would not be hunted down. So the new Chevalier de Montagne sailed to Quebec with his new-found relative, who had been posted there, and "spent three very pleasant weeks" before the ship sailed for France.

"There were a number of English officers," he wrote, "and each one had a mistress, and it was one long round of banquets and festivities. They were all very polite and kind to me and made sure always to call me M. de Montagne."

Col. Poulariez of the Royal Roussillon found him a white uniform with the blue facings of that regiment, entered him on the rolls as a Roussillon officer, and he sailed back to France, at English expense, as a Frenchman.

He travelled more comfortably than the leaders of New France. De Lévis had trouble with his baggage and that of Mme. Penisseault, who accompanied him. The English threatened, insultingly, to search his belongings for the missing flags of the French regiments. The general gave his word of honor that they had been destroyed — which was true — but added that they had been worn out and worthless, which was, by military standards, an enormous lie.

It took three flatboats to carry Bigot's effects and papers out to the ship provided for him and Mme. Péan. According to the surrender terms, these papers were not to be seized, or inspected. A further three boats carried Vaudreuil's belongings and those of his family to their ship, which was the best transport available. Altogether, twenty ships were needed to carry home the remnants of French rule. Their welcome in the homeland was uncertain, to say the least, but by the time they arrived few were in a condition to care what King Louis thought of them.

Storms battered the convoy most of the way downriver and bigger storms hit them off the Nova Scotia coast. Vaudreuil's ship struck a rock and had to be abandoned, while he and his damp possessions were moved to a smaller vessel. De Lévis' ship lost a mast and nearly sank, while Malartic's schooner ran aground. La Corne's transport did sink, and only the guerrilla leader and six others survived. Bigot was stormbound for days and Mme. Péan, the Pompadour of New France, became extremely seasick and ill-tempered. All of the senior officials complained loudly about the English food.

While they were suffering at sea, news of the capitulation reached Versailles, causing some annoyance but little dismay. "At last", sighed the real Mme. de Pompadour, "At last the King can get some rest." Voltaire, who had just published a slim book entitled "Candide", threw a party to celebrate "the loss of 15,000 acres of snow." His acreage may have been wrong but the cynic was consistent in the smallness of his thinking about the New World. It was shared by the French Court which, for a century and

Montreal after the fall of New France. British ships bob on the St. Lawrence while Mount Royal frowns in the background. Engraving by Thomas Patten.

(Royal Ontario Museum, Toronto)

a half, had sent heroes to Canada without enough common folk to support them.

Isaac Barré rode ahead of the storm and reached England with his news on October 3. The bonfires blazed once more, but the excitement soon died down. England was satiated with victories. Walpole professed to be bored by them. The feeling persisted that Canada had been won the year before, and India, a much more valuable prize, had still to be digested. It was three weeks — October 24 — before Pitt found time to write to Amherst, in a great flurry of capital letters, expressing "the universal Applause and Admiration at his masterly Plan which he had formed with such Application and Diligence."

The next morning King George II fell dead on his bedroom floor and Pitt was on his way out. The bland, priggish young George III and his Scots mentor, the Earl of Bute, would renounce his plans to smash France and would make peace as soon as possible.

👑 ⚜

When the news of Montreal's fall spread southeast pulpits were thumped once more in New England. Satan and savage idolators had been conquered by God and the King, with the help of Wolfe and Amherst. The howling wilderness would now be pushed back, more corn planted and more Protestant churches built. The cautious, coast-bound colonist could now fill his chest with windy liberty, stretch his limbs and advance inland.

James Murray foresaw the outcome — Murray the eager, far-from-brilliant general who was now the first British governor of Canada. As Malartic, with what was left of his regiment of Bearn, boarded his schooner for France, Murray asked him, "Do you think we will give Canada back to you?"

Malartic replied: "I am not so familiar with politics to see so far ahead."

"If we are wise", said Murray, "we will not keep it. New England needs something to rub up against. Our best way to give them that is by not retaining this country."

The two men parted friends, having fought fiercely in a campaign that had changed the face of a continent and cleared the way for a greater change, the birth of the United States of America.

Chapter 15

New Paths

The drama of Quebec ended with the two principals dead on stage while the supporting cast of heroes and villains wandered off. Some went into obscurity and some to jail, but many became principals in their own right. For they were remarkable men.

Governor Vaudreuil went to the Bastille, along with Bigot, Cadet and twenty other officials. They stayed there for a year before being brought to trial for fraud, and then spent a further two years awaiting judgment. The governor had with him his Negro servant, his books, and a fine stock of tobacco and wine. Bigot and Cadet also had servants, and were given special permission to go out to Mass — it being felt that they had particular need of repentance. Bigot prepared a written defense of his conduct that ran to twelve hundred printed pages and blamed everyone but himself for the ruination of the colony. He named Cadet as the archcriminal, aided and abetted by Vaudreuil and Montcalm. His charges against the dead general were so virulent that Montcalm's widow and mother tried to sue for libel. The lesser prisoners accused one another of lesser crimes, while agreeing to put most of the blame on Cadet. The roll of accused grew to fifty-five, including the twenty-three in the Bastille, and twenty-seven judges spent fifteen months examining the final papers.

Vaudreuil put up a dignified defense. He had been solely concerned with military matters and had nothing to do with finance or contracts. The sordid charges against him insulted his noble lineage and the honor of the armies of France. He must now speak out to defend the regular army officers who had fought and died for France, but were under suspicion.

Vaudreuil did speak out for them, although they were not on trial, and he was. He wrapped himself in the mantle of Montcalm and appeared in court as a soldier of France, innocent and ignorant of the civilian brigandage going on around him. It worked. He was acquitted and awarded the Grand Cross of St.

Louis, plus pensions of 12,000 livres. He retired to his family chateau where he died in 1778, aged eighty. He left a journal telling his story of the loss of Canada, but his family declined to publish it. In 1871, during the Franco-Prussian war, the chateau was in danger of falling into enemy hands and a Vaudreuil descendant burned the journal, creating the suspicion that it contained secrets better left untold.

Bigot was found guilty. The prosecutor demanded that he be made to kneel before the main gate of the Tuileries wearing only a shirt, a rope around his neck and a placard labelling him "Thief", and confess his crimes aloud before having his head chopped off. The court decided instead to confiscate all his possessions, fine him 1,500,000 livres and banish him from France for life. Evidently the court knew that he had hidden assets from which to pay the fine after all his visible possessions had gone. Bigot could always find money. While noble families scrambled to buy up the silver plate and other valuables from the chateau he had built for his retirement, he paid the fine and went to live comfortably in Switzerland. He died at Neuchatel about 1778.

Cadet, the butcher's boy who had out-swindled them all, startled the court by making a full confession. He was fined six million livres, which he paid cheerfully, and banished for nine years. The banishment was soon lifted and he moved freely between France and Canada. In his later years, as a great landowner with two daughters married into the old nobility, he sued the government for nine million livres in unpaid bills. But he remained a speculator, lost all his millions and died, bankrupt, in 1781.

Péan and Penisseault were fined enormous sums, which they paid. Only the minor thieves remained in jail.

General de Lévis discarded Mme. Penisseault (which, as it turned out, was fortunate for her) and married a wealthy Frenchwoman. He paid court to his friend Madame de Pompadour and was well received in society. If not exactly a hero, he was at least free of blame for the surrender, thanks to his gallant offer to fight to the death on St. Helen's Island. His friends in London persuaded Pitt to relieve him of his undertaking not to fight again in the current war and soon he was back in the field, battling against Britain's ally Frederick of Prussia. He became Marshal of France and Duc de Lévis, and died in 1787, aged sixty-seven, just in time to avoid the French revolution. But the revolutionaries guillotined his widow and two daughters and dug up and scattered his bones.

Bougainville, whose land exploits had been none too successful, took to the sea as a navy captain. He established a short-lived French colony in the Falkland Islands, then sailed to the South Seas and claimed Tahiti for France. He commanded the first French squadron to sail around the world and his two-volume account of the voyage established his reputation as an explorer and naturalist. But he remained a warrior, and took his revenge on the British. In 1781, he commanded the French fleet that forced the surrender of Lord Cornwallis at Yorktown. He later narrowly escaped being torn to pieces by a mob during the French Revolution. But he avoided the guillotine and survived to become a senator of France and a count of Napoleon's empire. At seventy-seven, he asked to command the French fleet that fought Nelson at Trafalgar, but was turned down. He died on his Normandy estate in 1811, aged eighty-two. An active man of many and varied talents, he is best remembered by the tropical flower he named bougainvillea.

De Ramezay collected almost all the blame for the surrender at Quebec. He wrote out an elaborate defense, but French officialdom forbade him to publish it because it would only lead to further explanations and contradictions by others involved — meaning, presumably, Vaudreuil. It was published one hundred years later. De Ramezay received a pension of only three hundred livres and died in 1781, a poor man serving in the hellish climate of Cayenne.

The guerrilla leader, St. Luc de la Corne, shipwrecked at Cape Breton on his way to France, made an epic 600 mile journey on show-shoes back to Quebec, where he joined the British. He led his Indian bands against the American colonists during the War of Independence, helped capture his American counterpart Ethan Allen, and was himself captured and exchanged. He allowed his Indians to scalp and torture at will and was described by an American as "that archdevil incarnate who had butchered hundreds — men, women and children — in the most inhuman manner." He was appointed to the first legislative council at Quebec, wrote one of Canada's earliest books, and died peacefully in 1784, aged seventy-two.

Johnstone became a chevalier of the Order of St. Louis in 1762 and settled in Paris to live on his small pension and to write his *Dialogue in Hades*, in which the shades of Wolfe and Montcalm discuss their tactics and mistakes. "It is now", he began, "that we can contemplate at leisure the errors and passions of men which rush like the waves of the sea and break themselves in pieces on the rocks . . . . " The Chevalier de Johnstone did not enjoy his leisure. He tried and failed to claim his heritage in Scotland, and the revolution swept away his French pension. "Death is to man the refuge of an unhappy life", he wrote, "and one may say that God, who is immortal, treats us with rigour in giving us life on conditions so annoying." He died in Paris around 1800.

Robert Stobo, the other Scots merchant's son, was no luckier than Johnstone. He fought under Monckton in Britain's war against France and Spain in the Caribbean, then returned to Quebec, where the garrison mutinied because their pay was cut by fourpence a day. He stood beside Murray as the general ordered the redcoats to demonstrate obedience by marching between two flagpoles. Murray threatened to kill every man who refused. There was a long, tense moment — then they marched, and the mutiny was over.

Before being posted to England, Stobo bought a 108-acre estate on Lake Champlain for 450 livres. His title was good at the time, but later both New York and New Hampshire claimed the area. Eventually it became part of Vermont. Stobo spent years wrangling with British and colonial bureaucrats, trying to get his land back. He cited his colorful war record and claimed to have given "very material intelligence" to Wolfe at Quebec. His supporters said he revealed the secret of the Foulon, but this was never established one way or the other. In 1770, at forty-three, Captain Stobo shot himself with his pistol in Chatham barracks. The coroner brought in a verdict of lunacy and he was buried in unhallowed ground.

James Cook, the laborer's son, attained a captain's commission in the Royal Navy. He visited Canada every summer for seven years to survey the St. Lawrence estuary and the coasts of Nova Scotia and Newfoundland. In the winters he returned to London to work on his charts and astronomical calculations. In 1768 he obtained the backing of the British Royal Society for the first of three great scientific voyages which gave Britain her claim to colonies in Australasia. On the second, he beat the universal menace of scurvy by forcing his sailors to take vitamins. Bougainville was always slightly ahead of him, reaching Tahiti before he did and completing his first circumnavigation of the world while Captain Cook was still at sea. But the scientific honors were even when Cook's career was cut short. In 1779, at the age of fifty-one, he was stabbed and drowned by angry natives in the shallow waters of Kealakekua Bay, Hawaii.

Jeffrey Amherst, final victor in the struggle for Canada, received the thanks of Parliament and the position of Governor-General of North America. But because he was Pitt's man and thus suspect in the eyes of young George III, he did not get the peerage he expected — only a knighthood and a bill for £522 for his induction into the Order of the Bath. In 1763 he was faced by a revolt of the western Indians, led by their chief Pontiac, which spread from Michilimackinac to the Ohio valley. His distaste for Indians flared up, and he proposed to kill them all by distributing blankets infected with smallpox. But before this venture into biological warfare could be tried, he was brought back to England to be commander-in-chief of the home army. King George had changed his mind about him and now proposed to present him with the enormous Canadian estates of the Jesuit order; but political enemies blocked this tremendous gift and he got the title, Earl Amherst, instead. His new coat-of-arms included an Indian waving a bloody scalp. He hung on to his command until he was nearly eighty, then retired as a field marshal to his estate in Kent, which he named Montreal.

Monckton, quietest of Wolfe's brigadiers, recovered from the chest wound he received at Quebec and swallowed his resentment towards Townshend for signing de Ramezay's surrender without showing it to him. "You are one of the Last Men in the World that could give me offence", he wrote. "I hope, My Dear Townshend that Malicious Tongues will not be Suffer'd to hurt me in your Opinion." He went on to lead the successful Caribbean expedition against Martinique and Havana, then returned to England as lieutenant general and Governor of Portsmouth, which he represented in Parliament. He never married, and died in 1782, aged fifty-six.

Townshend inherited his family's great estates, becoming master of Raynham, fourth viscount and later first Marquess Townshend. He was Lord Lieutenant of Ireland for five years, resigning when his beloved Charlotte died. In 1773 he appeared on the field of honor once more to fight a pistol duel with an old en-

Townshend in later life; painted by Mather Brown.

(Public Archives of Canada)

emy, the Earl of Bellamont. According to the Annual Register, he fired first, putting a pistol ball into Bellamont's stomach and nearly killing him. The Earl "discharged his pistol immediately after, without effect." The duel ended his active military career, but he was later proclaimed a full general and then field marshal. He died in 1807, aged eighty-three, having long since put Quebec out of his mind. When Murray wrote to him in 1773, telling him that he intended to publish his theory that Wolfe never intended to fight a general action, Townshend advised him to forget it. He said that if an account of the Quebec expedition were placed before him alongside a book about current operations at Tanjore in India, he would read about India first. Murray never wrote his story, but fired a sarcastic letter back to Townshend — "God forbid, My Lord, that I should interrupt your Amusements: Tanjour (sic) you may quietly Enjoy, while I am knocking my obstinate Scotch head against the Admiration and Reverence of the English Mob for Mr. Wolfe's memory."

In his five years as Governor, Murray had become fond of Canada and its people, whom he called "perhaps the bravest and best race upon the Globe." He treated them well — so well, in fact, that the newly-arrived English merchants complained that he discriminated against his own countrymen, and he was brought home to face a parliamentary inquiry. Although he was exonerated, he did not return to Canada. He left behind five large seigneuries which he had acquired after the fall of the French regime. He was Governor of Minorca when the American colonies rebelled, confirming his belief that the King had more to fear from the English-speaking settlers than the French. With no French presence to "rub up against" they were certain to go their own way. In 1781, he was forced to surrender Minorca to a besieging French army and was brought home once again, to be court-martialled for mismanagement of the island. Again, he was exonerated. He became a full general and died in 1794, at seventy-two. He never changed his opinions about Wolfe, the Canadians, the Americans, or anything else.

Admiral Saunders was knighted and given command of the Mediterranean fleet. Although he was at sea most of the time, he continued to hold his seat in Parliament, regularly gaining re-election in his absence. War with Spain brought fabulous prizes in captured treasure-ships, which officers and crew shared according to rank. The Hermione, for example, yielded twenty wagon-loads of riches. Saunders and two ship captains who captured her took £65,000 each; junior officers got £13,000 apiece, and every seaman £500. By 1766, when he went ashore to become First Lord of the Admiralty, Sir Charles Saunders was very rich indeed. He soon quarrelled with his government colleagues and left the Admiralty, but stayed in Parliament, barking disapproval of attempts to weaken the navy. At one point he threatened: "I shall go to Portsmouth on Thursday and will hoist my flag and go into my ship and never stir out of it while I stay in England . . . if I sail it will be war!"

His last recorded speech was on the Quebec Act of 1774, which, among other things, gave Canadians back their fishing rights. "Give up the fishery", the admiral growled, "and you will lose your breed of seamen." The following year he died of gout in the stomach and was buried in Westminster Abbey, near the Wolfe memorial. Walpole called him "that brave statue . . . with most unaffected modesty. No man said less or deserved more."

Bourlamaque pleaded with the French Court to let him go back to Canada and fight again. He had been Montcalm's closest friend, the man to whom the general turned in his dark moments.

He was honest and dignified; even in the hell's kitchen of Montreal in that final winter, no one had a sneer for Bourlamaque or a whisper of scandal about him. He had risked his life to save English prisoners from the Indians, so he felt the injustice of Amherst's insult to French arms. The British government had released him from his undertaking not to fight again in the war. He was a soldier, without private means, and he wanted to go back to avenge his friend. Given regular troops, ships and supplies, he said, he could win back the colony.

He may well have been right, but the fate of Canada was now being decided in the ornate chambers of the diplomats and in the counting-houses of Paris and London. The London merchants, unimpressed by the patriotic outbursts in the streets and alehouses, reckoned that possession of Canada meant, at most, a slight extension of the fur trade — and beaver hats were no longer the last word in elegance. The new King wanted to make peace with France, and this meant giving up some of his newly-won territory. A pamphlet, circulated in London, carried the argument that the French sugar island of Guadaloupe, also won by Britain, was far more valuable than Canada. It had a bigger population than Canada and produced as much sugar, rum, cotton and coffee as all the British Caribbean islands put together. Keep Guadaloupe, the pamphleteer said, and let Canada go. If the French are driven out of North America, the colonies will demand independence.

The French were thinking along the same lines. Guadaloupe had been more profitable and given less trouble. In a century and a half, Canada had cost the King millions of livres and returned no profit except to men like Bigot and Cadet, whose trial was still dragging on, with shocking revelations every few months. For a time it seemed that both Wolfe and Montcalm had died for nothing; neither side really wanted the land they had fought for.

Within three months, George III had acquired the throne of England, the rest of North America and the whole of India. He failed to grasp even the geography of his new possessions, remarking to surprised courtiers that the Canadian forts along the Ganges would have to be demolished. Pitt, who had spent so much blood and money to capture Canada, argued that the colony would expand and pay for itself. But Pitt was out of office, a gouty figure wrapped in black robes and dramatic sulks. One morning the King paid out £25,000 in bribes to Members of Parliament and the Commons vot-

Two idyllic views of Quebec in 1780 painted by the same Thomas Davies who painted the burning of Grymross in 1759.

(*The National Gallery of Canada, Ottawa*)

ed to end hostilities. The Treaty of Paris was signed on February 10, 1763, and the Seven Years War was over. Britain finally decided to keep Canada and abandon Guadaloupe — largely for the inglorious reason that British planters on other West Indian islands feared a drop in sugar prices. With Canada came all the territory east of the Mississippi, except the area around New Orleans. France renounced her claim to Acadia and gave up the St. Lawrence islands. She retained fishing rights around Newfoundland and the two tiny islands of St. Pierre and Miquelon.

And Bourlamaque, who wanted Canada, became Governor of Guadaloupe. He died there after a year, aged forty-seven.

George Washington, who had fired the first shots against the French at Fort Duquesne, led the Continental Armies to victory in the revolution that Murray and others had predicted. It followed a series of outstanding blunders by George III and his ministers — particularly Charles Townshend, whose mean little taxes infuriated the New Englanders — but it would almost certainly have happened anyway as the consequence of Wolfe's victory. The revolution might well have swept Canada, but for the cold, gray presence of Wolfe's quartermaster-general, Guy Carleton.

When he succeeded Murray as Governor at Quebec, he saw at once that the colony could never become a replica of the British possessions to the south. It was a feudal kingdom that had lost its king, but had no intention of changing its ways. English ideas of freedom and self-government had never penetrated there;

the Canadians expected to be ruled by their seigneurs and their priests; if they wanted freedom they took to the woods. Carleton promoted the Quebec Act of 1774 which, in effect, restored the old French system while adding some English seigneurs to run it. French civil law was restored, although English law applied in criminal cases. The seigneurial land laws were confirmed, the Church was allowed to collect tithes, and the Ohio frontier lands were returned to Canada. New France was re-established in all but name. British parliamentarian Edmund Burke called this "squinting at tyranny", but when the libertarian explosion blew the redcoats out of New England, most Canadians clung to their familiar tyranny and refused to join the revolution.

American armies, led by Benedict Arnold and Richard Montgomery, invaded Canada in 1775, capturing Montreal and besieging Quebec. Carleton escaped from Montreal, disguised as a fisherman, defeated and killed Montgomery — an old colleague who had fought with Wolfe and Amherst — and routed Arnold on Lake Champlain.

He left Canada to command British forces in America and in 1783 evacuated his beaten army from New York City. In 1786 he returned to govern Canada as Lord Dorchester and kept the Canadians loyal to Britain through the French Revolution. This done, he retired home to breed horses, and died in 1808, aged eighty-four. "Grave Carleton", as Wolfe called him, had preserved what Wolfe had won.

But not forever. For two centuries French Canada stood firm as the Rock of Quebec, while the tides of progress surged past. No immigrant ships arrived from France: it survived by its own remarkable birthrate, the "revenge of the cradle." The priests sheltered their flock from the anticlericalism of republican France and the Protestantism of the millions around them. Traces of the despotism of Laval, the great bishop and Talon, the great intendant, survived Carleton's gentlemen's government and lingered beneath the veneer of parliamentary democracy that was added when the feudal state became Lower Canada and then the Province of Quebec in the self-governing Dominion of Canada. The corruption of Bigot lingered, too.

Carleton had kept the land out of the United States by placing it in limbo. It was the kernel of the new British nation of Canada, but it could never become a part of Britain, France or

Victorian strollers pass the monument to Wolfe and Montcalm in Quebec. Lithograph by Sarony and Major.

(*Royal Ontario Museum, Toronto*)

America so long as it stayed frozen in the eighteenth century. Even as modern industry moved in, ravaging the forest sanctuaries and stripping the seigneurial soil, the black robes of the sallow missionaries seemed to blend with the shadows and the gleam of plumed helmets to reflect upon the waters. And the ancient grievances remained.

They remain to this day. A new generation of French Canadians has brought a new Quebec out of the musty tomb of New France. But the new Quebec is still different in language, faith and outlook from the rest of the continent. There is a growing separatist movement which would set up an independent republic. Sons of habitants have torn down the pillar on the Plains of Abraham inscribed "Here Died Wolfe Victorious". Angry tides still surge along the St. Lawrence. And angry men still seek the paths of glory there.

Bibliography

Alberts, Robert C. *The Most Extraordinary Adventures of Major Robert Stobo.* Houghton Mifflin, Boston, 1965.

Amherst, Jeffery *Journal, edited by J.C. Webster, 1931*

Bergeron, Léandre *The History of Quebec — A Patriote's Handbook,* N.C. Press, Toronto, 1971.

Boswell, James *The Life of Samuel Johnson,* London, 1791.

Bougainville, L.A. de *Adventures in the Wilderness: The American Journals of Louis Antoine de Bougainville 1756-60, edited by Edward P. Hamilton, 1964.*

Casgrain, the Abbé H.R. *Wolfe and Montcalm,* Toronto, 1905.

Clark, S.D. *The Social Development of Canada,* University of Toronto Press, Toronto, 1942.

Connell, Brian *The Heights of Abraham,* Hodder and Stoughton, London, 1959.

Corbett, Julian *England in the Seven Years' War,* Longmans, London 1907.

Costain, Thomas B. *The White and the Gold,* Doubleday, New York 1954.

Cowburn, Philip *The Warship in History,* Macmillan, New York, 1965.

Creighton, Donald *Dominion of the North, A History of Canada,* Macmillan, Toronto, 1964.

Davies, Blodwen *The Storied Streets of Quebec,* Montreal, 1929.

Doughty, A.G. *The Cradle of New France,* Quebec, 1908.

Doughty, A.G. and G.W. Parmelee *The Siege of Quebec (six vols.),* Quebec, 1901.

Duncan, David M. *The Story of the Canadian People,* Toronto, 1904.

Findlay, J.T. *Wolfe in Scotland,* Longmans Green, New York, 1928.

Frégault Guy *Francois Bigot, Administrateur française,* Montreal, 1948.

Grinnell-Milne, Duncan *Mad, is He? The Character and Achievement of James Wolfe,* The Bodley Head, London, 1963.

Harper, Col. J.R. *The Fighting Frasers,* DEV-SGO Publications, Laval, Que. 1966.

Hibbert, Christopher *Wolfe at Quebec,* Longmans Green, London, 1959.

Home, John *The History of the Rebellion in Scotland,* 1882.

Hughes, Maj-Gen B.P. *British Smooth-bore Artillery,* Arms and Armour Press, London, 1969.

Hutchison, Bruce *The Struggle for the Border,* Longmans, Toronto, 1955.

Jefferys, C.W. *The Picture Gallery of Canadian History (three vols),* Ryerson Press, Toronto, 1942.

Johnstone, Chevalier de *A Memoir of the 'Forty Five,* Paris, 1820.
— *A History of the War in Canada,* Aberdeen, 1871.

Knox, Capt. John *Historical Account of the Campaigns in North America (two vols.),* London, 1769.

Lawson, C.C. *A History of the Uniforms of the British Army (four vols),* Norman, London, 1961-66.

Lloyd, Alan *The King who lost America,* Doubleday, New York, 1971.

Maham, Capt. A.T. (USN) *Influence of Sea Power,* Sampson Low, 1889.

Mahon, R.H. *Life of General the Hon. James Murray,* London, 1921.

"Major Moncrief" (Major Patrick Mackellar) *Journal (see Doughty and Parmelee)*

Malartic, Comte de *Journal des campagnes au Canada,* Paris, 1890.

Milford, Nancy *Madame de Pompadour,* Pyramid Books, New York, 1953.

Montcalm, Marquis de *Journal (edited by Casgrain),* 1895.

Montresor, John *Journal of the Siege of Quebec (see Doughty and Parmelee)*

Morison, Samuel Eliot *The European Discovery of America. The Northern Voyages A.D. 500-1600,* Oxford, 1971.
— *Oxford History of the American People,* Oxford, 1965.

Murray, Hon. James *Journal of the Siege of Quebec,* London, 1871.

O'Brien, Vincent *The White Cockade,* Abelard-Schuman, London, 1963.

Parkman, Francis *Montcalm and Wolfe. The Decline and Fall of the French Empire in North America,* Boston, 1884.

Patterson, E. Palmer *The Canadian Indian, A History since 1500,* Collier-Macmillan, Toronto, 1972.

Plumb, J.H. *England in the Eighteenth Century. Pelican History of England,* London, 1950.

Prebble, John *Culloden, Secker and Warburg, London, 1961.*

Reid, J.H.S., Kenneth McNaught and Harry Crowe *A Source-book of Canadian History,* Longmans, Toronto, 1959.

Rutledge, Joseph Lister *Century of Conflict, Doubleday, 1956.*

Rogers, Major Robert *Journals, 1765.*

Ryerson, Stanley B. *The Founding of Canada, Beginnings to 1815, Progress Books, Toronto, 1960.*

Salmon, Edward *Life of Admiral Sir Charles Saunders, K.B., Pitman, London, 1914.*

Samuel, Sigmund *The Seven Years' War in Canada, 1934.*

Schull, Joseph *Rebellion, The Rising in French Canada, 1837, Macmillan, 1971.*

Stacey, C.P. *Quebec, 1759. The Siege and the Battle, Macmillan, 1959.*

Townshend, Lt.-Col. C.V.F. *The Military Life of Field-Marshal George, First Marquess Townshend,* John Murray, London, 1909.

Walpole, Horace *Memoirs of the Reign of George II, London, 1847.*

Warburton, G.D. *The Conquest of Canada, 1849.*

Waugh, W.T. *James Wolfe, Man and Soldier, Montreal, 1928.*

Webster, Dr. Clarence *Wolfe and the Artists, Toronto, 1930.*

Whitton, Lt.-Col. F.E. *Wolfe and the North American, London, 1929.*

Wolfe-Aylward, A.E. *The Pictorial Life of Wolfe, Plymouth, 1924.*

Wood, Col. W. *The Logs of the Conquest of Canada, Toronto, Champlain Society, 1909.*

Wright, R. *Life of Major-General James Wolfe, London, 1864.*

Wrong, George M. *The Fall of Canada — A Chapter in the History of the Seven Years' War, Oxford,* 1914.

INDEX

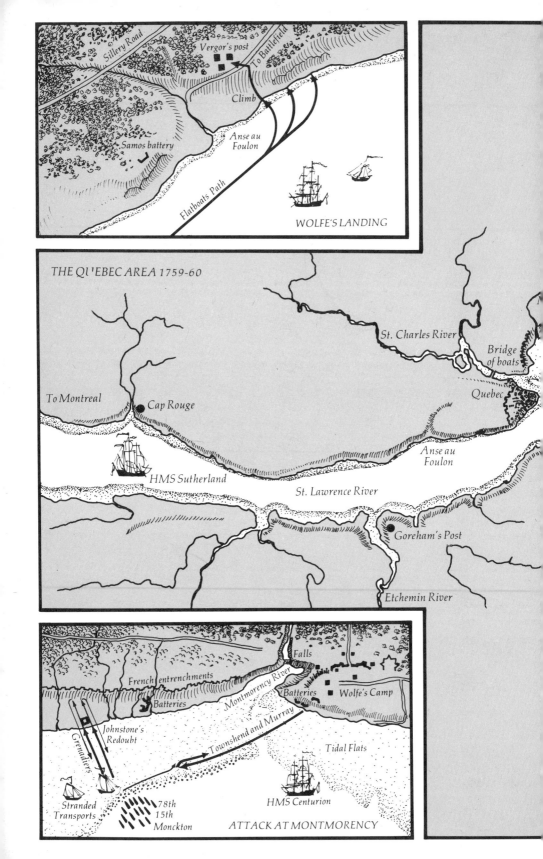

WOLFE'S LANDING

Sillery Road
Vergor's post
To Battlefield
Climb
Samos battery
Anse au Foulon
Flatboats Path

THE QU'EBEC AREA 1759-60

St. Charles River
Bridge of boats
Quebec
To Montreal
Cap Rouge
HMS Sutherland
Anse au Foulon
St. Lawrence River
Goreham's Post
Etchemin River

ATTACK AT MONTMORENCY

Falls
French entrenchments
Montmorency River
Batteries
Batteries
Wolfe's Camp
Johnstone's Redoubt
Grenadiers
Townshend and Murray
Tidal Flats
Stranded Transports
78th
15th
Monckton
HMS Centurion